Biographical Passages

Biographical Passages

Essays in Victorian and Modernist Biography

Honoring Mary M. Lago

Edited by Joe Law and Linda K. Hughes

University of Missouri Press
Columbia and London

Copyright © 2000 by
The Curators of the University of Missouri
University of Missouri Press, Columbia, Missouri 65201
Printed and bound in the United States of America
All rights reserved
5 4 3 2 1   04 03 02 01 00

Library of Congress Cataloging-in-Publication Data

Biographical passages : essays in Victorian and Modernist biography, honoring Mary
M. Lago / edited by Joe Law and Linda K. Hughes.
    p. cm.
  Includes bibliographical references and index.
  ISBN 0-8262-1256-5 (alk. paper)
  1. English prose literature—19th century—History and criticism.   2. Biography as
a literary form.   3. English prose literature—20th century—History and criticism.
4. Modernism (Aesthetics)—Great Britain.   I. Law, Joe.   II. Hughes, Linda K.
PR756.B56 B56 2000
820.9'492—dc21   99-048271

☉™ This paper meets the requirements of the
American National Standard for Permanence of Paper
for Printed Library Materials, Z39.48, 1984.

Designer: Stephanie Foley
Typesetter: BookComp, Inc.
Printer and binder: Edwards Brothers, Inc.
Typeface: Garamond

For Mary Lago, with gratitude and affection

Contents

Acknowledgments

For permission to reprint a portion of Julie Codell's essay that earlier appeared in the *Journal of Pre-Raphaelite Studies,* n.s. 5 (1996): 5–34, we are grateful to *JPRS* editor David Latham.

We also wish to thank Julianne Smith for research assistance, Jane Lago for biographical information on Mary Lago prior to her academic career, Stacia Neeley for completing the index, and Beverly Jarrett for her oversight of this project.

Biographical Passages

Joe Law and Linda K. Hughes

"And What Have *You* Done?"
Victorian Biography Today

Jürgen Schlaeger's impression of England is inextricably linked with that country's love of biography: "Wherever you go, wherever you are faces stare up or down at you as if crying: 'Look at me! Look at what I have done! And what have *you* done?' . . . The faces are in pictures and in portraits and on the covers of biographies. In common-rooms and banqueting halls, in stately homes, libraries, and bookshops, from monuments and in churches, literally thousands of faces seem to confront the visitor with the same everlasting questions." The accuracy of Schlaeger's phrase "literally thousands" is confirmed by Ann Thwaite's report that 2,164 biographies (that is, an average of more than forty a week) were published in Britain in 1990.[1]

Much the same situation prevails in the United States, as a visit to a bookstore of even moderate size demonstrates. A typical store (in this case, Books & Co., in Dayton, Ohio) helps to confirm Schlaeger's observations—and make Thwaite's number more credible. Located next to Bibles, the section devoted to biography fills eight floor-to-ceiling shelves with highly

---

1. Schlaeger, "Biography: Cult as Culture," in *The Art of Literary Biography,* ed. John Batchelor (Oxford: Clarendon, 1995), 63; Thwaite, "Starting Again: One of the Problems of the Biographer," in *The Art of Literary Biography,* ed. Batchelor, 205.

1

diverse contents. One shelf loaded with volumes about the British royal family is balanced by another reserved for the Kennedy family. Books about Lillian Hellman and Ernest Hemingway sit side by side, an enforced association both would have probably resisted in life; jacket photos of Whittaker Chambers and Leslie Abramson stare at each other across an aisle; Elie Wiesel and Rosie O'Donnell rub shoulders on a display table. Other volumes recount the lives of politicians, figure skaters, film stars, radio personalities, wealthy entrepreneurs, and retired generals.

But biographies are not confined to this specialized section of the store; generous complements of life stories appear everywhere. Literary criticism includes biographies of novelists, poets, essayists, and even a few literary critics. The sports section likewise contains lives of well-known athletes and coaches, living and dead, and the "true crime" division consists largely of the lives of notorious felons, the grislier their deeds the better. Biographies of composers, singers, pianists, conductors, dancers, film directors, actors, and others associated with the arts form a substantial part of the offerings in those sections, and volumes in a series called Lives of Notable Gay Men and Lesbians are housed, along with numerous memoirs, in the shelves devoted to gay and lesbian interests. Individual and collective biographies are an important component of the books grouped under the headings of African American and Native American culture. Prominent among the business books are the lives of the successful, whose stories trace their routes to wealth. Surely Samuel Smiles would be gratified to see the biographies of men and women such as Sam Walton and Mary Kay Ash, modern proof of the continuing efficacy of self-help. On the other side of the store, the areas stocked with books on history and war are so filled with the lives of individual men and women that the presiding deities of these sections could only be Emerson ("There is properly no history; only biography") and Carlyle ("History is the essence of innumerable biographies," or, more famously, "The history of the world is but the biography of great men").

The presence of these two nineteenth-century sages accords well with Schlaeger's feeling that all these published lives challenge their readers. The everlasting question he feels—"And what have *you* done?"—echoes the call to individual action offered so many times by Emerson, Carlyle, and their contemporaries. Eric Homberger and

John Charmley say that our continuing interest in biography suggests that this genre offers "at least the possibility, the hint of a surviving common culture."[2] This bookstore tour suggests more than a possibility, more than a hint. The unified self not only survives but positively thrives in contemporary biography, along with confidence in the ability of that self to act and to achieve. Postmodern doubts about agency and autonomy have had little impact on the practice of biography, particularly popular biography. That absence is noted with seeming chagrin by Schlaeger, who sees biography as fundamentally conservative in its loyalty to a "personality-oriented cultural mainstream."[3] This book, then, is dedicated to exploring points of convergence between Victorian and modern biography; it scrutinizes Victorian biography for precursors of trends familiar to turn-of-millennium readers, yet it also identifies recurrences of Victorian biographical practice in postmodern biography.

According to Richard Holmes, the two most successful biographies in English are Boswell's *Life of Samuel Johnson LLD* (1791), which has never been out of print, and Andrew Morton's *Diana: Her True Story* (1992), which sold two and a half million copies within three years of its publication.[4] Holmes's juxtaposition does indicate the enduring popularity of the form. To see a hint of a common culture in these two best-sellers might seem unlikely at first, particularly if we are to trace commonalities through the nineteenth century that separates them. Even without reference to publication dates, no one would immediately associate either book with Victorian biography; in their different ways, they seem worlds apart from the conventional image of the pair of black-bound, worshipful volumes crammed indiscriminately with heavily expurgated letters and diaries, the mode that prevailed roughly from Boswell until Lytton Strachey's *Eminent Victorians* (1918) made the emergence of modern biography possible. Although the descrip-

2. Homberger and Charmley, introduction to *The Troubled Face of Biography* (New York: St. Martin's Press, 1988), ix.

3. Schlaeger, "Biography," 63.

4. Holmes, "Biography: Inventing the Truth," in *The Art of Literary Biography,* ed. Batchelor, 15. Following the death of Princess Diana on August 31, 1997, she has been the subject of numerous additional biographies, including a brief one on *The British Monarchy,* the official Web site of the royal family <http://www.royal.gov.uk/family/diana.htm>.

tion is suspect, particularly in this crudely reductive form, it remains a familiar narrative describing the genre (see, for example, the entry on biography in *The Oxford Companion to English Literature*).[5] For at least the past quarter century, though, scholars have been demonstrating the many continuities between Victorian and contemporary biography. To reclaim Steven Marcus's phrase from Michel Foucault, we might well regard ourselves as "the 'other' Victorians" in the realm of biography, too.

Even superficially, nineteenth- and twentieth-century biographies increasingly look alike. Stuffed with corroborating materials, recent volumes have bulked up to resemble their Victorian ancestors. In the foreword to Ruth Hoberman's *Modernizing Lives,* A. O. J. Cockshut notes that the "impressionistic, and often unhistorical, sketches of Strachey and Virginia Woolf" have given way to "the biography dominated by documents, strong on facts, and wary of too much interpretation." That description sounds very much like Cockshut's own much earlier characterization of Victorian volumes, which he says reflect the period's "universal trust in documents." Those books are long, he explains, "because there is so much written evidence, and selective processes are suspect."[6] Robert Skidelsky's description of modern biographies is similar: "Truth is equated with length, with 'telling all,' with piling up detail on detail." However, he pursues the connection still further, arguing that scholarly biography is also becoming more "Victorian" in the way it approaches its subject. He claims that today's insistence on scholarship re-creates some of the economic conditions under which Victorian biographies were produced:

> Ironically, it is the requirements of scholarship, as much as anything else, which tethers contemporary biography to its Victorian ancestor. Original sources mean, in practice, the subject's private papers; the widow means the person or persons who control access to, and quotation from, those papers. Thus the contractual basis of the Victorian biography, in which the widow granted

5. Margaret Drabble, ed., *The Oxford Companion to English Literature*, 5th ed. (Oxford: Oxford University Press, 1985).

6. Cockshut, foreword to *Modernizing Lives: Experiments in English Biography, 1918–1939,* by Ruth Hoberman (Carbondale: Southern Illinois University Press, 1987), x; Cockshut, *Truth to Life: The Art of Biography in the Nineteenth Century* (New York: Harcourt Brace, 1974), 16.

the biographer access to family papers in return for his tact and discretion in their use, has been reinforced by the increased emphasis on "original research." There is also the prize to biographer and publisher alike for "first use" of original material. This in practice means as soon after the death of the subject as possible, when the pressure to be complimentary is also highest.[7]

Even when commercial pressures and the wishes of the "widow" play no overt role, modern biographies are shaped by many of the same forces as their earlier counterparts. The desire to provide exemplary lives, for example, underlies many a nineteenth- and twentieth-century publication. That purpose has been stated explicitly by many feminist biographers; even Liz Stanley, who complains of the uncritical practice of much feminist biography, accepts without demur the provision of "feminist heroes to stand alongside the more usual subjects of auto/biography" as an unquestioned goal of these works. Likewise, at a 1985 conference hosted by the University of East Anglia, a number of well-known biographers spoke of their work in terms that emphasize its didactic value. Michael Holroyd, for example, says that biographers "give the dead an opportunity of contributing to the living world" by serving as "examples of conduct." All possible candor is required if modern readers are not to "make ourselves unhappy by accepting impossible standards. . . . Allowing this truth to be posthumously given . . . may be as useful to posterity as donating kidneys and corneas." Similarly, Hugh Brogan asserts that biography can be "a profoundly civilising force" that rebukes historians, bigots, and "philistines of all sorts." At its best, it "can move us, amuse us, instruct us, and all in such a way that our sense of human solidarity is enhanced—it can even do this through the life of a monster, as Alan Bullock showed us in his book on Hitler."[8]

Not everyone seems happy with modern versions of this old function of biography. After acknowledging that biographers "are once

7. Skidelsky, "Only Connect: Biography and Truth," in *The Troubled Face of Biography,* ed. Homberger and Charmley, 8.

8. Stanley, *The Auto/biographical I: The Theory and Practice of Feminist Auto/ biography* (Manchester: Manchester University Press, 1992), 255; Holroyd, "How I Fell into Biography," in *The Troubled Face of Biography,* ed. Homberger and Charmley, 99–100; Brogan, "The Biographer's Chains," in *The Troubled Face of Biography,* ed. Homberger and Charmley, 111–12.

more in the business of writing exemplary lives," Skidelsky points to
what he sees as an important distinction:

> But now the example is the life itself, not what the life en-
> abled the person to achieve. Or, more precisely, the life *is* the
> achievement; what used to be called the achievement is now
> only one accompaniment, possible [*sic*] a minor one, of a style
> of living. Quite obviously on this criterion a much wider range
> of lives is opened up to biography, paucity of achievement in
> the traditional sense being no barrier to being written about;
> conversely, some hitherto biography-worthy subjects might find
> themselves "lifeless," because their (genuinely) blameless lives
> are no longer sufficiently exemplary to record; or because they
> imprudently failed to leave enough evidence of sexual or other
> unorthodoxy to make them suitable "role models" for the next
> generation.[9]

(In Skidelsky's reading, "And what have *you* done?" is evidently re-
configured as an uncomfortably provocative challenge.)

One need not accept Skidelsky's implicit attitude to acknowledge
his point about the wider range of lives now available in print and
their utility to previously silenced groups. However, using biography
to help define and legitimize groups of individuals is hardly a new
development of the identity politics of our own time. In a well-known
comment, Michel Foucault has asserted that modern homosexuality
was born in 1870: "the sodomite had been a temporary aberration;
the homosexual was now a species."[10] Biography played an important,
though circumspect, role in the emergence of this new species, and
life stories were central to the identification (both "scientific" and
personal) of homosexuality. One of the key Victorian figures in the
struggle to come to terms with this identity was John Addington
Symonds. At the end of his memoirs (written in 1889 but unpublished
until 1984), he briefly recapitulates his sexual history in the third person, concluding with this rhetorical question: "What is the meaning,
the lesson, the conclusion to be drawn from this biography?" In a note
appended to this passage in 1891, Symonds comments on his recent

9. Skidelsky, "Only Connect," 13.
10. Foucault, *The History of Sexuality,* vol. 1, *An Introduction,* trans. Robert
Hurley (New York: Pantheon, 1978), 43.

discovery of the autobiographies of "urnings" included in the work of German sexologists J. L. Casper, Carl Liman, Karl Heinrich Ulrichs, and Richard von Krafft-Ebing: "I . . . am now aware that my history is only one out of a thousand."[11] Although understated, Symonds's comment suggests something of the force this new awareness had on him; in even these brief case histories, the life itself may indeed have seemed an achievement to him. In 1892 he approached Havelock Ellis about the possibility of a volume on sexual inversion, and the two eventually decided to collaborate on the project. In addition to reviewing the current theories on the subject, they gathered case histories, calling on Edward Carpenter and Edith Lees (Ellis's wife) to obtain additional narratives. In *Sexual Inversion,* the book that was finally published in 1897, Symonds's own story appears as Case XVII.[12] Although abbreviated and narrowly focused, these biographies are clearly at the service of a larger agenda.

Works like *Sexual Inversion* were extremely rare and limited in circulation, but apologists of other sorts were much more common. The emergence of new professions, for example, called forth a number of biographical works that attempted, among other things, to gain recognition and respect for those fields. Paul Theerman's work with nineteenth-century biographies of scientists indicates the degree to which biographical materials were deliberately deployed to that end. In the political turmoil of the 1830s and 1840s, he writes, "scientists were self-consciously organizing and defining their public role." Among them was David Brewster, whose 1830 review of Charles Babbage's *Reflexions on the Decline of Science in England* contained this judgment: "Without expecting that any of our philosophers should be cabinet ministers or privy councilors or ambassadors, it might reasonably be supposed that, in a country like Great Britain, a variety of her public institutions would have furnished ample provisions for

11. *The Memoirs of John Addington Symonds,* ed. Phyllis Grosskurth (New York: Random House, 1984), 283, 281.

12. The collaboration was ended by Symonds's sudden death in 1893, and Ellis himself completed the book in 1895. Published in German in 1896, it was scheduled to appear in England in 1897 but was withdrawn and published later that year without Symonds's name. For an account of the genesis and reception of *Sexual Inversion,* see Phyllis Grosskurth, *Havelock Ellis: A Biography* (New York: Alfred A. Knopf, 1980), 172–90.

scientific men." Brewster's own biographical contributions might be seen as demonstrating scientists' fitness for public life. Among them are two dealing with a single figure: *The Life of Sir Isaac Newton* (1831) and *The Memoirs of the Life, Writings, and Discoveries of Sir Isaac Newton* (1855, 2 volumes). Between them, in 1841, came *The Martyrs of Science,* which included lives of Kepler, Tycho, and Galileo. The title alone suggests much about the goals of the volume in elevating the status of science and scientists.[13]

In other fields biography played a similar part in debates over the function of intellectuals in shaping their culture. Examining the emergence of history as a discipline, David Amigoni outlines the way J. R. Seeley used biography to increase its acceptance and enlarge its influence. The Regius Chair of History at Cambridge after 1869, Seeley believed history should be the foundation for teaching those who would become leaders, and he recognized the value of popularized lives of statesmen in preparing the larger public to accept "the authority of this knowledge."[14] That impulse shaped such works as Seeley's *The Life and Times of Stein* (1879) and the series called Twelve English Statesmen, published by Macmillan (1888–1905) under the general editorship of John Morley. Much the same may be said of Macmillan's English Men of Letters series, also under Morley's editorship, and of the many individual lives of artists, to take only two additional examples. Although every one of these books celebrated genuine accomplishments, they also legitimized the groups to which these individuals belonged.

Biographies of political figures were by no means limited to the sort of elected statesmen connected with the Macmillan series. The royal family was often the subject of such works, sometimes the authors of them as well. In early 1868, Queen Victoria published *Leaves from the Journal of Our Life in the Highlands,* which, in Stanley Weintraub's words, "fleshed out laconic old issues of the *Court Circular* for a public always eager for trivia about how royalty really lived."

13. Theerman, "National Images of Science: British and American Views of Scientific Heroes in the Early Nineteenth Century," in *Beyond the Two Cultures: Essays on Science, Technology, and Literature,* ed. Joseph W. Slade and Judith Yaross Lee (Ames: Iowa State University Press, 1990), 261.

14. Amigoni, *Victorian Biography: Intellectuals and the Ordering of Discourse* (New York: St. Martin's Press, 1993), 39.

That publication proved useful in shoring up the queen's waning popularity, her continuing isolation having raised questions about her role as monarch. Weintraub characterizes the book as a "public-relations triumph at a time when the Queen needed one." A sequel, *More Leaves . . .*, was published in February 1884. First printed in an edition of ten thousand, it sold rapidly, Mudie's rental libraries taking fifteen hundred copies, and new editions of five thousand copies were soon required. Dedicated "especially to the memory of my devoted personal attendant and faithful friend John Brown," the publication had some adverse consequences as well. The frequent mention of Brown renewed gossip about his role in the queen's life, particularly the speculation that he had grown enormously rich in her service, and there were also rumors that Brown had left a diary that would soon be published.[15]

Some earlier publications had been even more damaging. In early 1870, when the Prince of Wales was subpoenaed to testify in the Mordaunt divorce case, public attention was brought to the royal family's lifestyle, particularly the prince's extravagance. Later that year, *The Coming K—*, a "biographical" pamphlet claiming to be an exposé of the private life of the Prince of Wales, appeared in print, drawing upon "apocryphal stories current in Paris and in the London underworld"; furthermore, its deliberate parody of *Idylls of the King* counterpointed the mythic with the disappointingly real, contrasting ideal models of monarchy with tawdry practice.[16] Another pamphlet published at the same time (called *What Does She Do With It?*) renewed questions about the queen's reclusiveness, this time alleging that she was living like a miser and hoarding vast amounts of money.

A similar combination of prurient and political interests can be seen in a full-scale 1875 American biography of an English monarch. The full title of John Banvard's book hints at sensational exposures to come: *The Private Life of a King: Embodying the Suppressed Memoirs of the Prince of Wales, Afterwards George IV, of England.* Following

15. Weintraub, *Victoria: An Intimate Biography* (New York: Dutton, 1987), 383, 393–94.

16. Philip Magnus, *King Edward the Seventh* (New York: Dutton, 1964), 109. For a discussion of the parody, see John R. Reed, "Teasing the King," in *The Arthurian Revival: Essays on Form, Tradition, and Transformation,* ed. Debra N. Mancoff (New York: Garland, 1994), 61–71.

the author's name on the title page is the assurance that his testimony is supported "with corroborative authorities, drawn from the secret archives of the Chartists, and authentic documents in the British Museum." Banvard's real intent is suggested in the dedication to his "Southern fellow citizens . . . who once expressed a wish to be governed by a British Prince, in preference to submitting to the generous rule of our Federal Union." The preface spells out still more plainly Banvard's desire to use the life of George IV to show the inferiority of the monarchical system.[17] Still, there are enough hints and innuendo about the monarch's morals to engage the reader's interest on more than the political level. Despite Banvard's euphemisms and his serious purpose, it is not so far to today's interest in the royal family and their love lives, an interest that may also be turned to similar political ends.

Celebrity biography is, of course, a form of public gossip and as such carries the multivalent significance of gossip itself. As Patricia Meyer Spacks notes, gossip can range from intimate conversations that reinforce community to malicious attempts to shatter reputations to mere idle talk. The boundaries among these categories can be permeable. Thus, two or three intimate friends may deepen friendship by sharing interpretations of others' lives; but such acts can also function as empowerment, serving as "a resource for the subordinated (anyone can *talk;* with a trusted listener, anyone can say anything), a crucial means of self-expression, a crucial form of solidarity." Gossipy biographies about royals or other privileged celebrities, moreover, even the balance of power between reader and biographical subject, since, "as Roland Barthes has pointed out, the idea of being talked about implies threat, regardless of what specifically is said. 'Gossip reduces the other to *he/she*' . . . objectifying" the other.[18] The threat of lavishly public gossip, then, is a means of policing and constraining behavior—true not only of twentieth-century media celebrities whose lives are closely followed by gossip columnists and circumscribed by the threat of tell-all biographies that expose hitherto secret failings, but also of Victorian and twentieth-century royalty, biographies of whom

17. Banvard, *The Private Life of a King: Embodying the Suppressed Memoirs of the Prince of Wales, Afterwards George IV, of England* (New York: Literary and Art Publishing Co., 1875).

18. Spacks, *Gossip* (New York: Alfred A. Knopf, 1985), 5, 33–34.

mark out the limits of behavior acceptable to the reading public. Gossip's role of sustaining community, however, may be fulfilled by another form of biography—the eulogistic—which can allow reader and biographer to join in lauding values fundamental to a given community.

Today, such a configuration of the personal and political is often evident in the field of African American studies, which has grown steadily over the past thirty years. Sojourner Truth, Thurgood Marshall, Margaret Morgan Lawrence, Elijah Muhammad, Jervis Anderson, Martin Luther King Jr., Louis Farrakhan, and Willie Brown are only a few of the many African American figures whose lives have been examined recently in the larger context of race in American society. Of particular interest is *Thirteen Ways of Looking at a Black Man,* in which Henry Louis Gates Jr. employs the conventions of the collective biography to accomplish two ends: presenting the "narratives of ascent" of seven men, he simultaneously highlights their success and questions the monolithic identity of the "black man." A more old-fashioned, single-minded didactic intent is evident in such collective biographies as Sara Lawrence-Lightfoot's *I've Known Rivers: Lives of Loss and Liberation,* Kareem Abdul-Jabbar's *Black Profiles in Courage: A Legacy of African-American Achievement,* Martha Ward Plowden's *Olympic Black Women,* and Jessie Carney Smith's *Powerful Black Women.*[19] In volumes such as these, "And what have *you* done?" is transformed into an invitation to participate in the success they illustrate.

That same Victorian question echoes in many of the biographies influenced by the feminist movements of recent years. Homberger and Charmley associate much of this work with the nineteenth-century aim of providing exemplary lives, explicitly asking, "Who said that Victorian biography could never make a comeback?" However, their description of feminist biography is regrettably reductive: "feminist biography consists largely in the presentation of 'role models' among 'our foremothers, our sisters, our heroines.'" Their source for the

19. Gates, *Thirteen Ways of Looking at a Black Man* (New York: Random House, 1997); Lawrence-Lightfoot, *I've Known Rivers: Lives of Loss and Liberation* (New York: Penguin, 1994); Abdul-Jabbar, *Black Profiles in Courage: A Legacy of African-American Achievement* (New York: Morrow, 1996); Plowden, *Olympic Black Women* (Gretna: Pelican, 1996); Smith, *Powerful Black Women* (Detroit: Visible Ink, 1996).

phrase is a book review in *Feminist Studies,* from which they also quote Elizabeth Kamarck Minnich's statement that biographies of women by women "bring back to us . . . women we can now admire as friends."[20] Although shared anxieties and aspirations are important to women seeking wider public roles, as they are to the formation of African American or gay and lesbian identities, the singleness of purpose evident in such comments does suggest the danger inherent in focusing too exclusively on a single aspect of a subject's life. Addressing precisely this issue, Liz Stanley has warned biographers of the danger of simplifying contradictory accounts of their subjects, urging them to avoid the temptation of "playing God" and presenting the "real" Virginia Woolf, for example, instead of "accepting that all these competing truths and selves may be true." Stanley was not the first to be concerned with this tendency toward oversimplification. As early as 1980 Lynn Z. Bloom was warning of these dangers, which can distort the complexities of biographical subjects and homogenize female experiences. Examining recent studies of Elizabeth Barrett Browning as an illustration, Bloom was particularly critical of Mary Jane Lupton's work: "More from wishful thinking than from objective evidence, in feminist Lupton's procrustean view, Elizabeth . . . is seen as a closet feminist."[21]

A number of subsequent feminist biographies have been more successful in examining the contradictory motives and fissured personalities that characterize modern conceptions of subjectivity along with the gender norms and social constraints that have shaped women's lives. For example, Margaret Forster's 1988 biography of Elizabeth Barrett Browning notes the startling contrast between her liberatory politics and her treatment of her maid Elizabeth Wilson. (When documentary evidence proved inadequate to pursue the issue further in a biographical study, Forster turned to fiction, producing the thought-provoking novel *Lady's Maid*.)[22] To take only one other instance, the work of Jenny Uglow, particularly her biographies of George Eliot

20. Homberger and Charmley, introduction, xi–xii.
21. Stanley, *The Auto/biographical I,* 11; Bloom, "Popular and Super-Pop Biographies: Definitions and Distinctions," *Biography* 3 (1980): 230.
22. Forster, *Elizabeth Barrett Browning: A Biography* (London: Chatto and Windus, 1988) and *Lady's Maid* (London: Chatto and Windus, 1990).

and Elizabeth Gaskell, presents complex female subjects who can be neatly categorized only by distorting or ignoring the contradictory elements in their lives and thought. Part of the Virago/Pantheon Pioneers series, Uglow's volume on Eliot begins with an explicit refusal to pigeonhole her subject: "Eliot can never be drawn easily into the feminist net, whatever powerful currents we may sense beneath the surface of her novels." Informed by feminist principles but not limited by them, Uglow's comprehensive study of Gaskell contains an even more richly detailed examination of the "competing truths and selves" to be discovered in her subject.[23]

Still, all biographers surely must face the temptation of "playing God" or at least engaging in what Victoria Glendenning calls "author-theology." Although writing of her concern that the desire to find role models among writers of the past sometimes results in distortion, Glendenning issues a wry warning that extends beyond the life stories of writers: "We are all, as biographers, in the business of ancestor-worship, even when we demystify and demythologise."[24] At times it may seem that modern biographies do not so much demythologize lives as they *re*mythologize them for our own needs. That may account in part for our habit of returning repeatedly to the same biographical subjects. Holmes suggests that certain lives "hold particular mirrors up to each succeeding generation of biographers, almost as the classical myths were endlessly retold by the Greek dramatists, to renew their own versions of contemporary identity." The retelling need not be heroic, particularly if the age does not see itself as heroic. Homberger and Charmley see the "unmistakable brand of our culture" in our biographies: "we must have T. E. Lawrence raped and tormented, and F. Scott Fitzgerald asking Hemingway to have a look and tell him if his penis was adequate for manly duties with Zelda."[25]

In rewriting lives to fit our own needs, our culture follows a pattern familiar in Victorian (and earlier) biography. The case of Byron provides an especially telling example. The subject of some thirty

23. Uglow, *George Eliot* (New York: Pantheon–Random House, 1987), 2, and *Elizabeth Gaskell: A Habit of Stories* (New York: Farrar Straus Giroux, 1993).

24. Victoria Glendenning, "Lies and Silences," in *The Troubled Face of Biography*, ed. Homberger and Charmley, 61.

25. Holmes, "Biography," 19; Homberger and Charmley, introduction, xi.

biographies between 1801 and 1838,[26] Byron was characterized in a variety of ways, ranging from the generous, pious aristocrat of the anonymous *Narrative of Lord Byron's Voyage to Corsica and Sardinia* (1824) to the aristocratic seducer of John Mitford's *The Private Life of Lord Byron: Comprising His Voluptuous Amours . . . with Various Ladies of Rank and Fame* (1836). Such patently fictional accounts were only partially displaced with the appearance of Thomas Moore's "official" *Letters and Journals of Lord Byron with Notices of His Life* (1830). Later biographies called forth repeated reevaluations of the poet's life, among them Edward John Trelawney's *Recollections of the Last Days of Shelley and Byron* (1858) and Harriet Beecher Stowe's *Lady Byron Vindicated* (1870). The latter was particularly significant in making public allegations of Byron's incest, thus renewing and intensifying earlier discussions of Byron's sexual behavior. Stowe's work spurred further controversy—and further biographies. Even before the publication of Stowe's book, the ongoing talk about Byron had an impact beyond its conversational interest. In *Byron and the Victorians,* Andrew Elfenbein has demonstrated how some Victorian writers deployed the "life" of Byron in one of the master narratives of the era, the bildungsroman that showed the growth of the subject away from "a youthful, immature Byronic phase to a sober, adult 'Victorian' phase."[27] That narrative was enacted not only in those writers' fictions but in their public lives and careers; in effect, the remythologizing of the poet's life facilitated these other life stories.

Elfenbein's work grows out of his recognition of "Byron the celebrity," a term that denotes not a real person but a figure capable of being defined in various ways, though available "only through the marketing of cultural goods." While this description suggests the twentieth century, Elfenbein argues that celebrity originates in Victorian capitalism,[28] and his analysis of this nineteenth-century phenomenon points to still another important continuity between Victorian and modern biography. If "Byron the celebrity" indicates a new category in the nineteenth

---

26. Joseph W. Reed, *English Biography in the Early Nineteenth Century, 1801–1838* (New Haven: Yale University Press, 1966), 22.

27. Elfenbein, *Byron and the Victorians,* Cambridge Studies in Nineteenth-Century Literature and Culture, vol. 4 (Cambridge: Cambridge University Press, 1995), 76–77, 89.

28. Ibid., 47.

century, celebrity itself has become an institution today. Although one does not usually think of Byron and John Wayne together, it is instructive to set *Byron and the Victorians* beside Garry Wills's *John Wayne's America: The Politics of Celebrity.* Wills describes his book as "the story of a mythical figure in a make-believe industry," and his reference to the industry that produced this figure points up the link: like Byron the celebrity, John Wayne must be seen as cultural goods produced by (and available only through) the market. Wills traces the careful, deliberate development of this mythical figure, examining the way "minor myths" about Wayne furthered the "larger legend";[29] Wills's explicit concentration on Wayne's image suggests the book might aptly be subtitled "the biography of a simulacrum." Although other celebrities may not have the same degree of impact on "real life" as Wayne, their celebrity is manufactured and marketed—if the two activities can, in fact, be separated—in the same way. Celebrity biography affords consumers an opportunity to boost their social standing by associating themselves with the subjects of those biographies. In doing so, they continue an established Victorian pattern.

The essays in this volume, then, take up issues of Victorian biography and also key issues in twentieth-century practice that discernibly emerge from the prior century. The collection opens with contributions by two distinguished biographers. According to P. N. Furbank, the continuities between Victorian and modern biography are grounded in the craftlike nature of biography. As a craftsperson, the writer of a biography is denied certain freedoms available to the artist, that is, to the writer of fiction or even of autobiography. Despite that seeming limitation, biography is an intensely personal form of writing that is as much about the author's relationship to his or her subject (a form of trying on the subject's personality, Furbank speculates) as about the biographer's subject.

Michael Holroyd, another of the foremost biographers of the second half of the twentieth century, examines the divergent conceptions of biography of Lytton Strachey and Gerald Brenan. Although Strachey's practice of biography is usually regarded as iconoclastic, even revolutionary, and the beginning of "modern" biography, Brenan situates

---

29. Wills, *John Wayne's America: The Politics of Celebrity* (New York: Simon and Schuster, 1997), 31.

it "on the border-line between the new and the old." In " 'On the Border-line between the New and the Old': Bloomsbury, Biography, and Gerald Brenan," Holroyd demonstrates the affinities between Strachey's various biographical volumes and earlier work, pointing out that Brenan, too, was in many ways as much a traditionalist as a modernist.

Among Strachey's contributions to "new" biography was his emphasis on the inner, psychological life of his subjects and the centrality of that life to his subjects' accomplishments. As Holroyd points out, Strachey "smuggled deviant sexual behavior into our national heritage." Although Holroyd's remark extends beyond life writing, that heritage is particularly evident in biography. If Strachey's examinations of the impact of his subjects' sexuality on their lives and work were necessarily circumspect, his heirs have been able to approach that topic much more directly. Nowhere is that more evident than in biographies of Benjamin Britten. Following the composer's death in 1976, biographers have increasingly addressed the connections between Britten's life—particularly his homosexuality—and his music. In her essay, Mary C. Francis investigates the collaboration of Britten and E. M. Forster on *Billy Budd* (1951), arguing that the collaboration was a charged one despite each artist's admiration for the other and their shared enthusiasm for the project. Looking at these men's differing conceptions of homosexual love—and thus their necessarily diverging views of Melville's novella—Francis demonstrates that for Forster the opera became an opportunity to portray a positive homosexual relationship after a lifetime of stifling his desire to do so in his fiction, whereas Britten saw in the Vere-Billy-Claggart triangle the destructive power of love. This exposition of biographical elements not only sheds new light on the sometimes troubled collaboration of these two major twentieth-century artists but also helps account for some of the ambiguities that are part of the resulting score.

Julie F. Codell, in "Victorian Artists' Family Biographies: Hybridity, Professionalism, the Marketplace, and the Artist's Body," discusses the way biographies written by artists' families present their subjects in word and image. These works emphasize the social, domestic life of the artist rather than the professional life, using photographs of the artists and their studios, homes, and work to construct a normative Victorian figure that might be used in promoting sales of the artist's work. Codell's work demonstrates clearly that the "PR bio" is a Victorian invention, if one more readily associated with the era of late capitalism in the twentieth century—in part because the icon of lofty, genteel, and "manly" Victorian artist was so successfully reproduced and disseminated.

While Codell examines a wide range of Victorian artists' biographies, Debra N. Mancoff turns to the late work of a single painter, Edward Burne-Jones. She argues that many twentieth-century biographical interpretations of Burne-Jones's work are spurious, not because biographical analysis is necessarily suspect, however. If Codell shows the danger of taking life stories at face value, Mancoff shows the dangers of ignoring biographical documentation, which is at odds with some of the motives attributed to Burne-Jones in undertaking his late paintings. Mancoff thus suggests the continuing validity of the Victorian—and modern—insistence on careful analysis of primary documentation produced during the biographical subject's lifetime.

Our penultimate essay is at once an enactment of biography and a culminating link between Victorian and modern biography in the form of a biographical exploration of the postcolonial experience. Key contributions to understanding identity formations in the late twentieth century have come from theoretical work by Edward Said, Gayatry Spivak, Ashis Nandy, and others who have written on colonial legacies and postcolonial subjectivities. Anantha Sudhaker Babbili's meditation on his own passage from India to America, and of his family from Hindu faith to membership in the Anglican Church, at once answers to late Victorian celebrations of General Gordon and moves beyond the colonial-postcolonial dyad to suggest new ways of enunciating the postcolonial condition embedded in the genre of the life story.

The volume's concluding pages then provide a biographical overview of the scholar to whom this book is dedicated, Mary Lago, whose own work brings together so many of the concerns raised in this book.

P. N. Furbank

The Craftlike Nature of Biography

Ours is a flourishing age for biography; indeed people tend to say it is getting the edge over fiction. So this might be the moment for sober reflection on biography as a genre. Let me start with a suggestion that, if a shade drastic, could prove helpful. It is that we should recognize that biography is a craft, not an art.

For one thing, people come to a biography as they might to a car or a teapot, expecting certain things and likely to be disgruntled if they do not find them. A car is expected to have a steering wheel and a lighting system, a teapot is expected to pour, and these demands limit the freedom of their makers. Accordingly, fashions in the crafts change at a quite different, and much slower, rate than in the arts. In certain respects the shape of a spoon reached its perfection two centuries ago, and a modern spoon made on this pattern does not strike us as particularly quaint or outmoded. Similarly, a biography is expected to supply dates; information about family trees and about birth, marriage, and death; a chronological progression; and various other practicalities. Readers and critics, further, tend to speak, in Boileauesque fashion, as though there were "rules" as to how a biography should be written. They certainly would not do so nowadays in regard to a poem.

Accordingly, despite various superficial differences, a modern literary biography does not seem at bottom so very unlike a Victorian "Life and Letters." John Forster's *Dickens* does not strike the reader as positively archaic. Indeed it is not too easy to imagine an avant-garde biography, or at least a successful one. Modern biographers, like their predecessors, strive to provide their readers with what they expect and want, and they think of this not as pandering but as a point of honor. Of course, it takes away a little of their glamour as "artists"; but, after all, it is no degradation to be of the company of Chippendale and Cellini, Daimler and Lobb.[1]

It should be remembered, moreover, that what is true of biography is also true of history, which is equally craftlike. In fact, of course, the two overlap. For a historical biography is not essentially different in genre from a literary biography, or from a religious or political one; and what is true of a biography is true of all kinds of historical writing, that is, that the historian is not a free agent, able to mold his or her material just as he or she would wish. Whatever the mode or school of the history—and the gulf between a Ranke and a Macaulay, a Braudel and a Puret is pretty enormous—it is forced to respect the contingent and the accidental, the randomness of the archive and the obstinate arbitrariness of "what happened."

The point grows very clear when one thinks about historical narrative. There was a controversy on the topic not so long ago. In an article in *Past and Present*, Lawrence Stone claimed that historians, having for fifty years deserted historical storytelling in favor of structural analysis and the like, were beginning to grow disillusioned and to see virtues in the narrative method again.[2] It was not a very convincing article, for Stone had not given any serious thought to what a literary narrative is. Had he done so, he would have seen that a work of history, whether by Gibbon or Motley or Trevor-Roper or Simon Schama, can be called a "narrative" only by way of metaphor. For literary narratives are what historical "narratives" would like to be but signally cannot be—exemplary systems of causation. They are to be judged according to the infrangibility, subtlety, and profundity of their demonstration of what led to what. Now, obviously, this is possible only because a storyteller or novelist, unlike a historian, is free to invent his or her materials: he or she is exempted from the

1. The celebrated London bootmaker.
2. Stone, "The Revival of Narrative: Reflections on a New Old History," *Past and Present* 85 (November 1979): 3–24.

duty to report certain things simply because they in fact happened. In a successful narrative, as Roland Barthes once remarked, *post hoc* should be equivalent to *propter hoc,* and this would be a quite fatal aspiration for a historian.

The biographer is in good company, then, and need not be too resentful at my rule (about being a craftsperson rather than an artist). But anyway the rule is not quite an iron one, and there is one biography at least that breaks it. I mean Boswell's *Johnson.* It is impossible to refuse the word *art* to this work, and the reason is significant. It is because Boswell was, at least some of the time, actually creating his own material. I do not mean in the sense of inventing it, as a novelist does, but of causing it to happen, as when, for instance, he deliberately engaged Johnson in conversations, such as a famous one on predestination, which he knew would produce some intense reaction. Maybe, for all he knew, it would be a furious telling-off; but, artistically speaking, that would be a gain too.

The point at stake is artistic freedom, the freedom that a poet or a novelist takes for granted but that is normally denied to a biographer as to a historian. It would hardly be questioned that an autobiography may be high art, and this would be a function of the same freedom. An autobiography is permitted to approach its subject from any angle, to be governed entirely by a theme or a thesis, to be selective to the point of losing all resemblance to a biography. No practical or utilitarian considerations dictated that Sartre should give his biography *Les Mots* the shape that he did; and it is a strange reflection that some have attacked this magnificent work on the grounds that friends or relatives of Sartre tell a different story about him. I suppose a biographer of Sartre might do so too. This gives us an insight, not so much into the relativity of truth, as into the theory of genres.

Rousseau's *Confessions,* the only work of Rousseau's that I can manage to think a masterpiece, is another instructive case in point. It is governed by a plot, of a profound and altogether original nature. He is, he says, providing the reader with two separate subjects: the self that he was given by nature, and the self that he forged for himself. By nature, he tells us, he was idle, a liver-in-the moment, incapable of planning evil but prone to momentary temptation—so that the vice most natural to him was theft. When, however, after a revelation, he became a writer, he had to become "another man"—a most impressive figure, austere and full of stern moral effort, all very ancient-Roman. This was complicated by the fact that, or so he claimed, his close friend Diderot saddled him with a "hard" manner of writing that did not really come naturally to him. Thus he fully realized himself as a writer only when he had escaped from Paris and from the society of the *salons;* and, with perfect consistency, when he felt his career as a writer was at an end, he reverted to his old cheerfully idle and hedonistic self. This plot, whether true to life or not, is a work of genius, and is not of a kind that a biography could allow itself.

The point about artistic freedom came home to me recently in regard to Proust. A friend of mine said he could not understand Charles Swann's marriage to Odette: had Swann not fallen out of love with her by that time? was she not a shallow and ignorant creature, without a thought in her head, etc., etc.? It was a very reasonable worry, yet it seemed to me, and still seems, to be based on a wrong assumption—namely, that Proust had the duties of a biographer toward Swann. Better, surely, to say that "Swann married" belongs to a different novel from "Swann in Love": one in which, according to the Balzac system that Proust so much admired, he would reappear in a relatively minor role and be seen from a different angle. There would, evidently, be much that could be said about how Swann got married, and a biographer would feel obliged to say it. The freedom to profit artistically by not saying it was reserved for the avant-garde novelist.

My general thesis has, perhaps, some implications for the relations between biographer and subject. Let us think for a moment of literary biography. A literary biographer is a writer, just as his or her subject is, and this is bound to raise problems of envy and rivalry. How will his or her own prose strike the reader, when cheek by jowl with the subject's? It is a disturbing thought; and what a literary biographer has to avoid, at all costs, is competitiveness. Let a biographer of Oscar Wilde not indulge in dazzling witticisms; let a biographer of Stevenson not write racy prose.

It once struck me that the right model for the biographer might be a trainer. Here would be a very happy professional relationship. A boxer's trainer knows more about the champion, in some ways, than he does himself: his weight problems, his woman problems, his prefight neuroses, and the like. It is professional knowledge, intimate knowledge that he is paid to acquire, and having it need not entail the slightest embarrassment.

I think indeed this would be a good model, but only one to aspire to, not to hope of attaining. For a biographer is involved, more deeply than the trainer. I doubt if, during one's lifetime, one should write more than two or three biographies, of the detailed life-and-letters kind. To do more would begin to seem like promiscuity. I do not mean on grounds of loyalty, but for a more personal reason. For the biographer will in fact be writing, not so much about so-and-so, the famous novelist, explorer, or politician, as about himself or herself as so-and-so—will, that is to say, be trying out a new personality. He or she may not realize this till later, but the knowledge eventually seeps through and is hard to deny.

My theory that biography is a craft, not an art, is not contradicted by this, for success in a craft is a deeply personal affair. It is out of the depths of a personality and an individual sensibility that any craft-masterpiece, a Renaissance saltcellar or a good biography, springs; it is from here that it gets its coherence and livingness.

If readers and critics are allowed to have "rules" about biography writing, it must not be supposed they extend very far. They will have no bearing on what the biographer shall treat as significant in the subject's life, and this can have unexpected answers. In expansive works like Richard Ellmann's *James Joyce* or Ray Monk's *Ludwig Wittgenstein* the emphasis sometimes falls in odd places, but always, in some not obvious way, with perfect relevance. What one is describing here is a personal relationship.

One feels like quoting, though it is not quite the same thing, or rather it is a huge exaggeration of the same thing, from Thomas Carlyle's extraordinary tribute to Boswell:

> And now behold the worthy Bozzy, so prepossessed and held back by nature and by art, fly nevertheless like iron to its magnet, whither his better genius called! You may surround the iron and the magnet with what enclosures and encumbrances you please,—with wood, with rubbish, with brass: it matters not, the two feel each other, they struggle restlessly towards each other, they *will* be together. The iron may be a Scottish

squirelet, full of gulosity and "gigmanity"; the magnet an English plebeian, and moving rag-and-dust mountain, coarse, proud, irascible, imperious: nevertheless, behold how they embrace, and inseparably cleave to one another![3]

It is painful, of course, when the biographical relationship goes wrong, as it can do so easily. The temptation of possessiveness can be strong; and once let the idea take hold that the subject of the biography can do no wrong, that he or she needs to be excused all failures and defended against all enemies, and madness has crept in. The next thing will be vendettas: against hostile critics, perhaps, or worse, against someone—some Judas—in the subject's own entourage. A biographer needs very regular habits of soul-searching.

Then how nightmarish if one were to discover, halfway through writing a biography, that one found the subject detestable or unbearable. I have heard that this happened to a biographer of Sinclair Lewis, when many hundred pages were still to be written. I do not know how it all turned out, and I am not sure that I want to know.

As for biographers of the dirt-dishing or "fearless exposure" school, I wonder how they feel on looking back on their careers? One seems to picture them surrounded by bloodstained heaps of maimed novelists and slain poets, as in those paintings of eighteenth-century Portuguese monarchs, posed beside the spoils of their day's battue. It is an uncharming vision.

But to return to the "personal" quality of biography writing. It is for me an argument against multiple-author biographies—I mean, the kind where parts of the story are told by one author and other parts by others. The authors (a whole string of them) of the Voltaire Foundation's enormous, five-volume *Voltaire en son temps* (1988–1994) are a most distinguished band; but the fruit of their labors, though it tells one immensely about the eighteenth century, is not, one feels, a biography so much as a magnificent tomb. The man is somehow no longer there—as we used to be told, though wrongly, was also true of his other tomb, in the Pantheon.

3. Carlyle, "Boswell's Life of Johnson," in *Critical and Miscellaneous Essays* (1899; rpt. New York: AMS Press, 1969), 3:71. First published in *Fraser's Magazine*, no. 28 (1832).

What is missing, in fact, is not so much a man as a story. The point is, I think, important. The meaningfulness of a successful biography inheres in the story that the biographer has made out of the subject's life. A biographer is not a bard or a ballad maker, employed to embroider an already existing tale or myth. He or she is, on the contrary, employed to create a tale. Now this is work for a single person; it cannot really be done cooperatively. The point comes home to one with the multiple-author biography of D. H. Lawrence, commissioned by the Cambridge University Press. The author of the first volume, John Worthen, discussed the theory behind this enterprise at length, and much to his credit. To have three different people write the life would, he said, be "an explicit (even dramatic) acknowledgment that, however important the continuities, the Lawrence of the last years (for example) is so different from the 19-year-old who visited the Haggs Farm, that it sometimes seems only by accident that they share the same name." The book was, he said, to be "a new kind of biography," avoiding "deterministic" hindsight and the "genetic fallacy" (that is, explanation by origins).[4] Multiple authorship aimed to prevent the story line being rigged to serve a single interpretation.

I am inclined to think the reasoning of this is wrong in several ways. For one thing, the point about the different "Lawrences"—which may have some truth in it—would surely best be conveyed, indeed could only satisfactorily be conveyed, through the lens of a *single* consciousness? But more essentially, what is implied—in those references to "deterministic" hindsight and the "genetic fallacy"—is a distrust of story. It is no surprise, then, that this first volume at least, though full of absorbing, and often quite new and surprising, information, suffers from a lack of story. There is a kind of deltalike or running-into-the-sand effect, so that one loses the sense of where one is going. According to Worthen's criteria, of course, this should be good, should free us from the hegemony of a preconceived pattern or interpretation. But what this overlooks is that to lose story is to lose meaning: the meaning of a biography lies in its story.

What multiple authorship also seems to encourage, in practice, is an ambition to make the biography "complete," or at least as complete as

---

4. Worthen, *D. H. Lawrence: The Early Years, 1885–1912* (Cambridge: Cambridge University Press, 1991), xiv.

possible. This must mean a rather mechanical kind of completeness, because in any other sense "completeness" would be a meaningless concept; and with Worthen's volume it leads to what, to my mind, is a wrong and quite misguided practice—I mean, drawing upon fiction for biographical purposes. "I shall quote a good deal from *Mr. Noon,*" writes Worthen; "a biography of DHL which did not draw from it would be absurd." Even more thoroughly he quarries *Sons and Lovers.* The principle seems to be that, when something in *Sons and Lovers* is confirmed by real-life evidence, the biographer has a duty to cite this fictional version and incorporate it into his narrative; but, further, when real-life evidence about something is lacking but a fictional version is at hand, it should be given, biographically speaking, the benefit of the doubt. Thus, apropos of Lawrence's father's emotions upon the death of his beloved son Ernest, we read: "In the absence of any knowledge of Arthur Lawrence's feelings, it is appropriate to cite the reaction of Mr Morel in *Sons and Lovers* after the death of his son William; it may even be authentically Arthur Lawrence's."[5] But what if it were not Arthur Lawrence's, what if Arthur Lawrence had felt something altogether different? The biography would have incorporated a falsity, maybe with quite damaging effects. Biography can have a truth, and fiction can have a "truth," but the area between them is a no-man's-land into which, I would hold, one has no right to stray.

I have been thinking, mainly, about the leisurely, chatty, detailed kind of biography. There are, of course, also "Brief Lives," in the Plutarch, or Aubrey, or Samuel Johnson style, not to mention the ones in the *Dictionary of National Biography.* They form a large and important subject, though one I shall not discuss here. As for the ample, comprehensive style of biography, it would seem that its natural climate has been Britain, or at least Anglo-Saxondom. France, which has magnificent memorists, has never been much interested in biography (nor till very recently did she discover the index, a fact which may not be unrelated). One ponders why this should be, and I have a mild suggestion.

Let us consider the very sinister character that Fielding, in *The Life of Mr. Jonathan Wild the Great,* has given to the "biographer" who

5. Ibid., 382, 99.

tells Wild's story. "Before we enter on this great work," announced this biographer, "we must endeavor to remove some errors of opinion which mankind have, by the disingenuity of writers, contracted":

> For these, from their fear of contradicting the obsolete and ab-
> surd doctrines of a set of simple fellows called, in derision,
> sages or philosophers, have endeavoured as much as possible
> to confound the ideas of greatness and goodness, whereas no
> two things can possibly be more distinct from each other: for
> greatness consists in bringing all manner of mischief on mankind,
> and goodness in removing it from them.

It seems accordingly, he says, very unlikely that the same person should possess both qualities, and yet writers often make their "great" heroes the compliment of goodness into the bargain. They report, for instance, how Alexander, having scattered ruin and desolation over an entire empire, benevolently refrained from cutting the throat of an old woman and raping her daughters, "but was content with only undoing them." He hopes, he says, his reader will have the justice to admit that, in his life of Wild, he has not made this mistake, has nowhere treated the smallest spark of goodness in Wild as anything but a meanness and a sad blemish on his greatness.[6]

"Greatness," *gloire,* still tended in Fielding's day to be an idea associated with France, with the France of the Grand Monarch Louis XIV. It will be remembered how Fielding's disciple Thackeray, who inherited his outlook on this subject, drew a malicious set of pictures of the bald, toothless, potbellied Grand Monarch as he was when he got up, before his valet had got him dressed. "Greatness" calls for eulogy, and Fielding's imaginary biographer is evidently a professional panegyrist. But then, the eulogy, and in particular the speech a French Academician has to make about the previous occupant of his *fauteuil,* is a complex literary form, no mere sycophantic flummery in the style of pious obituaries or "authorized" royal lives. You may indeed have to be an Academician to understand these *éloges* fully, and they are often full of covert malice, but some have become literary classics.

---

6. *The Works of Henry Fielding* (Philadelphia: John D. Morris, 1902), 5:3–4.

The *Academie* and the *eloge* have colored French literary life, even for those who have despised them. (French writers have always maintained a haughtier public persona than English ones; they have had a stronger sense of performing in a public arena.) Could it be that, in France, biography has had its status put in question, its nose put out of joint, by the eulogy?

Michael Holroyd

"On the Border-line between the New and the Old"

Bloomsbury, Biography, and Gerald Brenan

In *The Modern Movement,* a volume that lists one hundred key books from England between 1880 and 1950, the critic Cyril Connolly described Lytton Strachey's *Eminent Victorians* as the first important publication of the 1920s—though, to be pedantic, it actually appeared in 1918. In short, it was, shall we say, rather ahead of its time. Connolly believed *Eminent Victorians* to be a revolutionary book. It was, he wrote in *Enemies of Promise,* "the work of a great anarch, a revolutionary text-book on bourgeois society written in the language through which the bourgeois ear could be lulled and beguiled, the Mandarin style." Nevertheless, as Connolly elsewhere acknowledges, "a writer who sought to interpret the present solely through the past cannot inspire the young."[1]

This perhaps is one of the reasons Lytton Strachey never inspired the young Gerald Brenan. "I was tongue-tied in his presence," Brenan wrote of Strachey. "The overriding impression that I got from listening to him was of his maturity." Brenan had notions of being a biographer in the 1920s but did not complete—did not really begin—his life of Saint Teresa.

1. Connolly, *Enemies of Promise* (Harmondsworth: Penguin Modern Classics, 1961), 59, and *The Evening Colonnade* (London: David Bruce and Watson, 1973), 287.

When he did return to biography late in life with a book on Saint John of the Cross, it was a very different form of biography from Strachey's. Indeed it defined one of their incompatibilities. All religion was "pernicious nonsense" to Strachey, whereas Brenan derived an aesthetic pleasure from religion. That was why, for example, Brenan was more responsive than Strachey to the poetry of T. S. Eliot. Brenan came to like Strachey's *Eminent Victorians,* but he responded to it, measured it, placed it rather differently from Connolly. "We are going I think to have a new age in English literature," he wrote to Strachey in 1921; "*E[minent] V[ictorians]* will then be on the border-line between the new and the old."[2]

Connolly placed Strachey among the new writers because of a particular moral achievement. It was Strachey, he believed, who had made nonconformity permissible again for the postwar generation after the long trauma of Oscar Wilde's imprisonment and exile. Brenan, a member of this postwar generation almost fifteen years younger than Strachey, was a natural nonconformist, and he took this achievement for granted. What troubled him about *Eminent Victorians* was Strachey's "Mandarin style." Was not this a dandified style imposing a premature limitation on contemporary writing—fencing it off into a small perfection instead of letting it out to find new forms? Where were the living seeds of the future in such a book as Strachey's? It went as far as it could in a certain direction, and then it stopped. "There is not a line in it that gives it away," Brenan complained to Strachey about *Eminent Victorians,*

> that allows one to penetrate into the workshops where it was made. Is it possible that it came into existence without any of those fevers of hope and despair and aridity and self-disgust that other authors have to put up with? . . . Books, even great ones, ought to show signs of human imperfection. . . . I prefer [James] Joyce to you: he does not taunt me, but leads me on, points to very far horizons, and shows me a way that leads there. He promises new discoveries, new methods, new beauties—you don't promise anything. You just are. A vision, clear, complete, and yet unattainable.[3]

2. Brenan, *Personal Record, 1920–1927* (London: Jonathan Cape, 1974), 90; Michael Holroyd, *Lytton Strachey,* vol. 2, *The Years of Achievement, 1910–1932* (London: Heinemann, 1968), 325.

3. Holroyd, *Strachey,* 2:325.

That last sentence points to another factor influencing Brenan's complex attitude to Strachey. During the 1920s he was deeply in love with the artist Dora Carrington, who, intermittently loving Brenan, nevertheless would always reserve her emotional priority for Strachey. Brenan had a clear vision of Carrington as a Beatrice to his Dante. In the romantic tradition, and because of Strachey, she was unattainable. The torment of this strange situation—strange because Strachey was homosexual—eventually drove Brenan to live in Spain, thereby extending the influence of Bloomsbury into the literature of the Spanish people. The famous journey that Strachey and Carrington and the man she married, Brenan's best friend Ralph Partridge, made to stay with Brenan in Granada in 1920—and which Strachey later told Virginia Woolf had been "DEATH!"—has always seemed to me to be a comic exploration of Brenan's and Strachey's incompatibility. But the remarkable thing about this incompatibility was that it did not put a stop to their respect for each other. It was true that on first seeing Strachey at Tidmarsh in 1919, Brenan had likened him to "a darkly bearded he-goat glaring at me from the bottom of a cave." But almost fifty years later he wrote to me that "as soon as I had got over my first shock, I felt his elegance and distinction."[4]

When parting from Carrington and Strachey, Brenan wrote in 1922: "It has been a great pleasure to me to have caught a glimpse at Tidmarsh of people who cultivate a free, happy and civilized life. Now that I have lost my part in it, I see all its attractions." And Strachey wrote to Brenan: "I hope you will go on writing. From the little I've seen of your work, it seems to me to differ *in kind* from everything else going about by writers of your generation. To my mind there is a streak of inspiration in it, which is very rare and very precious indeed . . . [and] never forget that, whatever happens, and in spite of all estrangements, you are loved by those you love best."[5]

It is a good exchange—not the usual reciprocal civilities of authors that Dr. Johnson considered one of the world's most risible spectacles, but Bloomsbury at its best. What Brenan considered to be Bloomsbury

---

4. Brenan, *South from Granada* (Harmondsworth: Penguin, 1987), 28; Brenan to Holroyd, September 14, 1966, quoted in Holroyd, *Lytton Strachey: The New Biography* (London: Chatto and Windus, 1994), 432n.

5. Brenan to Strachey, June 13, 1922, and Strachey to Brenan, June 15, 1922, quoted in Holroyd, *Strachey: New Biography,* 510, 509.

at its best was its refusal to allow sexual jealousy to dictate the moral code: the moral code that Strachey, in a letter to Carrington, sums up as "a great deal of a great many kinds of love."[6] Here was a message that could indeed inspire the young, and one that was very appealing to Brenan. The question I wish to ask is: did Brenan adhere to this Bloomsbury code, or was his judgment blown off course by jealousy?

Strachey's background was altogether different from Brenan's. He was one of the younger sons of a large and distinguished Victorian family, and his father, who was a general in the army, spent much of his career out in India. Lytton Strachey didn't look, or indeed sound, like the son of a nineteenth-century general. He looked and sounded an enfeebled character. In late Victorian society he was the complete outsider: homosexual, often ill, and not well-off. No one would have put much of a bet on Strachey's chances of being happy or successful. Yet there was far more toughness in him than the silent drooping figure suggested. He grew up determined to change the society in which he lived. And he did so, in a sense, by rewriting the past and setting the future on a new course. Discretion, he said, was not the better part of biography. And this is true. Biography, as opposed to history, has often been somewhat indiscreet, and that suited Strachey's temperament very well.

Strachey's home in London had been claustrophobic and his school-days miserable. But at Cambridge he found lifelong friends and be-came a far happier person, indeed a rather influential person. He joined a secret society known as the "Apostles" and was gradually transformed from an outcast into a member of an intellectual elite. He was particularly impressed at Cambridge by the philosopher G. E. Moore, whom he saw as another Plato and whose *Principia Ethica* he greeted as a new *Symposium*. From this book's publication in 1903, Strachey dated the beginning of the Age of Reason—in other words, the end of the Victorian Age. It was Moore's celebration of friendship and beauty that Strachey specially welcomed, for they were attributes that had been singularly lacking in his own childhood and adolescence.

---

6. Strachey to Carrington, March 23, 1917; see Jane Hill, *The Art of Dora Carrington* (London: Herbert Press, 1994), 31.

In his preface to *Eminent Victorians* Strachey wrote: "Human beings are too important to be treated as mere symptoms of the past. They have a value which is independent of any temporal process—which is eternal and must be felt for its own sake." Yet the four Victorians he chose for treatment were not independent of Victorian values. His portrait of Cardinal Manning, for example, was an exposé of the evangelicism that had been a defining characteristic of Victorian culture. Then, in removing Florence Nightingale from the pedestal where she posed as the legendary lady with the lamp, and replacing her with a twentieth-century neurotic, Strachey struck directly at the popular mythology of Victorian England. For Florence Nightingale was the incarnation of nineteenth-century humanitarianism, the movement which salved the conscience of the Victorians. Strachey's enmity toward his third eminent Victorian, Dr. Arnold, probably arose from his own unhappy schooldays. His target was not only the public school system, but the whole movement of orthodox Victorian liberalism. Of Dr. Arnold, the most influential teacher of the Victorians, Strachey wrote as follows: "Was he to improve the character of his pupils by gradually spreading round them an atmosphere of cultivation and intelligence? By bringing them into close and friendly contact with civilized men, and even, perhaps, with civilized women? By introducing into the life of his school all that he could of the humane, enlightened, and progressive elements in the life of the community? On the whole, he thought not." This is Strachey ironically contrasting, as it were, the lessons of G. E. Moore and of Bloomsbury against the pattern of education he had himself endured. Then finally we see General Gordon indulging his secret passion for fame and becoming a willing instrument, not of God, but of the imperialist faction of the British government. This was well recognized by Gerald Brenan's war-weary generation just back from the Great War, a generation sickened by the chauvinism of bishops and journalists who had been declaring that God was in the trenches on their side. So no wonder that *Eminent Victorians* was so popular in 1918. Evangelicism, liberalism, humanitarianism, education, and imperialism in the nineteenth century: these were Strachey's targets, and he struck them beautifully.[7]

7. Strachey, *Eminent Victorians* (Harmondsworth: Penguin Modern Classics, 1986), 10, 167.

In his preface to *Eminent Victorians* Strachey wrote that the historian "will row out over that great ocean of material, and lower down into it, here and there, a little bucket, which will bring up to the light of day some characteristic specimen, from those far depths, to be examined with a careful curiosity."[8] Strachey's biographical aquarium is full of odd fish and small fry. Robbed of their awful surroundings in the depths, they no longer appear the formidable creatures of sea-legend. With their comic grimaces, their futile perambulating to and fro, their crazy retinue of dabs and squids, they are turned into a comic spectacle. Only the good-natured uncompetitive sole, content to lie modestly in silence, is presented with any real affection.

The best example of these mild creatures is the figure of Lord Hartington in the essay on General Gordon. Strachey's description of his solid personality is full of imaginative humor. "He was built upon a pattern which was very dear to his countrymen," Strachey wrote.

> . . . In Lord Hartington they saw, embodied and glorified, the very qualities which were nearest to their hearts. . . . His fondness for field sports gave them a feeling of security; and certainly there could be no nonsense about a man who confessed to two ambitions—to become Prime Minister and to win the Derby—and who put the second above the first. They loved him for his casualness . . . for his hat. It was the greatest comfort—with Lord Hartington they could always be quite certain that he would never, in any circumstances, be either brilliant, or subtle, or surprising, or impassioned, or profound. . . . Above all they loved him for being dull. As they sat, listening to his speeches, in which considerations of stolid plainness succeeded one another with complete flatness, they felt involved and supported by the colossal tedium. . . . They looked up, and took their fill of the sturdy obvious presence. The inheritor of a splendid dukedom might almost have passed for a farm hand. Almost, but not quite. . . . One other characteristic . . . completes the portrait: Lord Hartington was slow. He was slow in movement, slow in apprehension, slow in thought and the communication of thought, slow to decide, and slow to act.[9]

Strachey has been accused of being a debunker. It is an interesting word, *debunker.* Although now pejorative, it was an American

8. Ibid., 9.
9. Ibid., 246–47.

colloquialism that originally meant someone who took the bunkum or humbug out of a subject—not such a bad thing, after all. No historian had written quite as he wrote. What Strachey did was to introduce literary caricature into historical biography. He also turned the nineteenth-century cult of aesthetics into a twentieth-century weapon of revolt. His homosexuality defined his treatment of a number of his subjects, from General Gordon in *Eminent Victorians* to the Prince Consort in his *Queen Victoria*.

The suggestion that he write a biography of Queen Victoria had come from a professor of English literature at Oxford University called Walter Raleigh. "We want your method for some stately Victorians who have waited long for it," Raleigh wrote to Strachey. "First the great Panjandrum—Victoria herself. This is obvious."[10]

Queen Victoria was a great challenge to Strachey. Thirty-five years earlier, in 1886, Bernard Shaw had demanded a new class of royal biography. "The truth is that queens, like other people, can be too good for the sympathies of their finite fellow-creatures," Shaw wrote. "A few faults are indispensable to a really popular monarch. . . . What we need now is a book entitled 'Queen Victoria: by a Personal acquaintance who dislikes her' . . . . The proper person for the work would be some politically indifferent devil's advocate who considers the Queen an over-rated woman and who would take a conscientious delight in disparaging her."[11]

Such conscientiousness was widely expected from Lytton Strachey in the 1920s. Among contemporary biographers he was the outstanding devil's advocate, and though he had not been a personal acquaintance of the queen, he had acquired "private information," referred to in his footnotes, from his godfather's widow, Lady Lytton, who had been one of the queen's ladies-in-waiting. He had no political ideology, but what other writer of nonfiction could so disparage a public reputation by linking it incongruously to the subject's private life, especially to the sexuality of that private life? He was anxious,

---

10. Holroyd, *Strachey: New Biography,* 440.

11. George Bernard Shaw, "The Year of Jubilee," *Pall Mall Gazette* November 16, 1886; collected in *Bernard Shaw's Book Reviews Originally Published in the "Pall Mall Gazette" from 1885 to 1888,* ed. Brian Tyson (University Park: Pennsylvania State University Press, 1991), 214.

he told one of his cousins, not to make Victoria appear "ridiculous" since she was a "great queen." At the same time he wrote to his brother James that "it's quite clear that Queen Victoria was a martyr to analeroticism." The test lay in steering "the correct course between discretion and indiscretion"—that is, providing an indiscreet subtext to the royal panoply of the narrative.[12]

Queen Victoria is presented as a romantic novel beneath the surface of which moves a current of subversive irony. Strachey's Victoria is a woman who is dependent on men. Although shrewd, she had none of the political genius of Queen Elizabeth. Her deepest happiness came from her marriage to Albert, the Prince Consort, which forms the central panel of the biography. Strachey shows her as being swept off her feet by a violent sexual upheaval which he describes in highly charged romantic language: "Albert arrived; and the whole structure of her existence crumbled into nothingness like a house of cards. He was beautiful—she gasped—she knew no more. Then, in a flash, a thousand mysteries were revealed to her."[13]

Although the prince was a mirror of manly beauty in the eyes of the queen, his constitution was not strong, and "owing either to his peculiar upbringing or to a more fundamental idiosyncrasy," Strachey wrote, "he had a marked distaste for the opposite sex." By this Strachey intended to indicate that Albert was a secret homosexual. This is the key to several passages that point to Albert's melancholy and isolation. Strachey sees in Albert something of his own loneliness. His Prince Consort has the power of arousing an idolatry that does not answer his emotional needs—like Strachey aroused in Carrington. But unlike Strachey the prince could not turn elsewhere for companionship. This was his "curious position," which Strachey describes as follows:

> The husband was not so happy as the wife. In spite of the great improvement in his situation, in spite of a growing family and the adoration of Victoria, Albert was still a stranger in a strange land. . . . Victoria idolized him; but it was understanding that he craved for, not idolatry. . . . He was lonely.

12. Holroyd, *Strachey: New Biography,* 490.
13. Lytton Strachey, *Queen Victoria* (London: Collins, 1958), 100.

The fascination of this marriage for Strachey becomes clear when he asks: "was he the wife and she the husband?" and answers, "It almost seemed so."[14] What pricked Strachey's curiosity was Victoria's underlying ascendancy. It is only when we see her through the eyes of her declining husband that we are made to feel a repugnance. Otherwise there is a growing feeling of tenderness for the queen, especially in old age, which may be attributed to Strachey's having associated her with his mother.

His portrait proved the truth of Bernard Shaw's assertion that "a few faults are indispensable to a really popular monarch." The biography inaugurated a new and legendary view of the queen—a whimsical, teasing, half-admiring, half-mocking view that found in Victoria a quaintly impressive symbol of a quaintly impressive age.

It was a worldwide success. Strachey had not only re-created the queen but also revolutionized the art of historical biography by show-ing that it could be adapted to one of the *genres* of fiction. He had dedicated the book to Virginia Woolf. But the romantic novel after which he had shaped his narrative was already a debased form of fiction and very different from anything Woolf herself was attempting in her novels. This, and the enviable popularity of *Queen Victoria,* made Woolf critical of the book. She had been unable to finish it, she told Gerald Brenan. Brenan had been ready to criticize the book himself. Strachey's style, he claimed, gave him the sensation of treading on limp linoleum. But in the face of Virginia Woolf's hostile criticism he found himself defending it. For no one, he felt, could seriously deny that Strachey was readable. His writing went down so smoothly you were hardly aware you had digested anything at all. Brenan himself preferred something meatier. He preferred Proust and Joyce. But when he discussed *Ulysses* with Virginia Woolf, she told him that she was put off by its modernist male cliquishness, its clever cheap coarseness, which made her own writing, by comparison, suddenly seem so ladylike. As for Strachey, he told Brenan that he could not find a single intelligent sentence in *Ulysses,* while E. M. Forster complained that the book covered everything in filth. Nothing demonstrated more vividly to Brenan the limitations of Bloomsbury. It was the limitation of skepticism. They valued truth and mocked pretension, and they

14. Ibid., 103, 129.

could provide what Brenan called "the most brilliant and fantastic conversation that one can hear anywhere in England." Nevertheless, they were narrow in their enthusiasms, often conservative in their tastes, self-protective, and cautious. That was why "I was always divided in my attitude to 'Bloomsbury,' considered as a group," Brenan recorded in his autobiography.[15] He wanted something bolder and more original.

Something bolder and more original was what both Virginia Woolf and Lytton Strachey were aiming for in the late 1920s. Instead of being confined by their culture, they were experimenting with ways of leaving the polite world, mingling gender and time, and challenging the public with deviant fantasy. Both *Orlando* and *Elizabeth and Essex* derive from private emotional experience—Virginia's love affair with Vita Sackville-West and Lytton's with Roger Senhouse—and the two books are curiously intertwined. *Orlando*'s beginnings in the sixteenth century overlapped with the period of Strachey's history, and presented an aging Queen Elizabeth very similar to the queen in *Elizabeth and Essex* as well as an eponymous hero who, with his "strength, grace, romance, folly, poetry, youth," inevitably brings to mind the earl of Essex.[16]

Virginia and Lytton had each urged the other to go for something new. After *Queen Victoria,* Virginia recommended her friend to try to write for the theater. After *Mrs. Dalloway,* Lytton had said that Virginia should take on something wilder: "a frame work that admits anything, like *Tristram Shandy,*" was how he phrased it. Both books were eventually judged to be comparative failures, or at least not among their authors' important works. Virginia was pleased that in "dashing off *Orlando* I had done better than he had done." Lytton's comparative failure, she eventually decided, was due to the confining nature of biography itself. In her essay "The Art of Biography" she used *Queen Victoria* to show what biography could do, and *Elizabeth and Essex* to show what it could not do. "In the *Victoria* he treated biography as a craft; he submitted to its limitations," she wrote. "In the *Elizabeth and Essex* he treated biography as an art; he flouted its limitations."

15. Brenan, *Personal Record,* 156–57.

16. Virginia Woolf, *Orlando: A Biography* (Oxford: Oxford University Press, 1992), 24.

This theory solved the problem of how such a remarkable intellect as Strachey's, with its suppleness and flickering wit, had not achieved something more powerful. It also supported the deconstructive thesis of her own biographical pastiche—that the "riot and confusion of the passions and emotions" could not be fitted into a biographical form and that, as George Gissing had written, "the only true biography is to be found in novels."[17]

This too was Brenan's belief. His biographer Jonathan Gathorne-Hardy quotes a letter in which Brenan writes, "Only poetry can give immediacy—prose biography just satisfies curiosity." And in his autobiography Brenan confesses, "What I had really wanted was to be not a prose writer but a poet." But then so did Lytton Strachey want to be a poet. Brenan's biography of Saint John of the Cross is his attempt at a poetic biography; and *Elizabeth and Essex* is Strachey's experiment at shaping biography in the form of dramatic poetry. This was his response to Virginia Woolf's having urged him to write for the theater. The biography is constructed as a five-act Elizabethan drama and is based on *Antony and Cleopatra*. Essex leaves and returns to his queen as Antony leaves and returns to Cleopatra; and like Antony he dies a violent death. Elizabeth is no Cleopatra, but each in her fashion was "a lass unparalleled," the queen of England's variations of mind and temper making a dramatic equivalent to the "infinite variety" of the queen of Egypt. In Strachey's picture of Sir Robert Cecil we have a close approximation to the calculating Octavius. Shakespeare closes *Antony and Cleopatra* with the triumph of Octavius; in the carefully weighed passage with which *Elizabeth and Essex* ends, Strachey employs another device from the Elizabethan stage, showing Cecil brooding over the destiny of England and the future of his own family. Whenever possible, Strachey treats his readers as direct onlookers—that is to say, as an audience. He tries to transform every source—letters, diaries, documentary accounts—into visual material, and writes in places as if giving directions to a group of actors, using the spoken words and also providing instructions as to how they

---

17. Holroyd, *Strachey: New Biography*, 607; *The Diary of Virginia Woolf*, vol. 3, ed. Anne Olivier Bell, assisted by Andrew McNellie (London: Hogarth Press, 1980), 234; Woolf, *Collected Essays*, vol. 4 (London: Hogarth Press, 1967), 223; see *Journal of the British Institute in Paris* 24/25 (autumn 1997/spring 1998): 7.

should be delivered. ("There was a pause; and then the high voice rang out," and "She stopped, and told them to stand up, as she had more to say to them," and then "Pausing again for a moment, she continued in a deeper tone.") No wonder it was adapted for the stage and became a film and the inspiration for Benjamin Britten's opera *Gloriana*.[18]

Elizabeth and Essex shows the justice of Brenan's view that Strachey's work lay "on the border-line between the new and the old." In *Eminent Victorians* Strachey had used the old essay form of the Victorian belletrist to provide a new analysis of Victorian moral values. In *Queen Victoria* he had followed a somewhat discredited form of fiction writing to uncover a startlingly novel reinterpretation of recent royal relations. In *Elizabeth and Essex* he combined the pattern of a sixteenth-century drama with the modern insights of Sigmund Freud.

Elizabeth and Essex was dedicated to Lytton's brother and sister-in-law, James and Alix Strachey, who had by the midtwenties established themselves as, in Freud's words, "my excellent English translators."[19] During the 1920s psychoanalysis gradually permeated Bloomsbury. Virginia Woolf's brother Adrian Stephen and his wife, Karin, became analysts; and the Hogarth Press published the Stracheys' translations of Freud. In *Elizabeth and Essex* the Freudian thesis was a method of deepening the general pattern of Shakespearian predestination by adding a stream of unconscious inevitability to the mood of sixteenth-century fatalism. Strachey had come to accept the general premise that infant sexuality and the adult operation of the sex instinct infiltrate human thought and action. He used Freud's ideas concerning father-daughter relationships to account for the underlying attitude of Elizabeth to Essex's execution. He sees, rising within Elizabeth, the spirit of her father, Henry VIII, who had executed Elizabeth's mother.

"You seem, on the whole, to imagine yourself as Elizabeth," Maynard Keynes wrote to Strachey after reading the book, "but I see from the pictures that it is Essex whom you have got up as yourself."[20] In

---

18. Jonathan Gathorne-Hardy, *The Interior Castle: A Life of Gerald Brenan* (London: Sinclair-Stevenson, 1992), 505; Brenan, *Personal Record,* 71; Strachey, *Elizabeth and Essex: A Tragic History,* chap. 16.

19. Sigmund Freud, *Collected Papers,* vol. 3, quoted in Holroyd, *Strachey: New Biography,* 609.

20. Holroyd, *Strachey: New Biography,* 612.

fact, Strachey seems to have seen Essex through the queen's eyes as the sort of person he desired to be. But there are those who, prolonging the Freudian thesis and believing Strachey's manhood to have been thwarted by the female-dominated atmosphere of his home, identify Elizabeth with Strachey's mother and himself with Essex.

What seems true is that Strachey's Elizabethanism is a personal evocation peopled by phantoms who acted out instincts that four hundred years later had receded into our subconscious—a never-again land with which we are connected by residual memories and into which we are invited deliciously to lose ourselves.

When Strachey left the Victorians for the Elizabethans his manner changed. "We are aware for the first time disagreeably," wrote the American critic Edmund Wilson, "of the high-voiced old Bloomsbury gossip gloating over the scandals of the past as he ferreted them out of his library." *Elizabeth and Essex* added to Strachey's reputation as a liberator of biographical forms, but the atmosphere of the book was thin. There are few ironical flashes from the author of *Eminent Victorians:* for the most part Strachey is "whipping the flanks of the language," as Virginia Woolf observed, "& putting it to this foaming gallop, when the poor beast is all spavins & sores." Yet the book had an extraordinary pace, glitter, and attractiveness, as well as a compelling subtext. It was an instantaneous success. In the United States and Britain it created a record in the sales of a serious biography, and it was translated into almost twenty languages.[21]

Strachey brought out one more book in his lifetime. *Portraits in Miniature* appeared in May 1931, some eight months before his death, and was, in the words of Edmund Wilson, "one of Strachey's real triumphs." Even Virginia Woolf admitted it was "rather masterly in technique, and the essays read much better together than separate." They read better together because there is a theme that runs unobtrusively through them, tracing, in France and England, town and country, the evolution of the modern world from the sixteenth to the nineteenth century. In *Eminent Victorians* he had pulled down the mighty from their high places; in *Portraits in Miniature* he raised up the victims of history—obscure pedants and pedagogues, crackpots,

21. Wilson, *The Shores of Light* (London: W. H. Allen, 1952), 553; *Diary of Virginia Woolf,* 3:209.

biographers, and other square pegs and odd birds—and treated them with humorous tenderness. They range from Sir John Harrington, who was led by his sensitive nose to become the inventor of the water closet, to Strachey's predecessor in biography, that assiduous muddler in love and literature John Aubrey, seeking after Apparitions and Impulses, and transmuting "a few handfuls of orts and relics into golden life."[22]

All these characters had been swept from the mainstream narrative of history presided over by the "Six English Historians" who appear at the end of the book, and who themselves have largely vanished as mainstream characters of the times. Because their reputations have lapsed, their faiths decayed, their arguments been buried in the dust, their troubled spirits do not vex the twentieth century. They have become the subjects of historical burlesque, and breathe the pure air of comedy and pathos. "A biography should be either as long as Boswell's," Strachey wrote, "or as short as Aubrey's." In *Portraits in Miniature,* Strachey showed his mastery as a biographical miniaturist.[23]

How has Strachey's reputation survived since his death? In the 1950s it rested on a revaluation made by Noel Annan, who argued that the Great War seemed to have severed the 1920s from the past. "The profound emotional impact of the horror and the slaughter," Annan wrote, "convinced many that the values which held good before the war must now by definition be wrong, if indeed they were not responsible for the war. A society which permitted such a catastrophe to occur must be destroyed, because the presuppositions of that comfortable pre-war England were manifestly false." Searching for a way in which to regard conduct and replace Victorian values, the 1920s came to see it either through the eyes of the Fabians, led by Bernard Shaw and Beatrice Webb, or through the eyes of the Bloomsbury Group, led by Lytton Strachey and Virginia Woolf.[24]

The Fabians believed that equality of income, when linked to the abolition of the English class system, would lead to a better life for

22. Wilson, *Shores,* 553; *The Diary of Virginia Woolf,* vol. 4, ed. Anne Olivier Bell and Andrew McNellie (London: Hogarth Press, 1982), 26.

23. Strachey, *Biographical Essays* (London: Chatto and Windus, 1948), 16.

24. Lord Annan's most comprehensive critique is to be found in his introduction to *Eminent Victorians* (London: Collins Classics, 1959), 9–17.

all. Bloomsbury had a different formula. Personal relationships plus aesthetic sensibility equaled the good life for them. This good life was based on freedom and individuality and the sense not to exploit these privileges. They did not disagree with the Fabians, but they had a different set of priorities.

Strachey was a good example of this individualist philosophy. By the end of the 1960s his name had become something of a cult among the hippies. The historian Piers Brendon has suggested that, "with his pacifism, his homosexuality and his bohemianism" as well as his anticipation of the plea "Make love, not war," Strachey was one of the patron saints of the "flower power" generation.[25]

According to Dr. Samuel Johnson, fame is a shuttlecock that needs determined play from the opposite side of the net to keep it in contention. Strachey has, by this rule, been blessed with powerful enemies. In the early posthumous years these enemies were led by the redoubtable Dr. Leavis, of Downing College, Cambridge, who informed his students that Strachey had been responsible, through his malign influence on Maynard Keynes, for the outbreak of the Second World War.[26]

It is the reward of a successful ironist to be acclaimed in such a grand style. In his book, *A History of the Modern World,* which was published in 1983, the journalist Paul Johnson describes Strachey as "a propagandist of genius" who aimed at an intellectual takeover of the twentieth century. In Johnson's pages we see Strachey organizing the Bloomsbury coterie until it grew into a mafia "far more destructive to the old British values than any legion of enemies." Strachey's influence reaches "upwards and downwards by the 1930s to embrace the entire political nation," Johnson wrote. For in Johnson's view Strachey destroyed the virtues of patriotism and left behind an emptiness that became the homosexual recruiting ground at Cambridge for Soviet espionage.

Now, in the 1990s, I also see Lytton Strachey as a subversive and challenging figure—but in a far more positive way. There can be no doubt that he revolutionized the writing of biography. He smuggled

25. Brendon, "Strachey: Short and Sharp," *Now!* [London], February 29, 1980.
26. Paul Johnson, *A History of the Modern World* (London: Weidenfeld and Nicolson, 1983), 29, 106–71, 347.

deviant sexual behavior into our national heritage with his subtle reassessments of Elizabethan and Victorian times, and he extended his influence over modern behavior with his extraordinarily free and tolerant lifestyle. Gerald Brenan, to an extent, was part of that lifestyle, as was Virginia Woolf, and their reactions to Strachey were to some extent parallel. Virginia Woolf was envious of his quicker success and larger sales, but at the same time she loved him and counted him one of the few important people in her life. In her comments to friends she had few good words for Strachey's books. Only after his death did she find a way of writing about them generously and without insincerity.

Gerald Brenan was not so much envious as jealous of Strachey. As Jonathan Gathorne-Hardy reveals, he felt a sense of rivalry that emerged as an attack not on Strachey but on Strachey's idol, the historian Edward Gibbon. In 1951, when he published *The Literature of the Spanish People,* he saw that, by way of praise, several reviewers compared his book to Strachey's *Landmarks in French Literature.* This cannot have pleased him. For much of his life he had little good to say of this early work of Strachey's. But then, like Virginia Woolf, his critical opinion rose and latterly he began to see merit in it.

Although he was fascinated by the modernists, Brenan chose more traditional forms in which to write: the essay, the picaresque novel, history, and romantic autobiography. His work stands "on the border-line between the new and the old," as Strachey's does. As he explored this territory, discovering how fertile it was for his talent—for what Strachey had called his "streak of inspiration"—so he began to understand Strachey's own achievement better. It was this understanding, I believe, that helped him to overcome old jealousies and, somewhat to his own surprise, to keep the aesthetic code of Bloomsbury.

Mary C. Francis

"A Kind of Voyage"

E. M. Forster and Benjamin Britten's *Billy Budd*

Toward the end of his career E. M. Forster embarked for the first time on a collaborative project, the 1951 opera *Billy Budd,* with music by the composer Benjamin Britten. Although it was not to be an entirely peaceful collaboration, *Billy Budd* provided both artists with a vehicle for what they most wanted to say to society at that moment. Thirty-four years apart in age, the two men were in very different stages of their careers, and ultimately each sought to say something different in the opera. *Billy Budd* weaves together the differing visions of two artists, two humanists, two homosexuals with deeply conflicted relationships to their public.

Forster's love for music is evident from his various writings, though he modestly qualified his musical expertise: "Although I've got this deep devotion to music, I know nothing at all about its technical requirements."[1] He was an amateur pianist and frequent concert-goer, with a taste for the musical monuments of the nineteenth century. Beethoven was a particular favorite, as numerous mentions in his writings and entries in

1. Benjamin Britten, Eric Crozier, and E. M. Forster, "Talking about *Billy Budd,*" BBC Radio 3 broadcast, November 8, 1960 (unpublished typescript housed in the Britten-Pears Library, Aldeburgh), 9.

his commonplace book attest.[2] Beethoven's music makes an important appearance in *Howards End,* where the reactions of various characters to Beethoven's Fifth Symphony reveal something of the inner life of each. Similarly, in *A Room with a View,* Beethoven's piano music is Forster's key to part of Lucy's inner world:

> It so happened that Lucy, who found daily life rather chaotic, entered a more solid world when she opened the piano. She was then no longer either deferential or patronizing; no longer either a rebel or a slave. The kingdom of music is not the kingdom of this world; it will accept those whom breeding and intellect and culture have alike rejected.[3]

Beethoven (and music generally) emerge from *A Room with a View* in particular as a vehicle for those emotions that are stronger and more honest than those usually acknowledged in the domesticated settings of Forster's novels. Music, which connects Forster's characters with their true selves, is on the side of those emotional connections between individuals that are so valued by Forster in all his writings.

Forster's veneration of Beethoven is not surprising given the prominent role Beethoven and his works have played in the construction of the artist as supreme individual in Western culture. More than any other composer in the western canon it is Beethoven who has become the emblematic "heroic" individual, the artist who must strive against the invisible fetters of conventionality to assert a singular vision. The importance of being an individual and of drawing strength from bonds between individuals is crucial to Forster's worldview—hence his famous formulation pitting loyalty to friends against loyalty to the state.[4] Beethoven, and music generally, play a part in the completion of that ideal in Forster's life and thought.[5]

2. Forster, *Commonplace Book,* ed. Philip Gardner (Stanford: Stanford University Press, 1985); see, for example, 95, 111, 253.

3. Forster, *A Room with a View,* ed. Oliver Stallybrass, Abinger Edition (London: Edward Arnold, 1977), 29.

4. "What I Believe," in *Two Cheers for Democracy* (New York: Harcourt Brace, 1951), 68.

5. It is interesting to compare Forster's high regard for Beethoven with Britten's distinct lack of enthusiasm. Of the *Coriolanus Overture,* which Forster greatly admired, Britten said: "What a marvelous beginning, and how well the development

The man whom Christopher Isherwood praised as "the anti-heroic hero" shared several mutual friends with Britten. Forster, born in 1879, was a generation older than Britten (born in 1913) and acted as a kind of father figure and model to several younger homosexual writers and artists. These younger men—Wystan Auden, Isherwood, the South African novelist William Plomer, Britten, and Britten's life companion, the tenor Peter Pears—were among those trusted friends who read Forster's unpublished novel *Maurice*. Forster felt them to be a sympathetic and understanding audience; they all shared the experience of being homosexual in a hostile society.

Forster's homosexuality is an inescapable factor in his biography as an artist, though his own acknowledgment of his sexuality did not extend as far as the public face of his art. The explicitly homosexual *Maurice* remained unpublished in Forster's lifetime, as did various short stories he wrote on homosexual themes. Fairly early in his long life the connection between the lived life and the art became frayed to the point where Forster ceased to publish novels. According to his biographer, P. N. Furbank, Forster "himself sometimes gave a much more practical reason for giving up novel-writing: namely, that being a homosexual, he grew bored with writing about marriage and the relations of men and women." In the opinion of Philip Brett, "Forster's acceptance of his homosexual nature, although on the one hand it caused him to stop writing fiction, had on the other strengthened his resolve and ability to be true to himself and his feelings."[6] While he continued to write homoerotic short stories and completed the novel *Maurice,* Forster's public voice did not address homosexual themes.

Like Forster, Britten was officially closeted all his life, though his lifelong relationship with Peter Pears was played out in open sight of

---

in sequence is carried out! But what galled me was the crudity of the sound; the orchestra sounds seem often so haphazard." Regarding the Op. 111 piano sonata (with which Lucy makes such an impression on Mr. Beebe in *A Room with a View*), Britten was even more forceful, calling parts of it "grotesque." See Murray Schafer, *British Composers in Interview* (London: Faber and Faber, 1963), 119. Britten held Mozart in the highest regard, while Forster thought Mozart "did not go so far" as Beethoven ("The C Minor of That Life," in *Two Cheers for Democracy,* 126).

6. Furbank, *E. M. Forster: A Life* (New York: Harcourt Brace, 1978), 2:132; Brett, "Salvation at Sea," in *The Britten Companion,* ed. Christopher Palmer (Cambridge: Cambridge University Press, 1984), 134.

the world throughout their long professional life together.[7] Britten's work for the stage prior to the collaboration with Forster revolved around the theme of the outsider at odds with his society, such as the ostracized title character of *Peter Grimes* (1945) and (in a comic vein) the awkward protagonist of *Albert Herring* (1947), who is mocked and belittled for his inability to break free of his mother's apron strings.[8] It is easy to see how Britten, as a conscientious objector and a closeted homosexual, would feel drawn to the plight of the outsider. Discussing *Peter Grimes* in a rare interview, Britten described the story of the outcast Peter Grimes as being parallel to the situation he and Peter Pears were in at the time he wrote the opera (1942–1945): "As conscientious objectors, we were out of it."[9] He could well have substituted "homosexuals" for "conscientious objectors."

After Britten's death Philip Brett broke the silence that had surrounded the open secret of Britten's homosexuality to interpret *Peter Grimes* as an allegory of homosexual oppression in modern society.[10] Only this explicit breaking of the silence halted the mechanism of the open secret, since no one had openly interpreted Britten's operas, even the later ones that involved more explicitly homosexual relationships, in this light during his lifetime. Britten himself said little about his operas, leaving them to speak for themselves. Music, famously resistant to specification in western culture, allowed Britten to invest his critique of society (and later, the homoerotically charged relationships in his operas) with very public passion. But a passion expressed in music could be safely ignored or attributed to other sources by listeners disinclined to confront the subtexts of the operas. Thus Britten and his public were able to collaborate in perpetuating the open secret. Forster, whose craft relied on the specifying medium

7. Pears, a tenor, created many of the leading roles in Britten's operas, including Captain Vere in *Billy Budd*. He cofounded the Aldeburgh Festival with Britten, and the two were recital partners throughout their professional lives.

8. Although stories of outsiders obviously had resonance for a homosexual, more explicitly homosexual elements have been discerned in both operas, most notably in the work of Clifford Hindley, who reads *Albert Herring* as a "coming out" story. See "Not the Marrying Kind: Britten's *Albert Herring*," *Cambridge Opera Journal* 78 (July 1994): 99–126.

9. Schafer, *British Composers,* 119.

10. Brett, "Britten and Grimes" and "Postscript," in *Benjamin Britten: Peter Grimes* (Cambridge: Cambridge University Press, 1983), 180–89, 190–96.

of words, was never able to simultaneously present and camouflage his view in the same way.

In many ways, the collaboration between Britten and Forster was a meeting of minds. Both were successful and respected artists who nonetheless felt themselves to be outsiders by virtue of their sexuality. Both criticized British society as essentially unprepared to acknowledge the importance of the artist's role.[11] As artists, both focused primarily on the bonds between individuals. The ethics of Britten's operas are Forsterian, in the sense that relationships between individuals, and above all relationships founded on love, are the most important element of the operas. But in crucial respects Forster and Britten differed in their views of human relationships. Forster's characters are often granted the ability to overcome their shortcomings and mistakes to claim loyalty to a loved one (one thinks of the marriage of Lucy Honeychurch and George Emerson, the union of Maurice Hall and Alec Scudder, the mutual devotion of the Schlegel sisters), or at least awaken to regret over their inability to do so. By contrast, Britten has a tendency to portray the destructive side of love. In Britten's operas Forster's ideal inner life of connections between people is threatened not so much by the Wilcoxian outer life of "telegrams and anger" as by the destructive seeds that are found within love itself.

The *Billy Budd* collaboration had a long prehistory. Britten already knew and admired Forster. Forster's novels are mentioned in Britten's letters and diary entries, including a 1942 letter to Enid Slater that describes *Where Angels Fear to Tread,* which Britten was evidently rereading: "I have wasted hours reading it since it arrived, & love it as much as ever. God—what a cruel book, but how funny, & how damnably real."[12]

Forster was in the background of Britten's career as an opera composer from the beginning. Britten and Pears had gone to the United States in 1939, following in the footsteps of Auden and Isherwood. Like Auden and Isherwood, Britten came in for much criticism. The

11. Forster, "The Duty of Society to the Artist," in *Two Cheers for Democracy,* 95–100; Britten, *On Receiving the First Aspen Award* (London: Faber and Faber, 1964).

12. Britten to Slater, November 23, 1942, in *Benjamin Britten: Letters from a Life,* ed. Donald Mitchell and Philip Reed (Berkeley: University of California Press, 1991), 2:1101.

British establishment did not take kindly to its best young prospects in the arts abandoning their home on the eve of war. Unlike Auden and Isherwood, Britten returned in 1942, and this change of heart was due to unintended intervention on Forster's part. While in California, Britten encountered an article of Forster's in an old issue of the *Listener* about the poet George Crabbe. Crabbe hailed from the same part of England as Britten himself, and Forster's evocative writing about the North Sea coast of Britten's childhood provoked a profound change of heart in the young composer.[13] He decided to return to England. But Forster's article about Crabbe not only inspired Britten's return; it also introduced him to the subject of his first successful opera. By choosing Crabbe's poem *The Borough* as inspiration for *Peter Grimes,* Britten found an outlet for his ambivalence toward the society he had chosen to rejoin.

As the younger of the two artists, Britten looked up to Forster, but Forster also admired Britten's work. Although he was emotionally committed to the canonical works of the nineteenth century, Forster gamely defended new music as well. It may have been new music such as Britten's that inspired Forster to write,

> A piece of contemporary music, to my ear, has a good many sudden deaths in it; the phrases expire as rapidly as the characters in my novel, the chords cut each other's throats, the arpeggio has a heart attack, the fugue gets into a nose-dive. But these defects—if defects they be—are vital to the general conception. They are not to be remedied by substituting sweetness. And the musician would do well to ignore the critic when he admits the justice of a particular criticism.[14]

In 1944 Forster went to hear Britten and Pears at a wartime National Gallery concerts performance of Britten's *Michelangelo Sonnets;* he so admired the performance that he bought the recording of the work. Forster also admired the opera that he had unwittingly inspired, and his admiration of *Peter Grimes* brought him and Britten closer together.

13. Schafer, *British Composers,* 116.
14. Forster, "The Raison d'Être of Criticism in the Arts," in *Two Cheers for Democracy,* 121. This remark is worth noting in light of the disagreements that would arise over Britten's music for *Billy Budd.*

Their mutual admiration and the operatic links between them are evident from the fact that Britten dedicated his 1947 opera *Albert Herring* to Forster and inscribed Forster's copy, "For my dear Morgan / a very humble tribute to a very great man / Benjamin B 1948." Forster was invited in 1948 to participate in the Aldeburgh Festival, which Britten and Pears had founded as an outlet for their music in their new hometown, the very town where George Crabbe had produced the original "Peter Grimes." Forster lectured on Crabbe at the festival, comparing Crabbe's poem to the libretto of the opera. At the end of his lecture he hinted at his interest in the operatic version of Crabbe by outlining "what an opera on Peter Grimes would have been like if I had written it." Forster claimed that his version "would certainly have starred the murdered apprentices. I should have introduced their ghosts in the last scene, rising out of the estuary, . . . blood and fire would have been thrown in the tenor's face, hell would have opened and on a mixture of *Don Juan* and the *Freischütz* I should have lowered my final curtain."[15] While Forster's comments on the opera go on to demonstrate his understanding of Britten's theme of the outcast, Forster's version of *Peter Grimes* as modeled on a grand opera such as Weber's *Der Freischütz* indicates the extent to which his ideas about opera were rooted in the century of his birth.

It seems unlikely that Britten could have missed the hint about Forster's interest in writing a libretto. Soon after the 1948 festival, Forster and Britten were discussing the possibility of collaborating on a new opera in their letters. Britten wrote to his friend Erwin Stein of the possibility "that E. M. Forster (who's staying here now) will collaborate with Eric [Crozier] & me on the next opera—opera needs a great human being like him in it—which is a dazzling prospect."[16]

Forster was at first hesitant to accept the commission to write a libretto. His experience as a dramatist was limited to a handful of plays that never saw the stage, and he had never collaborated on a major project.[17] The aid of a third party was proposed, and Eric Crozier was brought on to assist Forster. A cofounder of the Aldeburgh Festival

15. Forster, "George Crabbe and Peter Grimes," in *Two Cheers for Democracy,* 171–86.

16. Britten to Stein, August 25, 1948, quoted in Humphrey Carpenter, *Benjamin Britten: A Biography* (London: Faber and Faber, 1992), 270–71.

17. Furbank, *Forster,* 2:178, 199.

and the English Opera Group with Britten and Pears, Crozier had collaborated with Britten on other operas: as producer of both *Peter Grimes* and *The Rape of Lucretia* and as librettist of *Albert Herring*.

The initial hurdle for the collaboration was the lack of a satisfactory subject. The idea of a comedy was considered, perhaps in light of the recent *Albert Herring* and Forster's own skill at producing comedies of manners, but Forster declared himself against the idea.[18] Britten seems to have mentioned Melville's *Billy Budd* in a letter to Forster written in November 1948. Forster was later to recall that the idea of doing an opera on *Billy Budd* "suited me at once." In his Clark lectures, which were published as *Aspects of the Novel*, Forster had called *Billy Budd* "a remote, unearthly episode."[19] The title character, a handsome and naive young sailor, attracts the obsessed attentions of the master-at-arms, John Claggart, who vows to destroy Billy. Claggart risks the death penalty for false witness by falsely accusing Billy of mutiny. But when the charge is made before Captain Vere, Billy, unable to defend himself verbally, strikes and kills Claggart. Vere, despite his own feelings toward Billy, has Billy hanged for the crime of murder.

The complex implications of the tale fit well with the preoccupations of both artists. The fact that Billy's fate rests on the dynamic of the relationships among Billy, Claggart, and Vere is in keeping with both Britten's and Forster's tendency to focus on individual relationships. *Billy Budd* was for both Forster and Britten the most direct and public treatment of the homoerotically charged relationships between men they had produced. For Britten this was a midcareer development, a move from his treatment of outsiders like Peter Grimes toward plots more inextricably linked to homosexual/homosocial relationships. For the older Forster the project was a late chance to achieve something he had not done in his published writing: publicly address the idea of homosexual love. Britten's music would provide Forster's words with a cloak of emotional significance without pinning them down to a single, potentially dangerous interpretation, hence creating a relatively safe arena for those words.

18. Mervyn Cooke and Philip Reed, ed., *Benjamin Britten: Billy Budd* (Cambridge: Cambridge University Press, 1993), 45.

19. Britten, Crozier, and Forster, "Talking about *Billy Budd*," 1; Forster, *Aspects of the Novel* (New York: Harcourt Brace, 1955), 142.

The degree to which Forster and Britten were convinced that Melville's novella was their subject is vividly conveyed by Crozier's account of his introduction to the idea. He was asked to come to Britten's home in Aldeburgh at the very beginning of 1949. Upon arrival, he was handed a copy of the novella and left alone to read until he had finished the entire story.[20] It was evident to Crozier that Britten and Forster were convinced they had found their subject: "Their eagerness for a favorable verdict was all too plain." He felt compelled to point out the difficulties that the story presented. Given that from the start Forster had his heart set on a "grand opera mounted clearly and grandly," Melville's story did not seem an obvious choice to Crozier. Years later, in interviews with Humphrey Carpenter for a biography of Britten, Crozier was able to state publicly what must have been a primary concern for the creators of the opera in 1948: "Whether a big opera could be done for a place like Covent Garden with no women at all involved . . . and with this inherently homosexual subject."[21]

But Crozier's objections went by the wayside in the face of Forster and Britten's mutual determination to take up *Billy Budd*.[22] The libretto was begun under the influence of the collaborators' determination to make the opera as historically accurate as possible. Forster did research on naval history from his home at King's College in Cambridge, and he and Crozier took a trip to Portsmouth to visit Nelson's flagship, the *Victory,* to better acquaint themselves with the layout of a typical vessel from the period of the French wars.[23] Forster began work immediately on the libretto; he was able to send a rough version of Vere's opening lines (what became the prologue of the opera) to Crozier in January 1949.

20. The version he was given was William Plomer's 1946 edition.
21. Crozier, "Staging First Productions I," in *The Operas of Benjamin Britten,* ed. David Herbert (London: Hamish Hamilton, 1979), 32; Forster to. Britten, December 20, 1948, in *Selected Letters of E. M. Forster: Volume Two, 1921–1970,* ed. Mary Lago and P. N. Furbank (Cambridge: Harvard University Press, 1985), 235; Carpenter, *Benjamin Britten,* 282.
22. Throughout the collaboration Crozier would play a crucial role, but the major decisions were made by Forster and Britten. Forster to the end insisted on Crozier's being given equal billing as librettist, but Crozier always stressed his role as the "technician" who guided Forster's writing into a theatrically viable form and made certain historical accuracy was upheld as much as possible. See Crozier, "Staging," 32.
23. Forster to Crozier, February 10, 1949, in *Selected Letters,* 236.

Throughout the spring, Forster and Crozier corresponded and occasionally traveled to Aldeburgh to work on the libretto at Britten and Pears's house. Once the project had begun, Forster was keen to be at work on the libretto as much as possible. The seeds of disturbance within the collaboration lay partly here, for Britten was at work finishing other pieces during this period and did not actually begin writing down the music for *Billy Budd* until January of the following year. This was typical of Britten, who usually contemplated the subject of each of his operas for quite a while before actually writing down any of the music.[24] In February, Forster wrote to Crozier that he was willing to give up a lecture tour in the United States to work as much as possible on the libretto: "That opera is much the most important bit of work which I see before me and I would sacrifice much to it."[25] Forster did not understand why Britten did not immediately begin writing as well. In March, Forster and Crozier spent two weeks at Britten's house in Aldeburgh working on the libretto while Britten worked on other projects; the three of them would meet several times during the day to review the progress of the libretto together.

During this period of intensive work on the libretto, Crozier detected signs of conflicted feelings toward the project on Britten's part. In letters to his fiancée, Nancy Evans, Crozier noted a period of depression for Britten coinciding with the work he and Forster had undertaken. On March 16, Crozier had evidently talked things over with Britten and reported to Evans that Britten "was going through a period of revulsion against *Billy Budd*, from a misunderstanding

---

24. Britten usually composed "in his head" weeks and months in advance and then wrote music out very quickly. This was the case with *The Rape of Lucretia* and *Albert Herring,* the two chamber operas that preceded *Billy Budd,* as well as *Gloriana* and *The Turn of the Screw,* the two operas that followed the collaboration with Crozier and Forster. All these operas were works in progress for about a year, but in each case the music was not actually written down on paper until a few months (or even weeks) before the premiere: "Usually I have the music complete in my mind before putting pencil to paper. That doesn't mean that every note has been composed, perhaps not one has, but I have worked out questions of form, texture, character, and so forth, in a very precise way so that I know exactly what effects I want and how I am going to achieve them" (Schafer, *British Composers,* 123). Britten reiterated in the 1960 BBC broadcast, "I remember very clearly that all my interest and emotions at that point were focused on *Billy Budd*" (8).

25. Forster to Crozier, February 10, 1949, in *Selected Letters,* 236.

about the purpose of the story, and he wanted to give the whole thing up. But now he has come through and he sees that his feeling was muddled, and with that change everything has improved—health, temper, outlook, work on the symphony, and spirits."[26] There is no telling what prompted Britten's conflicted feelings about the project, or whether Forster had any part in the discussion that ensued to put Britten's spirits back in order (though Crozier's use of the very Forsterian word *muddle* to describe Britten's state of mind is suggestive). It may well have been that he was beginning to grapple with the implications of having chosen a story with more overtly homosexual implications than anything he had produced before.

Various commitments, including the Aldeburgh Festival in the late spring of 1949 and a concert tour of the United States with Pears in the fall, kept Britten busy, and he continued to work at completing other composition projects. By August 1949 Forster was expressing his concern that Britten did not seem to be ready to focus on the *Billy Budd* project. But by January 1950 Britten was "at work in the vulgar sense of that word," as Forster said in a letter to the composer—actual notes were being written down on paper. Although it seems that Forster's misunderstanding about Britten's working method was now cleared up, a much larger hurdle was about to present itself. A premonition of trouble came in January when Forster came to Aldeburgh to convalesce after a prostate operation. Forster's desire to participate in Britten's process of creation temporarily interfered with the composer's concentration in some way, for he wrote to Pears that he was "in a bit of a muddle over Billy" and had temporarily halted the newly begun process of writing out the music.

For Britten it was very important to oversee the creation of the libretto. In one of the few interviews Britten gave he stated very plainly that he "had to" help shape his libretti: "I couldn't ask anyone to prepare a libretto for me without being in on it myself from the start."[27] But as Forster was to discover, this was not necessarily a

---

26. Quoted in Carpenter, *Benjamin Britten,* 283–84.

27. Schafer, *British Composers,* 115. The testimony of all of Britten's librettists, especially William Plomer and Myfanwy Piper, who prepared more than one libretto for him, confirms this. See also Crozier, "Staging," and Ronald Duncan, *Working with Britten* (Welcombe Bideford: Rebel Press, 1981) and "The Problems of a Librettist," *Composer* 23 (1967): 6–9.

reciprocal process between composer and librettist. Britten wanted to be able to shape the libretto but did not expect his librettist to have a hand in shaping the music. Britten's first full-length libretto had been written by Auden, another musically educated writer. Besides their initial collaborations at the GPO Film Unit where they met in 1936, Auden collaborated with Britten on a song cycle, *Our Hunting Fathers,* before writing the libretto for Britten's first stage drama, *Paul Bunyan.*[28] In their collaboration on *Paul Bunyan,* Britten was still very much dazzled by the more worldly and autocratic Auden. But the experience seemed to have taught Britten very quickly that he needed to work with more pliable librettists in order to have the desired control over the finished work.[29] Auden, a slightly older and far more confident artist at the time of *Paul Bunyan,* was too inhibitingly self-assured for Britten to dominate.

After his experience with the independent Auden, Britten had a different librettist for each of his operas. Often collaboration with the increasingly demanding Britten heralded the beginning of the end of a friendship. Auden and Britten eventually had a falling out. The left-wing playwright Montagu Slater wrote the libretto for *Peter Grimes* (after Isherwood turned down the commission). But when Britten wanted changes made to the libretto Slater was slow to comply, and the poet Ronald Duncan was brought in to make alterations. Duncan was then asked to write the libretto for Britten's next venture, *The Rape of Lucretia.* But he also quarreled with Britten and was superseded by Eric Crozier. Crozier, too, fell from favor after his work on *Albert Herring* and *Billy Budd.*

28. For detailed accounts of their collaborations, see Donald Mitchell, *Britten and Auden in the Thirties* (Seattle: University of Washington Press, 1981), and Edward Mendelson, *Early Auden* (New York: Viking, 1981).

29. Later, Auden himself came to appreciate this position when he returned to the world of opera to write the libretto for Stravinsky's *The Rake's Progress.* As Auden eventually put it in "Notes on Music and Opera," "The verses which the librettist writes are not addressed to the public but are really a private letter to the composer. They have their moment of glory, the moment in which they suggest to him a certain melody; once that is over, they are as expendable as infantry to a Chinese general: they must efface themselves and cease to care what happens to them" (*The Dyer's Hand* [New York: Random House, 1962], 473). (Coincidentally Auden's collaboration with Stravinsky took place around the same time as that between Forster and Britten, and the two operas premiered in the same year.)

Forster would also prove to be a one-time collaborator. Like Auden, Forster was inclined to stake his artistic integrity on the libretto to an extent that made it difficult for Britten to have his way; Forster was too authoritative, too respected by Britten to be dominated. It was not until the advent of the novelist William Plomer, and later Myfanwy Piper, that Britten was to find librettists with whom he could work repeatedly. Plomer, who was part of Forster's circle of London friends, was to be Britten's librettist for *Gloriana* (which followed *Billy Budd* in Britten's operatic output) and the "parables for church performance" written in the 1960s.[30] Plomer had more peaceful collaborations with Britten, since he seemed to understand and accept Britten's need to have the upper hand in operatic collaboration.

Once Britten recovered from the blockage that Forster's visit brought on, activity picked up and proceeded throughout the spring of 1950. But a serious disagreement arose between Britten and Forster in April, when the composer played through parts of the opera for the first time. Forster wrote to his friend Bob Buckingham, "I have had my first difference of opinion with him—over the dirge for the Novice. He has done dry contra-puntal [*sic*] stuff, no doubt original and excellent from the musician's point of view, but not at all appropriate from mine. I shall have a big discussion when the act is finished." Britten was almost pathologically sensitive to criticism, and Forster's opinions on what was musically "appropriate" were not welcome. Nor was Forster's worrying about Britten's dedication of his creative powers to the opera lost on Britten, who wrote to Crozier, "As you probably know I'm having a bit of a worry with Morgan, who can't quite understand my method of work! Please tell him, if you get a chance, that I *always* do twenty things at once, & that there'll be a good chance of the opera being done in time!"[31]

Evidently Britten did not express his discomfort with the older man's criticism directly. When Forster heard more of the opera in November

---

30. These works—*Curlew River* (1964), *The Burning Fiery Furnace* (1966), and *The Prodigal Son* (1968)—were short music dramas intended to be performed in church settings. Plomer, who had lived in Japan, urged Britten to attend a performance of Noh theater when he went to Japan in the late 1950s. Britten was very impressed by *Sumidigawa*, the Noh drama he saw, and this play became the inspiration for *Curlew River*.

31. Forster to Buckingham, April 23, 1950, and Britten to Crozier, August 29, 1950, quoted in Cooke and Reed, *Benjamin Britten: Billy Budd*, 59, 60.

1950, he did not hesitate to write Britten regarding what he saw as the flaws in the way Britten had conceived John Claggart's monologue in which he vows to destroy Billy Budd:

> It is *my* most important piece of writing and I did not, at my first hearings, feel it sufficiently important musically. The extensions and changes you suggest in the last lap may make all the difference for me, besides being excellent in themselves. With the exception of it, all delighted me, most wonderful.
>
> Returning to it, I want *passion*—love constricted, perverted, poisoned, but nevertheless *flowing* down its agonizing channel; a sexual discharge gone evil. Not soggy depression or growling remorse. I seemed to be turning from one musical discomfort to another, and was dissatisfied. I looked for an aria perhaps, for a more recognizable form. I liked the last section best, and if it is extended so that it dominates my vague objections may vanish. "A longer line, a firmer melody"—exactly.[32]

These sentences conjure up the complexities and problems of Britten and Forster's collaboration. Reading this passage one cannot fail to notice that what Forster emphasizes is waiting to be realized in the text is the sexual nature of Claggart's feelings toward Billy Budd. There is no evidence that Britten disagreed with the idea that there is a sexual element to Claggart's feelings toward Billy. But it is clear from what ensued after Forster sent the letter that Britten did disagree with Forster's conception of their roles within the collaboration. The emphasis on the possessive in the first sentence is an indication of just how strongly Forster felt about the libretto. This was more than a collaborative project; on some level for Forster it was *his* work, of an importance comparable to his fiction. He clearly did not think that Britten's music fit the ideas that his words were trying to communicate. Forster's conception of the librettist's role included not only providing the text but also helping to guide how the music was to fully realize the text.

Britten required words, not musical opinions, from his librettists, and he reacted badly to the criticism. The effect of the criticism was exacerbated by an estrangement at the end of 1950 when Britten and Crozier visited Forster in Cambridge. A perceived slight caused Forster

32. Forster to Britten, early December 1950, in *Selected Letters,* 242.

to respond harshly to Britten, and Crozier had to try to make peace between his collaborators. Forster's diary for December 1950 includes a reflection on this incident that reveals some ambivalence about Britten: "I am rather a fierce old man at the moment and he is rather a spoilt boy, and certainly a busy one."[33] In the process of peacemaking, Crozier, who had more experience with Britten's psychological needs as a creator, suggested that the revisions Forster was hoping for be put off until later. Britten eventually did make changes to Claggart's monologue, mostly to lengthen the final section of the aria, which Forster had found more to his liking.[34] Forster's "lack of enthusiasm" did not leave Britten's mind for the remainder of the collaboration.[35]

Differing interpretations of Melville's story probably contributed to the tension that developed between Forster and Britten. Although they approached Melville with united enthusiasm, it is clear from how Forster and Britten reshaped the novella and how they reflected on it later that they disagreed in important ways about the interpretation of the story. They certainly differed in their views of the three main characters, and from this stemmed the most central contrast in their opinions. For Forster the story is one of salvation effected through homosexual love; for Britten it is a darker tale of how love can bring about the destruction of the loved one. Forster's words and Britten's music bear out the conflicts in their interpretations.

The composer and librettist's struggle over the appropriateness of the music for Claggart's monologue is a telling symptom of the differences between the way Forster and Britten viewed Claggart, and the implications of Melville's story in general. If Claggart is pure evil for Forster, then clearly Forster did not hear what he expected in Britten's music. The music Britten did produce and his reaction to being criticized point to a different interpretation of Claggart. Conventional musical indicators of a "villain" are occasionally present, particularly in the use of the lower registers of the orchestra. But only at the

---

33. Quoted in Furbank, *Forster,* 2:285.

34. Several months after Forster's disastrous letter, these changes were made "grudgingly." Philip Reed, "On the Sketches for *Billy Budd,*" in *On Mahler and Britten: Essays in Honor of Donald Mitchell on His Seventieth Birthday,* ed. Philip Reed (Woodbridge: Boydell Press, 1995), 242.

35. Britten to Marion Harewood, March 16, 1951, quoted in Cooke and Reed, *Benjamin Britten: Billy Budd,* 63.

end of the aria does Claggart's vow, "I will destroy you," ring out with the kind of determination Forster evidently expected throughout. Claggart is not, for Britten, a symbol of pure evil with a trumpeting relish for wickedness, but a man, bitter and trapped by his feelings for Billy, which he cannot ever gratify. The "musical discomforts" Forster heard are Britten's interpretation of the "sexual discharge gone evil": an ordinary human love cramped and turned destructive.

In his discussion of *Billy Budd* in *Aspects of the Novel,* Forster emphasizes the allegorical aspect of Melville's characters. For him Billy "has goodness of the glowing aggressive sort which cannot exist unless it has evil to consume." Correspondingly, "Claggart is evil," and in him "evil is labeled and personified instead of slipping over the ocean and around the world."[36] In the discussion Britten, Crozier, and Forster held on BBC radio about the opera in 1960, Forster makes the point again that for him Billy and Billy's goodness were the main issue: "I tend to think Billy the central figure. He names the opera, and I think I consider things from his point of view. And incidentally, this question of goodness, and of making goodness interesting is one that does hold me very much, because I think if only writers were able enough . . . that you could make goodness very interesting; and I was very anxious to do that over Billy as far as I could." By contrast, in the same broadcast Britten stressed his attraction to "emotional content" and "the characters themselves and the conflicts between the characters."[37]

Forster's remarks on the importance of Billy show clearly the nature of the disagreement between the composer and the librettist about the main emotional and moral focus of the story. When asked which character he viewed as the focus of the opera, Britten replied: "I must admit that [it was] Vere, who has what seems to me the main moral problem of the whole work, round whom the drama was going to center."[38] Forster admitted during the broadcast that Vere is "the only character that is truly tragic," but he still returned at the end of the broadcast to Billy's importance to him: "I think, when I think of the play, before anything else, I think of Billy." Whereas Britten found

---

36. Forster, *Aspects of the Novel,* 141, 142.
37. Britten, Crozier, and Forster, "Talking about *Billy Budd,*" 4, 5.
38. Ibid., 5.

Vere to be the heart of the story, Forster viewed Vere as being in need of "rescue" from Melville.[39] In describing the role of the librettist as an adapter, Forster spoke of the main problem being "how to make Billy, rather than Vere, the hero. Melville must have intended this; he called the story *Billy Budd,* and unless there is strong evidence to the contrary one may assume that an author calls his story after the chief character. But I also think that Melville got muddled and that, particularly in the trial scene, his respect for authority and discipline deflected him. How odiously Vere comes across in the trial!"[40]

The conflict over whether Vere or Billy is properly the main character in the opera (or which of them deserves to earn the listener's sympathy) is related to a deeper conflict between Forster's and Britten's views of the story. For Forster the opera was a chance to portray a true salvation through homosexual love: the devoted Billy is Vere's savior, mounting the gallows willingly to preserve Vere's authority. Philip Brett once compared *Billy Budd* to Forster's own *Maurice,* in which Billy plays the same role as Alec Scudder in saving Vere/Maurice: "The intellectual Captain Vere is saved by the love of his handsome sailor Billy—with less reason perhaps, and certainly more poignancy, for Vere still orders his destruction." Forster's letter to Britten regarding the execution scene make his view clear: "Billy's last cry ["God bless Captain Vere!"] is insoluble. . . . It was compassion, comprehension, love. Only Vere understood it, and it had the supernatural force inherent in something which only one person understands. I wish it could have been purely musical. Since we have to use words, Starry Vere seems better than Captain Vere, but the really wrong word is 'God.' Who but Billy, at such a moment, could bless?"[41] Forster and Crozier thus changed Billy's final words from "God bless Captain Vere!" to "Starry Vere, God bless you!"

Forster's libretto augments the savior-Billy already present in Melville's execution scene, in which Billy blesses Vere as he goes to his

---

39. "The rescuing of Vere from his creator being no small problem" was how Forster described it to Lionel Trilling in a letter of April 16, 1949 (*Selected Letters,* 237). He also spoke of "rescue" to William Plomer in a letter, quoted in Furbank, *Forster,* 2:284.

40. Forster in the *Griffin* of September 1951, quoted in Cooke and Reed, *Benjamin Britten: Billy Budd,* 29, n. 6.

41. Brett, "Salvation at Sea," 136; Forster to Britten, August 8, 1951, quoted in Cooke and Reed, *Benjamin Britten: Billy Budd,* 67.

crucifixion-like hanging. Forster's Billy is given a final monologue the night before his execution, in which he reflects on his fate and Vere's: "We're both in sore trouble, him and me, with great need for strength, and my trouble's soon ending, so I can't help him longer with his. Starry Vere, God bless him—and the clouds darker than night for us both." This is far beyond the powers of Melville's simpler, more fatalistic sailor. Forster's Billy thinks of his captain in his last hours, and the notion that he could "help" Vere is striking, given that Vere has ordered Billy's death. Forster goes out of his way to show Billy's thoughts dwelling on Vere, preparing the way for "Starry Vere, God bless you" at the moment of execution. The final words of Billy's monologue emphasize the strength he has found on the eve of his death: "I've sighted a sail in the storm, the far-shining sail that's not Fate, and I'm contented. . . . I'm strong, and I know it, and I'll stay strong, and that's all, and that's enough."

Presumably Forster's Billy gains his strength from his brief encounter with Vere after Claggart's death, when Vere announces the death sentence to Billy. Melville famously did not describe this encounter, and Forster and Britten chose to preserve this crucial ellipse in the story. Forster withdrew words, as Melville had, and Britten's music alone inhabits the space between Vere's announcement that he will convey the sentence and the following scene, in which Billy delivers his final monologue. As the music lacks the power to specify what happens in the interview, Billy's assertion of his strength, and the veiled indication that his connection to Vere is the source of that strength, partly fills the gap.

Unlike Forster, Britten made no explicit statements about the relation between Vere and Billy or about what transpired between them in their final (and only) interview. And insofar as the music is left to "speak for itself," the music that accompanies Vere's conveyance of the sentence to Billy "says" even less than it might.[42] Britten deliberately

---

42. However, many scholars have tried to find an interpretation for the enigmatic passage that accompanies the interview. See, for example, Arnold Whittall, "Twisted Relations: Method and Meaning in Britten's *Billy Budd*," *Cambridge Opera Journal* 2 (1990): 145–71; Clifford Hindley, "Britten's *Billy Budd*: The 'Interview Chords' Again," *Musical Quarterly* 78 (1994): 99–126, and "Love and Salvation in Britten's *Billy Budd*," *Music and Letters* 70 (1989): 363–81; Barry Emslie, "*Billy Budd* and the Fear of Words," *Cambridge Opera Journal* 4 (1992):

eschewed any traditional musical signifiers at this point in the opera; the music is simply thirty-four triads, played by the orchestra in a sequence of different orchestrations and levels of dynamics. Melody, which in western music often can convey the sense of a positive or negative emotion, is absent, and harmonically the passage is a series of juxtapositions rather than progressions.

But there are other musical indications that Britten did not share Forster's view that Billy's love for Vere could save the captain. The music Britten wrote for Billy's two superior officers suggests similarities in the way Vere and Claggart relate to Billy, and it creates a great deal of ambiguity about Vere's ultimate salvation. Rather than giving Claggart larger-than-life "evil" music, Britten focuses on him as a man unable to escape a destructive homosexual obsession and then gives much of the same music to Vere, particularly after Claggart is dead. Almost as soon as Claggart's death is confirmed, Vere begins to use the key of F minor that had been strongly associated with Claggart. Several of Claggart's vocal lines are adopted by Vere during the trial scene, including the melody (and words) from the beginning of Claggart's aria, "O beauty, o handsomeness, goodness." Britten could scarcely have been equating these two characters by accident. While he must have agreed with Forster that Vere is attracted to Billy, Vere's musical similarities to Claggart suggest that Vere, like Claggart, is compelled to destroy the object of his love. By giving Claggart's music to Vere after Claggart's death, Britten suggests that Vere is taking on Claggart's mission to destroy Billy—which indeed he does.

The music of the opera's epilogue shadows Forster's idea that Billy's final words bless and save Vere with further ambiguities. Forster has Vere echo Billy's final monologue in the epilogue, but he also returns to the words of the prologue, "I am an old man now." Britten's response to this is to return to the music of the prologue, slowly rolling back the huge orchestral fortissimo that had accompanied Vere's echo of Billy's monologue to reveal the military drums that had accompanied Billy's execution. These remain; Billy's death is not easily dismissed by Britten. The stripping away of the orchestra leaves

---

43–59; Brett, "Salvation at Sea"; Donald Mitchell, "A *Billy Budd* Notebook," in Cooke and Reed, *Benjamin Britten: Billy Budd,* 111–34; and Shannon McKellar, "Re-Visioning the 'Missing' Scene: Critical and Tonal Trajectories in Britten's *Billy Budd*," *Journal of the Royal Musical Association* 122 (1997): 258–80.

Vere's harmonically equivocal line, which echoes the opening of the opera both in its words and in its notes. This quiet ending could be a peaceful closure—or it could be Vere about to begin the prologue (and the entire opera) again, endlessly returning to experiences he will never fully understand.

In the 1960 BBC broadcast Forster remarked that, "after all, when the composer wants to show a good character, he can give you good music." Britten, in clarifying that Forster must mean "music which depicts goodness" rather than music of quality, points out that "what one person thinks is good doesn't necessarily seem the music of goodness to someone else." Any search for which view of the drama, Forster's or Britten's, prevails in the finished work will inevitably break down on the fundamental ambiguity of the music. As Britten pointed out in the same BBC broadcast, "Isn't this surely what always happens with a parable? That people argue indefinitely about what the allegory is? In fact everyone's right and everyone's wrong."[43]

Whatever their disagreements, both Britten and Forster had taken an important artistic step in dramatizing the homoerotically charged triangle of Melville's novella. Britten went on to choose several more operatic subjects involving relationships between men that are implicitly or explicitly homoerotic. The vaguely threatening relationship between Miles and Peter Quint in *The Turn of the Screw* (1954), Oberon's desire for the Indian boy in *A Midsummer Night's Dream* (1960), and Aschenbach's consuming infatuation with the boy Tadzio in *Death in Venice* (1973) are striking examples of Britten's willingness to portray on stage what he could not publicly acknowledge as a part of his own life. Britten said little about his operas during his lifetime, leaving the ambiguity of the music to stand unencumbered.

In the years following his collaboration with Britten, Forster went on to a small but satisfying revival of his powers of fiction writing. In the summer of 1956 he took up a fragment that had been published as an "Entrance to an Unwritten Novel" by his friend J. R. Ackerley in the *Listener* in 1948 and transformed it into the powerful short story "The Other Boat."[44] The two protagonists of "The Other Boat" are much closer to Claggart and Billy than to Vere and Billy, in that

43. Britten, Crozier, and Forster, "Talking about *Billy Budd*," 6, 14.
44. Furbank, *Forster*, 2:301–2. The story is included in *The Life to Come*, a posthumously published collection of short stories.

their homosexual affair ends not in salvation for the aristocratic, white Lionel and self-sacrifice for the half-caste Coco, but with their mutual self-destruction. It is interesting to note a diary entry of P. N. Furbank, Forster's biographer, on this story: "Said he [Forster] thought the tragic theme of 'The Other Boat'—two people made to destroy each other— was more interesting than the theme of salvation, the rescuer from 'otherwhere,' the generic Alec. That was a fake. People could help one another, yes; but they were not decisive for each other like that."[45] Perhaps his work with Britten, and his experience of their disputes over the fates of Vere, Billy, and Claggart, led Forster to a darker view of love, similar to the view that so many of Britten's operas exemplify.[46] However, one would not want to propose an extreme change of heart on this issue. Part of Forster's return to fiction after *Billy Budd* was a revision of *Maurice* that made the final union of Maurice and Alec concrete and explicit.

Recalling the *Billy Budd* collaboration a decade later during the BBC broadcast of 1960, Forster said, "In writing my part of the libretto, in the collaboration, I felt quite different to what I felt while writing other things. Completely different. I was on a kind of voyage."[47] However profoundly Forster and Britten may have differed over the story of Vere, Claggart, and Billy, Forster recognized the collaboration for what it was, a unique chance to produce a work of art that addressed the possibility of homosexual love, even redemptive homosexual love. He wrote to Britten after the premiere of the opera: "You and I have both put into it something which lies deeper than artistic creation, and which we both understand. It could never have got there but for both of us. I hope to live and write on it in the future, but this opera is my Nunc Dimittis, in that it dismisses me peacefully, and convinces me that I have achieved."[48]

---

45. Quoted in Furbank, *Forster,* 2:303.
46. Indeed, Britten's next two operas, *Gloriana* (1953) and *The Turn of the Screw* (1954), center on love relationships between a powerful figure similar to Vere and a less powerful figure similar to Billy in which the less powerful object of love is ultimately destroyed.
47. Britten, Crozier, and Forster, "Talking about *Billy Budd*," 9.
48. Forster to Britten, December 9, 1951, in *Selected Letters,* 246.

Julie F. Codell

Victorian Artists' Family Biographies
Domestic Authority, the Marketplace,
and the Artist's Body

R ichard Altick argues that "English biography in the
nineteenth century was a rich but unstable compound
of history, journalism, eulogy, inspiration and material
suitable for the study of the mind." A hybrid genre, Victorian biography took many forms: the "compilation," "life and
letters," "reminiscences," "memoirs." Altick points out that literary biographies throughout the Victorian period discursively
intersected with current events, theories of the creative mind,
critical judgments, aesthetics, theories of personality traits,
and the equation between character and work.[1] Although the
development of the biography was complex and asymmetrical, as Altick demonstrates, realism increasingly replaced or
modified didacticism and hero worship, as biographical narratives struggled to order and thematize voluminous, heteroge-
neous details and multiple sources of information for Victorian
readers who consumed quantities of "collective lives, biographies in series and biographical dictionaries."[2] Yet biographies
for boys and girls, as well as those intended for adults, still

1. Altick, *Lives and Letters: A History of Literary Biography in England
and America* (New York: Alfred A. Knopf, 1965), 181, 193, 196.
2. Ira Bruce Nadel, *Biography: Fiction, Fact and Form* (New York: St.
Martin's Press, 1984), 13.

maintained their moral and socializing themes: self-sacrifice for public good, the lone individual struggling against family or the social order, the priority of hard work and dedication over personal gain.[3]

Examining in detail a number of artists' family or domestic biographies written between 1890 and World War I, I will argue that their authorship by the artists' widows and children exploited the hybridity of Victorian biography to assert a domestic authority necessary to the construction of an artist compatible with Victorian social values.[4] From the 1890s to World War I, these posthumous biographies may have been the last appeal from a fading Victorian art world whose principal representatives were dying out: John Everett Millais, Ford Madox Brown, John Hungerford Pollen, William Richmond, Charles West Cope, Richard Redgrave, Edward Burne-Jones, George Frederick Watts, William Quiller Orchardson, Thomas Woolner, and William Morris.[5] These artists had been very successful, and all lived long, prosperous lives. Their biographies mixed autobiographical content (letters, diaries) with a biographical narrative and a unique visual paratext of photographs that represented the abstract issue of artists' sociality through images of the artists' body and domestic environments.[6] I will argue further that the new discipline of art history and the changing professional status of artists after 1880 offered family biographers ways of presenting information (such as appended mini-catalogs) and

3. Martha Vicinus, " 'Tactful Organising and Executive Power': Biographies of Florence Nightingale for Girls," in *Telling Lives in Science: Essays on Scientific Biography,* ed. Michael Shortland and Richard Yeo (Cambridge: Cambridge University Press, 1996), 203–6.

4. Dozens of artists' lives, autobiographies, and biographies were written in the last quarter of the Victorian period, many in series created by popular publishers (George Bell, Macmillan, Adam and Charles Black, and various periodicals).

5. The subjects of these biographies are obviously male; while female artists wrote autobiographies as well (see Pamela Nunn, ed., *Canvassing: Recollections by Six Victorian Women Artists* [London: Camden Press, 1986]), there was no cottage industry in posthumous biographies of women artists by their widowers or children. Possible reasons include the economic independence of their husbands and the assumed contradictions for women artists between their domestic and professional roles. The culturally subordinate relationship of author to subject in these biographies and the domestic, rather than professional, authority of the biographers may have made such biographies seem inappropriate for widowers.

6. For presentations of these, see Paula Gillett, *Worlds of Art: Painters in Victorian Society* (New Brunswick: Rutgers University Press, 1990).

policing meanings of the concept *artist* in order to confirm Victorian aesthetic values in the face of new and foreign modernisms.

The very hybridity of Victorian biographies offered an opportunity to shape the meaning of *artist*. These authors increased the hybridity, introducing photos, illustrations, and appendixes of lists of works produced, exhibited, and purchased and a visual para-text of images of the artist, fellow artists, patrons, homes, studios, families, and works of art.[7] Although the numbers of reproductions varied from 317 (Millais) to 4 (Redgrave) and even none (Cope), most of these biographies contained about 40 to 50, mostly photographs. In John Guile Millais's biography of his father, some images (Millais's Uffizi portrait and portraits of Gladstone and Tennyson) are privileged full-page photogravures, not half-page illustrations in the text; reproduced paintings vary in size, another indication of privileging certain works. I will analyze these biographies' intertwined verbal and visual modes of representation within the context of Victorian notions of artistic professionalism and sociality. The bricolage of these biographies raises issues of privileged knowledge undergirding domestic authority in contrast to professional authority. Their seemingly jumbled and discontinuous narratives faceted artists into social, professional, national, and moral beings, creating interstices from which their authors could employ their domestic authority to define and defend the artist.[8]

---

7. Victorian biographical literature included the most traditional genre of artists' biographies, the collective biography that strung brief artists' biographies together into a "history" of art. Initiated by Vasari, who was much studied, criticized, and corrected by the Victorians, this genre was frequently taken up in England and, when not used for purely didactic lessons, turned into an encyclopedia or biographical dictionary. For a brief survey, see Richard Altick, "Writing the Life of J. J. Ridley," in *Nineteenth-Century Lives: Essays Presented to Jerome Hamilton Buckley,* ed. Laurence S. Lockridge et al. (Cambridge: Cambridge University Press, 1989), 26–58. There were also biographical dictionaries, such as dictionaries of women artists, including those by Walter Shaw Sparrow (1905) and Ellen C. Clayton (1876). Despite the increasing realism of biographical narratives, by the end of the century artists' lives were still used to exemplify characteristically Victorian virtues of hard work and nationalism, as in Henry Ewart's *Toilers in Art* (New York: Thomas Whittaker, 1892), part of a series on great men and women. This was a very enduring genre!

8. In many details, these family authors also followed the institutional biography modeled on Plutarch and promoted most energetically by Samuel Smiles

Reacting to Victorian forms of biography, Harold Nicolson in 1927 rather desperately insisted on clear boundaries between history, anecdote, and literature: "we must above all distinguish 'pure' from 'impure' biography; and having thus narrowed down the art of biography to a recognisable and distinct form of narrative, we must indicate what elements go to render any particular biography either 'good' or 'bad.'" He distinguished biography from "journals, diaries, memoirs, imaginary portraits, or mere jottings of gossip and conversation" and considered extraneous to a good biography "an undue desire to celebrate the dead, or a purpose extraneous to the work itself, or an undue subjectivity on the part of the biographer." Post-1890 biographies of recently dead Victorian artists, until now largely ignored despite the growing scholarship on Victorian life-writings, were perhaps the most impure biographies possible, by Nicolson's definition, and they contained all three faults he outlined: they celebrated the dead, used the artist's life to demonstrate a social role for the artist, and were undoubtedly very subjective. The importance of domestic sociality was ignored by Nicolson, who considered such information impure. Earlier writers on biography, however, such as James Stanfield, argued that biography should reveal "the transactions . . . the private hours . . . the secret propensities, enjoyments, and weaknesses of celebrated persons," all designed to increase "our sympathy in proportion to our intimacy with the object held up to us . . . with the touches of affection and interest," although he, too, cautioned against subjective moral judgments of biographical subjects.[9]

This intimacy was common in Victorian biographies, but by the 1890s biographers had to intervene against new notions of artists'

(see Nadel, *Biography,* 17–21; Altick, "Writing," 44–45): suppression of unpleasant information, structural topoi (genealogy, childhood, early display of talents, domestic tranquillity, public success), and preference for evaluation of the subject over strictly factual narrative, though now introducing the photographic "text" as a test of realism to highlight moral character. Following conventions, they embedded letters, diaries, memoirs by the dead artist, and comments by the artist's professional colleagues into their narratives. The ratio of primary documents to narrative varied: some included many letters and diary entries, while others provided full-scale narratives and cited documents sparingly.

9. Nicolson, *The Development of English Biography* (London: Hogarth Press, 1927), 8–10; James Field Stanfield, *An Essay on the Study and Composition of Biography* (1813; rpt. New York: Garland, 1986), 131, 133–35.

bohemianism, degeneracy, sexual ambiguities, and the mysteries of the studio. Radical commercial changes in production and reproduction (new exhibition venues, the trade in mass prints, new professional societies, and new consumers) conspired to encourage a new economic and worldly subjectivity for the artist. The artists' biographies I will examine unashamedly placed their subjects on pedestals, but their worshipful attitude served to veil one central but troubling topic: the dominance of the marketplace in artists' lives and careers. The widowed authors of these hybrid biographies had a stake in the market values of artworks by the dead artists. After all, this value was their inheritance. Artists' deaths result in a reevaluation of the market values of their works, and a high market value was worth writing for. Walter Bayes in his 1931 revisionist biography of the Romantic painter J. M. W. Turner argued,

> Painters, then, offer to writers a device for earning an occasional cheque. Writers in return build up an immense assumed value of painting. An artist's works are catalogued and his price increases at once. Monographs are written on him and reviews of the monographs. The advances in price are chronicled and, like the serpent feeding on its own tail, the chronicle provokes a further advance . . . a famous work of art is seen magnified through a halo of words, blurred in a mush of tricolour printing. . . . Is it any good raising the question of its quality? None at all unless you raise also the question of its authenticity. . . . A picturesque personality, a biography rather highly coloured in its episodes, are of great advantage to the artists, or again to be more exact, of advantage posthumously to the owners of the work.[10]

Artists' biographies were also inflected by the new discipline of art history, which helped separate professional from domestic authority and veil market values through an "objectivity" embodied in the form of catalogs and photographs of works that determined authenticity, provenance, and price. Building on Foucault's theories of disciplines, David Amigoni argues that the second half of the nineteenth century was marked by attempts to professionalize new academic disciplines, such as modern history and literature, and one strategy for this was to create authoritative interpretations of biographies to restructure,

10. Bayes, *Turner: A Speculative Portrait* (London: Geoffrey Bles, 1931), 5–7.

professionalize, and legitimatize disciplines.[11] Nicolson's insistence on purity participated in this academic policing of meanings. A burgeoning art history offered strategies with which to construct an objective, authoritative representation of the issues of professionalism, sociality, and labor. Surprisingly, family authors appropriated these "objective" strategies to sustain their domestic authority without sacrificing their subjects' professional legitimacy; for Victorian readers the construction of the artist required a synthesizing of discrete social, domestic, and professional selves.

Antecedents

Speculating on the imaginary biography of William Thackeray's character J. J. Ridley in *The Newcomes,* Altick imagines a relationship between the novel and the growing Victorian interest in artists and their lives. Before midcentury, artists' biographies were few compared with other forms of biographical literature, including voluminous collections of "lives" (such as Allan Cunningham's *Lives,* 1829–1833) modeled on Giorgio Vasari's paradigmatic collective biographies. Altick effectively describes biographers' strategies to make their subjects either more interesting or more acceptable in the first half of the nineteenth century, such as the use of themes of paranoia and self-destruction in some midcentury artists' biographies, themes not used by late-century family biographers. However, as Altick notes, Ridley fulfills a Victorian didactic ideal of an artist who satisfies public taste, succeeds through that formula, works very hard, and comes from humble circumstances.[12]

While midcentury artists' biographies by family members shared some features with later Victorian biographies, several antecedent works differed significantly from later biographies in the presentation of the artist.[13] Perhaps one of the strangest of the Victorian artists'

11. David Amigoni, *Victorian Biography: Intellectuals and the Ordering of Discourse* (New York: St. Martin's Press, 1993).

12. Altick, "Writing," 28, 32–37, 40, 42–43.

13. These common themes are moralizing and hygienic presentations; use of the subject's voice whenever possible; heroic representation; modeling of self-

biographies is the 1858 *Struggles of a Young Artist: Being a Memoir of David C. Gibson by a Brother Artist* (William MacDuff, who is never identified in the book). Gibson (1827–1856) fulfilled the romantic moral drama of an artist's tormented life: debauchery, sudden conversion to goodness, struggles with poverty, hard work, dedication to art, and an early grave. MacDuff began his biography with the artist's conventional education pitted against his desire to draw "what he saw or felt," combined with his desire to paint with a romantic rebelliousness. Despite fluctuating fortunes and wasted youth, Gibson was saved because "his study of Art was prosecuted vigourously." Finding patrons, Gibson returned to London but was led astray in politics and in morals:

> Profligacy, drowned and deadened conscience—that conscience that was once so full of delicate sensibility. . . . The Bible was scoffed at . . . night after night in the filth of the purlieus of Drury Lane and the Haymarket, revelling with degraded and degrading minds, making himself the song of the drunkard. . . . As infidelity followed debauchery—so, in the natural order of things, wild Utopian dreams as to Chartism and socialism—the equality of rights and division of property—tracked the footsteps of their elder sisters. . . . Every wretched heresy of the Owen school seemed ready to complete the wreck and disorganization of his moral nature.[14]

---

help behavior; concerns with the readers' edification; attention to formative experiences of childhood, parentage, residence, early exhibitions of talent; unalloyed mixtures of sources (letters, diaries, direct quotations, judgments from others); the theme of perseverance in the face of handicaps, often used for biographies of artists, writers, and scholars; and focus on the person rather than the art (Altick, *Lives,* 82–110). My examination of midcentury artists' biographies does not include many relevant works by near relations or very close friends: pre-Victorian works such as William Hazlitt's study of Northcote (1830), John Thomas Smith's study of Nollekens (1828), William Hayley's life of Romney (1809), and Victorian examples including Charles Leslie's biography and "memoirs" of John Constable (1843), Tom Taylor's study of Haydon (1853), and Anna Elizabeth Bray's biography of Thomas Stothard (her first husband's father; 1851). In "Writing the Life of J. J. Ridley," Altick offers a fine survey of this early biographical literature. I do not refer to Rev. John Romney's biography of his father, George Romney, which is not only pre-Victorian (1830), and thus has much in common with eighteenth-century conventions of biography, but was also written largely to refute Hayley's biography of Romney and thus had an unusual rhetorical motive.

14. J. F. MacDuff, *The Struggles of a Young Artist: Being a Memoir of David C. Gibson by a Brother Artist* (London: James Nisbet, 1858), 4, 18, 48–49.

Gibson's attempts to exhibit were thwarted by "the fashionable groups" who failed to appreciate a young artist's hard work and anxieties. Gibson retreated to the Highlands and found one patron, "an honest, hard-working baker in Kirkcaldy, who, from a pure love of art, had tried to foster his genius." Finding some exhibition success, Gibson was nevertheless tormented by his "chequered life" and filled with remorse. On the brink of success, he died.[15]

John Seddon's life of his brother Thomas (1858) was also a moral tale, although almost all of the text consisted of Thomas's letters. Among the letters were brief commentaries by John Seddon underlining the message to

> shew to those who are now struggling in the arduous path of art, how with a noble and unselfish aim one has toiled and trod in the same before them; that, seeing sometimes his "footprints" in the way, they may "take heart again" in their discouragement; and, above all, that they may learn, with him, to hold art, and success, and all things, but secondary to the one thing needful, and seek, as he did, to forward humbly by their work, as best they may, the cause of their Saviour.[16]

In the course of his professional training, the artist went to Paris in 1841 to study ornamental art, but France corrupted him: "he contracted a taste for pleasure and dissipation, which unnerved his mind," though he retained his "habitual conscientiousness." Seddon established a Workingman's College that initially enrolled two hundred workers, joined professional societies, and traveled to scenic areas to sketch and exhibit. Still, he was "overborne by besetting sins . . . he too often gave way to the impulses of his natural love of excitement and pleasure, and did what his conscience afterwards reproved. . . . 'But my heart is desperately wicked; . . . help me to bow in resignation to Thy will.'" Suffering serious illness at thirty, he had a conversion experience and, upon recovery, determined to work hard. His chosen subject, biblical landscape, turned his mind to God: "Art's highest vocation is to be the handmaid to religion and purity, instead of to mere animal enjoyment and sensuality." Seddon found this same

15. Ibid., 73, 93, 178.
16. Seddon, *Memoir and Letters of the Late Thomas Seddon, Artist* (London: John Nisbet, 1858), v–vi.

mission in Pre-Raphaelite art, especially the paintings of Holman Hunt, his traveling companion.[17]

In these cases the biographer's authority was legitimated by intimate knowledge of the subject's character on which to establish the artist's ultimate goodness. Letters and primary documents bore witness to the moral and religious contents that eclipsed their professional activity. Artists were subject to art's inherent moral temptations, but art could also save the artist. Early deaths confirmed the biographies' stoical theme of the futility of worldly attachments.

William Bell Scott's biography of his brother David, though also concerned with the artist's moral character, focused on his professional life. David moved in artistic circles, established a Life Academy in Edinburgh, and devoted himself to history painting, the most ideal and least remunerative genre of Victorian art. David's diary detailed operations of the art world of British and American artists living in Rome: artists' networks, professional meetings, discussions of sales and critical reviews, long hours in the studio, the combined web of social and professional behaviors, and shared professional strategies, such as the lucrative practice of having paintings lithographed. Scott's biography relied heavily on his brother's diary and notes, but there is more authorial narrative here than in Seddon's, and less moralizing than in the other two biographies. Scott dwelt more on his brother as an intellectual, rather than only a moral, type for the artist:

> The artist, whose genius is simply imitative of the outward, or whose power mainly lies in such imitation, has been again and again found wanting by the philosopher and the literary critic; and although his works are those that give to pictures their popular and commercial value, a higher intellectual character is wanted to support the dignity of art and of the artist. He must be in himself greater, not less than his works; his life and his labours must be one.[18]

The disparity between public perception of the artist and the artist's hard work and difficult life is a central theme of this biography. Scott appealed to the public, whom he addressed directly as "you," to

17. Ibid., 3–4, 13–14, 16, 127.
18. Scott, *Memoir of David Scott, R.S.A.* (Edinburgh: Adam and Charles Black, 1850), v–vi.

respect painters for their moral and intellectual gifts. He chastised the English public for thinking art was only "an embellishment and pleasing luxury." David's moral character was a central topic, but in the context of professional demands. We are assured through family history that David descended from good yeoman stock and behaved like a regular boy—he was interested in cockfights and pranks— while also displaying early artistic talent. William commented on the self-absorption that the artist's letters reveal: "the insatiable *me* sees nothing but obstacles in the *not me* . . . a noble nature struggling up in to the light. . . . Difficulties, pains, and venturing, are among the elements, not only of Christian, but of intellectual progress." Scott as author lamented the life of the "sensitive man" doomed to despair because "high art of an original kind, and on an adequate scale, is not required by any desire in the public mind . . . that the high art we now have is of the revival kind, and aims at foreign standards, or merely academic excellences." The moral character of his subject is revealed in his perseverance in the outmoded genres of history painting and allegory: "The history of our country of late years is a history of its finances," an era harmful to those artists not inclined to business matters. Scott outlined two kinds of artists, those in line "with the entire frame of the world" and thus successful, and those out of step, who, like his brother, failed.[19]

The romantic suffering artist was soon to be replaced by the successful Victorian artist, whose life and career dominated the last quarter of the nineteenth century. This more professional emphasis was anticipated by Wilkie Collins's biography of his father William (1848). This two-volume biography, while attending to the artist's upstanding moral character and dedication in the face of financial difficulties, focuses almost exclusively on the training, practice, and pursuit of an artistic career. Collins is an apologist for the Royal Academy, whose uneven art education was the subject of much debate and lament by artists, especially its poor training in draftsmanship. Nevertheless, the academy is presented as a nurturing, prodding, idealist institution.[20] Collins is frequently described as a genius, as well as a conscientious,

19. Ibid., 28, 5, 9–12, 53, 183, 188, 54, 208, 189, 192.
20. Collins, *Memoirs of the Life of William Collins, Esq., R.A.,* 2 vols. (London: Longman, Brown, Green, and Longmans, 1848), 1:31–33.

industrious worker, and his reprinted diaries almost entirely record his studio practice and work habits. Pictures produced and their buyers are recorded in the narrative, which follows Collins's career year by year. The biography concludes with a list of the pictures Collins painted annually, along with their exhibition sites, prices, and buyers, and a list of the engravings made from Collins's paintings, the latter an indication of the artist's popularity. These lists point in the direction of a more objective emphasis on professional productivity and such concerns as provenance and market value, interests that dominate late-nineteenth-century artists' biographies.

The Artist's Degeneration, J. M. W. Turner, and Samuel Smiles

Questions about the moral nature of the artist remained, however, and the image of the Victorian artist still had to address this issue. Art was popularly associated with "the sensuality which is often considered part of it," as John Henry Newman wrote in an 1855 letter,[21] and the artist as a deviant subject began to appear in increasing numbers of studies after 1880. Degeneracy was associated with Pre-Raphaelitism, French Impressionism, and Postimpressionism and thematized in the literature of degeneracy in "the image of the artist as morally, physically, and mentally degenerate."[22]

The literature of degeneracy was also a literature about the ties between genius and madness, a distinctly nineteenth-century controversy. The eighteenth-century notion of genius was of a person whose activities combined faculties of rational judgment, sense, and memory and was conditioned by education, tradition, and conventions. The Romantics, however, willingly labeled themselves mad or

21. Quoted in Anne Pollen, *John Hungerford Pollen, 1820–1902* (London: J. Murray, 1912), 258.

22. Patrick Bade, "Art and Degeneration: Visual Icons of Corruption," in *Degeneration: The Dark Side of Progress*, ed. J. Edward Chamberlin and Sander L. Gilman (New York: Columbia University Press, 1985), 226; William Greenslade, *Degeneration, Culture, and the Novel, 1880–1940* (Cambridge: Cambridge University Press, 1994), 123.

near mad and cultivated the neurotic personality in public. They emphasized imagination and its allied faculties of intuition, spontaneity, and creativity to construct a genius whose power lay primarily in originality, including resisting or overthrowing conventions. In the eighteenth century genius was a category of superiority, competing with wealth and birth, but more democratic and meritocratic. By the late nineteenth century its implications had changed dramatically and its associations were primarily with the arts.[23] The roots of these associations were Romantic theories of artistic creation as involuntary and outside the conscious control of artists. The promotion of artistic creativity as a kind of possession probably appealed to Romantics (such as Poe, Byron, Shelley, Keats), themselves economically dispossessed by changing patterns of patronage that threw them on the mercy of the market. In response and defense they mystified their processes and claimed the power to tap into sources of inspiration denied ordinary mortals. Two generations later this mystical appeal was turned into a complex set of explanations for the proximity of genius and insanity.

British contributors to the growing literature of degeneracy after midcentury included Francis Galton, who in *Hereditary Genius* (1869) formulated a "hereditary theory of genius in which he postulated that all differences in human abilities, from the idiot to the great man, constitute deviations from the normal or average ability." Other authors who contributed to the belief in and "scientizing" of the pathology of geniuses in England were Henry Maudsley and Havelock Ellis. These authors followed the initiators of this pathologizing literature, Cesare Lombroso and Max Nordau, whose popular works were repeatedly translated and reprinted in England (nine English editions of Nordau's *Degeneration* were published between 1895 and 1900). As George Becker points out, "The stereotype of the mad genius reached an apex of popularity at the turn of the twentieth century (1880–1920)."[24]

Among the theories propagated was that "genius constituted a state of instability or disequilibrium in psycho-physical organization," a

23. George Becker, *The Mad Genius Controversy: A Study in the Sociology of Deviance* (Beverly Hills: Sage Publications, 1978), esp. 24–31, 56.

24. Cesare Lombroso, *The Man of Genius* (London: Walter Scott, 1891); Max Nordau, *Degeneration* (London: William Heinemann, 1895); Becker, *Mad Genius*, 29.

condition that included not just mental insanity but also a propensity to "moral insanity."[25] According to Lombroso, "genius is a true degenerative psychosis belonging to the group of moral insanity." Degeneracy was considered a biological phenomenon, too, as it was handed down through generations, though counteracted by the believed failure of geniuses to produce offspring. Drawing on literature from antiquity through the nineteenth century, Nordau determined that shared characteristics of genius and of insanity constituted an "anthropological family," including both moral and physical signs, many of which were considered feminine. Among the moral signs were hysteria, vanity, self-preoccupation, impulsiveness, vagabondage, extreme and inconsistent behaviors, an exquisite and perverted sensibility or hyperaesthesia often resulting in paranoia or depression, originality ("genius divines facts before completely knowing them"), fondness for special words, misoneism (a hatred of originality in specialties other than one's own), skepticism, pessimism, ennui, inability to act, fear of others, and mysticism. The major physical signs included irregular teeth, beardlessness, small size, squinty eyes, asymmetrical facial features, protruding ears, rickets or lameness, pallor, emaciation, left-handedness, sterility, unlikeness to parents or national type, precocity, somnambulism. Nordau argued, for example, that Verlaine's "asymmetric skull and Mongolian face" revealed "an impulsive vagabond and dipsomaniac."[26]

Degeneracy was characterized by morbid contempt for traditional customs and morality, including conventional representational practices and a tendency to regress into, and imitate, the past. Artists were especially prone to infection from both environment and heredity, since for Nordau "illness is disturbingly linked to the creative process."[27] Even Georgiana Burne-Jones treated her husband's ill-

25. Becker, *Mad Genius,* 37–38.

26. Lombroso, *Man,* 333; Becker, *Mad Genius,* 99; Nordau, *Degeneration,* 35, 126; Greenslade, *Degeneration,* 122.

27. Daniel Pick, *Faces of Degeneration: A European Disorder, c. 1848–c. 1918* (New York: Cambridge University Press, 1989), 18. Nordau's English examples of degeneracy embraced the Pre-Raphaelites, especially Burne-Jones, who joined a disparate immoral band, including Wagner, Ibsen, and Zola, among others. Other English studies of degeneracy include J. F. Nisbet, *The Insanity of Genius* (1891), and Francis Galton's *Hereditary Genius* (2d ed., 1892). Havelock Ellis translated Lombroso's *L'uomo di genio* in 1891 and wrote *The Criminal* (1890), in

ness as "one of the understood influences of his life . . . as with other sensitive natures, body and mind acted and reacted on each other"; some critics, including Camille Pissarro, described Burne-Jones's paintings as "too sick."[28] While certain biographical conventions remained standard—genealogy, childhood, schooling, marriage, and family life—biography's discursivity took on added signification in the context of post-1890 discussions about art and artists, further fueled by the trial of Oscar Wilde, who, according to the press, seemed to prove Nordau's contentions. At Wilde's trial "the moral question was deemed inseparable from the aesthetic." Nordau condemned Wilde as degenerate even before the trial.[29]

One important distinction to emerge from these debates was between talent and genius, a distinction introduced in the mid-eighteenth century. Genius was a force of mystery, madness, and danger, while talent encompassed social order, training, and predictability: "the achievements of the talented man are conscious, anticipated, slightly original, voluntary; the creations of the genius are semi-conscious, inspirational, spontaneous, highly original." Another author argued that "talent implies discrimination and a talented person is usually clever, and of good judgment; a genius is often erratic, unreliable, unstable, and irresponsible. . . . They are dreamers and persons incapable of appreciating circumstances at their proper value and incapable of finding opportune adaptations."[30] In this context, the family biographies' insistence on their subjects' labor, orderly social and domestic lives, financial successes, and willingness to take on portraiture and illustrations to earn a living resonates with this distinction between genius and talent.

Domesticating artists meant presenting them as socially controlled and conventional figures of talent, not raging geniuses, Romantics, or bohemians who lived outside the norm and exemplified unacceptable behavior. It is not surprising, then, that artists' biographers conser-

---

which he perpetuated the link between Verlaine and criminality. See Greenslade, *Degeneration,* 120–33.

28. Burne-Jones, *Memorials of Edward Burne-Jones,* 2 vols. (1904; rpt. London: Macmillan, 1986), 2:3; Bade, "Art," 225.

29. Pick, *Faces,* 20–21; Greenslade, *Degeneration,* 123.

30. Schwarz, 1916, and Armstrong-Jones, 1914, quoted in Becker, *Mad Genius,* 59.

vatively replicated conventional biographical structures and topics—
work ethic, family life, physical normality, and economic productivity.
In this context, photographs of artists and their families conveyed
multiple meanings in response to images of degenerate physical and
moral traits. Photos revealed artists as appealing gentlemen with "normal bodies" and facial expressions. Photos of parents and grandparents assured that the artist's ancestors were not mad and that the
artist resembled them; photos of children proved that artists were
not impotent, a final stage of degeneracy. Images of large homes and
studios signified material success and paterfamilial roles. Family life in
word and image "proved" artists' heterosexuality, potency, domestic
orderliness; material success demonstrated that in the struggle for
survival, artists could struggle with the best of them and thus could
contribute to the species' well-being, since those well blessed were
considered the hope of the "race."[31]

In this regard, family biographies opposed the image of the artist
that dominated Victorian fiction. As Bo Jeffares has demonstrated,
artists were popular figures in Victorian fiction and were characterized in a variety of ways, from handsome, romantic bohemians with
glowing eyes and flowing hair and beard to dandified figures, graceful
and seductive (George Moore, *A Modern Lover,* 1883), often dressed
in brown velvet (Thackeray's Clive Newcome). More interestingly
they were portrayed often as without a stake in society (Geraldine
Jewsbury, *The Half Sister,* 1848): disheveled, oddly dressed, spiritual,
emotional, sloppy, unmarried. Characteristics of artists in fiction were
their inability to handle money, which they squandered, and a tendency to playful behavior in the studio rather than hours of labor.
Artists were defiant of conventional social norms, unmarriageable to
respectable ladies, antimaterialist, uneconomical, and cut off from the
world by devotion to art. Artists' morality was further eroded by visits
to Paris, of course.[32]

Another troubling feature was the studio, a space often believed
to be as much beyond domestication as the artist. In novels they
worked in untidy, sequestered studios "full of strange odours, full

31. Pick, *Faces,* 19.
32. Jeffares, *The Artist in Nineteenth-Century English Fiction* (Atlantic Highlands: Humanities, 1979), 52–74.

of shadows, enticements" (Morley Roberts, *Immortal Youth,* 1896) and behaved like libertines, engaged in sexual liaisons with their working-class models (Thomas Hardy, *Pursuit of the Well-Beloved,* 1892; Rudyard Kipling, *The Light That Failed,* 1891). Fictional studios were described as chaotic, tobacco stained, junk-filled, debris-strewn, with untended hearths (Mary Anne Hardy, *The Artist's Family,* 1857)— the complete entropic antithesis of the orderly Victorian home and hearth. Studios proclaimed "a totally unorganised, relaxed—indeed, almost an organic—attitude to life." The studio was a bachelor's haven frequented by working-class models and the site of parties and "smokers" attended by other male artists. The studio was male and messy; the home was female and orderly. These fictionalized homes and studios expressed "an overwhelming concern for what was emotionally exciting and visually attractive, rather than practically viable and soberly secure."[33]

In late-century biographies, however, studios were photographically sited in the artist's home; while signifying male work, they were nevertheless well kept and metonymically parallel to other rooms in the house. Georgiana Burne-Jones quoted her husband's reaction to Du Maurier's *Trilby,* which he loved: "his artists are like artists and his studios are real studios. Terrible stuff even the best novelists make of studios, and the strange life of them, with its *innocent lawlessness*" (italics mine). The visually confirmed proximity of studios to homes (with images of working artists and wives present in the studio) offered "factual" evidence of the studio as a proper workplace and a domesticated site, and probably demystified it to many who never entered a studio. After all, the home as a civilizing force, as Samuel Smiles defined it, offered "domestic purity and moral life" and provided family pleasures, self-respect, comfort, "breathing space, and room for separation of sexes."[34]

Central to this domestic ideal was attention to detail. Cleanliness, for example, demanded attention to little things that to Smiles bespoke "an atmosphere of moral and physical well-being." This so-called trivia, banished by Nicolson from biographies, represented concepts

33. See Jeffares, *Artist,* 36–38, 62–63.
34. Burne-Jones, *Memorials,* 2:243; Smiles, *Workmen's Earnings, Strikes, and Savings* (1862; rpt. New York: Garland, 1984), 55.

dear to many Victorians beyond their anecdotal value. Details served to commemorate Victorians' various economies—domestic, personal, and labor.[35] Small things—an early drawing, a sense of humor, a note from the artist, a memory of an expression or dinner party conversation—were not trivial but revealed true character and properly individualized the subject with a sense of order. Biographies filled with quotidian details were sites of mutually reinforcing domestic and professional economies that constructed a professional *and* a socially acceptable artist. These details formed a meaningful history, not simply a chaotic, anecdotal chronicle of events. Departing from Altick's assumptions about trivial details, "decorous domesticity, full of harmless jottings on the comings and goings of titled visitors," I would argue that domestic "trivia" assured the authority of the widow as a witness to the artist's domestic sociality. I suspect that modernism's hostility to such details in modern biography criticism, furthermore, served to disqualify the widow from her authorial role in hopes of replacing her with an "objective," "professional," masculine biographer trained in modern academic disciplines.[36]

Samuel Smiles in *Thrift* argued that the best human virtues "are intimately related to the right use of money, such as generosity, honesty, justice, and self-denial," while the worst human vices were related to the abuse of money. Furthermore, Smiles argued that one worked "for the benefit of those who are dependent upon us. Industry must know how to earn, how to spend, and how to save." Artists' visible success, then, demonstrated their proper use of money and thus their virtuous character as thrifty and as breadwinners. For Smiles, indefatigable work was the most important moral contribution artists could make as models of behavior, and he offered many examples of artists from England and the Continent who exemplified hard labor, persistence, and often success. In ideal circumstances, they were also married. In these biographies, then, images of large studios and artists working in them combined values of industry and success, while appended lists of paintings implied for their owners savings-as-future-earnings from appreciated market values. The Smilesian virtue of labor

35. Samuel Smiles, *Thrift: A Book of Domestic Counsel* (1875; rpt. London: Murray, 1907), 179–80.
36. Altick, *Lives,* 239.

was thematized in narratives or embedded diary entries by artists recording working practices and long studio hours and in photos of studios. Images of the artist at various stages of his life created a cathartic investment for the reader. After all, Smiles argued, biography served to model behavior.[37]

One biographical subject seized the Victorian imagination and challenged the symbiosis between work and home: J. M. W. Turner, recognized as one of England's greatest Romantic artists, was acknowledged as less than an ideal role model morally and socially. His undomesticated character was a central theme in Victorian biographies of him, a problem that did not trouble popular biographies of Reynolds or Hogarth. Victorian characterizations of Turner ranged from Ruskin's construction of a suffering genius despised by all and struggling against great odds, an echo of the Romantic sufferer, to Thornbury's recognition of Turner's success from the very start of his career—he was the youngest artist ever admitted to the Royal Academy, and he left a prosperous life's legacy of £100,000. Kenelm Foss described Victorian biographies of Turner as "Victorian in manner and nauseatingly so in moral inference. While grudgingly admitting that Turner was the greatest landscape-seascape painter of all time, they suggest that it happened in spite of the fact that he was mean, unsociable, unwashed, intemperate, and the father of at least five illegitimate children. . . . They likewise deplore the fact that this immortal was no gentleman."[38]

In his 1879 biography, Philip G. Hamerton, art critic, etcher, and editor, turned Turner's "dual life" into a virtue. He strategically described Turner's character at the *end* of his biography after 350 pages on his career and interpreted Turner's eccentricities as typically English:

> He was one of the most eccentric Englishmen who ever lived, *a perfect British original.* . . . In many respects the eccentricities of Turner had an excellent effect upon his art . . . his *prodigious fertility.* . . . He who wrought them could not conform to the customs of "good society." . . . [H]e got up early in the morning as laborers and blacksmiths do, he *worked at his trade all day.* . . .

37. Smiles, *Thrift,* v–vi; see also Samuel Smiles, *Self-Help* (1859; rpt. London: Murray, 1958), 168–204, 350.

38. Bayes, *Turner,* 3–8; Foss, *The Double Life of J. M. W. Turner* (London: Richards Press, 1938), v.

He invited nobody to dinner at his own house in Queen Anne Street. . . . [T]he rule of his life was to shut himself up when at home, and keep his movements secret when he went out. These eccentricities, which look so unsocial, were merely the habits of a workman who protected his own peace. . . . [H]e *never cared for money* in comparison with his art. (italics mine)

Turner was torn, in Hamerton's view, between desiring a public reputation and privacy: "Whilst planning schemes for attaining the utmost possible notoriety, he lived in hiding like an insolvent debtor." Hamerton argued that a liberal education would not have made Turner a better artist but instead might have dampened his visual gifts. Turner's physical appearance and behavior were also quintessentially English—"unprepossessing appearance, short and thick-set, with coarse features and the general appearance of the skipper of some small merchant craft . . . the style and manner of the lower middle class . . . [his incapability] of saying kind and polite things in an easy and graceful way . . . [were all] exaggerations of English characteristics" which included hard work ("his power of toil"), plain dressing, reticence, both thrift and generosity, and an inability to express emotion. Defending Turner's sexual liaisons and acknowledging that public attacks on these were more in reaction to his lovers' being lower class than to their being his lovers, Hamerton argued that Turner was no more immoral than most and lived simply and temperately despite a reputation for drinking. Turner's handling of money, a matter of much biographical discussion, was defended against accusations of stinginess ("exacting in money matters") with examples of his generosity, especially his schemes for helping starving artists.[39]

Finally, aware of the model of the domesticated Victorian artist, Hamerton raised the issue of Turner's domestic happiness: "he never knew the happiness of marriage. . . . [A] happy marriage . . . would probably have brought him into more natural relations with the human species. . . . Turner had no home in that dreary, dirty mansion in Queen Anne Street. And what are wealth and fame as motives for exertion in comparison with love and duty?"[40] Hamerton's ambivalence was expressed in his linking Turner's genius with his unsavory

39. Hamerton, *The Life of J. M. W. Turner, R.A.* (Boston: Roberts Brothers, 1879), 364–75, 380–82.
40. Ibid., 392–93.

characteristics through national identity, while concluding that marriage would have improved what a liberal education would not!

Hybridity, Visual Texts, and Domestic Authority

Artists' biographies written by their families answered Hamerton's Victorian questions: their families assured readers that the artists inhabited
domesticity; photos offered up their bodies as gentlemanly (unlike
Turner's physique) and English and their studios as domesticated,
public spaces, more in line with the institution of Show Sunday
than with the popular image of the solitary, eccentric, and immoral
genius. Other vital issues—handling of money, sociability, dress—
were implied by the images of artists at work, in middle-class dress
and in comfortable environs, and social enough to hunt and fish with
wealthy patrons, repudiating the Victorian notion that genius was unfit
for social or domestic life.[41]

Late-century biographies shared Victorian traits of the genre in
addition to those featured in their antecedents: fascination with minute
details of daily life; homogenized themes of hard work, manliness,
and success, as in the "prudential" biography, which initially focused
on subjects from industry, the military, and entrepreneurship. Family
genealogies created the artist out of a combination of genetics and
environment. These books were often expensive, long (four hundred
to six hundred pages in two volumes), with embossed covers that
embodied the ostensible artistic aura to appeal to laypeople, middle
class or above, and to appear "arty" while also participating in the
commercial popularity of the genre.[42]

Artists' lives as artists shared a general pattern: public school life
and Sass's Academy, which trained students for the Royal Academy

41. Altick, *Lives,* 107.
42. Ibid., 88. Most of these biographies appeared shortly after the artists' deaths:
"The lapse of time between interment and the publication of the first memoir
became ever shorter" throughout the century (ibid., 186). In some cases, children
were more critical of their fathers than wives were of their husbands: Hilda Gray
describes her father's procrastination, and John Guile Millais hints at resentments
toward his father. I am grateful to my colleague Joseph Lamb for sharing his
observations about these differences with me.

schools; the academy schools; a prize or two at the academy; the requisite artistic pilgrimage to Italy; leisure activities, such as fly-fishing and hunting, both identified with the well-to-do classes; taking up portraiture, the most lucrative genre and one in which artists' contacts networked across the upper and middle classes; and a London residency for the development of social networks. Descriptions of genealogy and school days were part of the broader tradition of middle-class life writings and thus situated artists in the mainstream. Such conventions were vital to artists' respectable self-presentation: even the socialist Walter Crane began his autobiography with a display of his families' heraldry and argued that character was hereditary.

Above all, artists figured as models of success. The romantic suffering of the midcentury biographies evaporated before these narratives of success. The son of the much heroized and popular John Everett Millais cited his father's early difficulties, including vituperative critical attacks, as preliminary to his father's ultimate successes: "The work of those early days was but the prelude to achievements that have since made his name famous. . . . They were simply years of self-education, of hardship and drudgery, in which the foundation of his future success was laid."[43] In fact, Millais's early Pre-Raphaelite style was abandoned later for abbreviated brushwork, and his rich symbolism thinned in favor of popular amorous narratives and historical genres.

The themes of success and sociality were most evident from the biographies' photos. Borrowing from Erving Goffman's sociology of self-representation and his concept of the "veneer of consensus," I am arguing that reproductions established artists' social and moral credentials and that these credentials proved more legitimating than aesthetics. Goffman's "veneer of consensus" is defined as a socially acceptable view of the situation, and this veneer, if established, integrated the artist into society. Thus, attention to social status and respectability in artists' self-presentations was vital for attracting patrons during artists' lives, and so these attributes were invoked by their families to attract buyers and sustain reputations postmortem. John Hungerford Pollen's hunting is mentioned in his daughter's biography of him. The son of Charles West Cope expurgated his subject's diaries

---

43. John Guile Millais, *The Life and Letters of Sir John Everett Millais,* 2 vols. (New York: Longmans, 1899), 2:1–2.

to highlight accounts of fly-fishing trips while only summarily noting Cope's successes in the art world. Even fly-fishing was a career event: in 1870 Cope was invited to fish by Lord Beresford-Hope, whom he sat beside at the Royal Academy banquet, that professionally vital, annual mingling of artists and wealthy patrons. Cope's wide-ranging, prolific artistic activities were treated as business and civic enterprises, free from the mystique of artistic creativity common to Romantic predecessors.[44] Social events brought forth clients. The biographers' cataloging of social activities marked the artist as a social being, not the stereotypical avant-garde loner. In a very speculative art market, sociability was crucial to success in life and in afterlife.

One central theme of Hilda Orchardson Gray's biography of her father, Sir William Quiller Orchardson, was the social equality of artists: "I always consider, and suppose my Father taught me, that artist-folk are the equals of anybody from Princes down to Plumbers. . . . At any rate his manners to a charwoman were as charming as to a duchess." Orchardson's life was filled with parties, billiards, banquets, foxhunting, and musical soirees. He was so successful that he built a large studio and house and sent his daughter to a celebrated girls' school. To mark every worthy occasion—being considered for Royal Academy president in 1896 or getting a degree from Oxford—Gray included letters from colleagues and patrons praising her father. She did not shrink from describing his religious skepticism, for example, perhaps to portray him in all his "human" facets. She even described her father's flirtations and her mother's unjealous response, confident that her husband was faithful to her. This example emphasized both her father's masculinity and his domesticity.[45]

Gray also referred to her father's professional life, including his artistic practices. When narrating his professional activities she called him Orchardson, while he was "Father" in the domestic context, thus maintaining a boundary between the two spheres. She compared him to his contemporaries, assuming an authority for herself in this sphere: "When the perfect president if imperfect painter [Leighton]

44. Anne Pollen, *John Hungerford Pollen, 1820–1902* (London: Murray, 1912), 43, 294–95; Charles Henry Cope, *Reminiscences of Charles West Cope* (London: Richard Bentley, 1891), 271.

45. Gray, *The Life of Sir William Quiller Orchardson* (London: Hutchinson, 1930), 244, 118, 132, 126–27.

died, Millais was his natural successor; he . . . with the possible exception of Orchardson was certainly the greatest painter of his day."
Upon Millais's death, Orchardson had to decide whether to run for
the presidency of the Royal Academy, but he declined out of love
for his wife: "Ambition, or love and long life to the loved one? Love
prevailed and my Father stood aside and voted for Briton Riviere;
Poynter was elected." Her mother's diary contained much information
about her father's artistic practices, thus here, too, blending domestic
and professional spheres, reflected in the photo of both parents in
the studio (Figure 1). Gray cited names of prominent patrons and
commissioned portraits, several of which, including the royal family's
group portrait, were reproduced along with the family's patriotic, pro-
English observations on the Boer War.[46]

Orchardson was depicted in his studio beginning with the frontispiece portrait now in the Uffizi (an "official" portrait, it was probably
the frontispiece because its intended site put Orchardson in the canons
of the great), in a photograph with his wife in the studio reading as
he paints, and in the final image of him in his studio working on
his last painting shortly before his death. Of his Uffizi portrait, his
daughter wrote that it was painted by invitation and "shows him as a
worker, the man of action, the keen observer, himself exactly as he
was when working."[47] Her interpretation enforced the professionalism
of his image. In all of these photos he has a palette in one hand and
a brush in the other and stands straight and solid in front of a canvas
on an easel. In the photo with his wife (Figure 1), he looks at his
palette as she reads her book, and they form a complementary pair,
she seated and reading with legs crossed, he standing with feet wide
apart in front of an empty canvas but turned gazing intently at his
palette as if about to begin painting. In all photos he wears a suit
without a smock, more a gentleman than a worker. Other images are
of his best-known works and their preparatory drawings and of his
wife, daughter, and patrons.

Like Gray, other authors struggled with the issue of how much of
the profession to include for their general readership. Charles West
Cope included technical information on painting in his diary, but his

46. Ibid., 132, 215–16.
47. Ibid., 245.

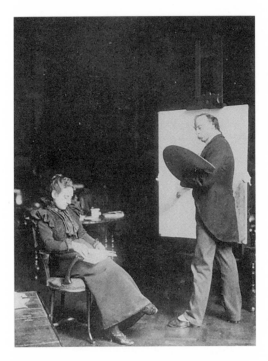

Figure 1. Orchardson and his wife in his studio. From Gray, *Life of Orchardson,* facing 332.

son repressed these sections of Cope's diary because he considered technical information to be only of passing interest—indicating his appeal to a general readership, rather than to other artists. Cope's son inserted letters from artists or patrons to enhance his narrative with presumably more objective evaluations.[48] Clearly his role was to boast of his father's artistic achievement through other authorities and to edit the diaries so as not to overshadow Cope's social role with a concern for his artistic practices, a balance maintained in Cope's own paintings: he specialized in domestic scenes, which sold well, and was dubbed the "Poet-Laureate of the Nursery."

Artistic achievement was always coordinated with public, civic, and familial matrices. Artists were presented as congenial, clubby, dutiful, accepting, and hardworking. In the context of the Victorian separation of spheres, the emphasis on the public nature of artistic behavior—homosociality, national popularity, material success, and

48. Cope, *Reminiscences,* 266.

exemplarity—masculinized the image of the artist as breadwinner and professional. The theme of work was overdetermined by exhaustive lists of exhibited paintings in the appendix, frequent comments by the narrator about the tireless efforts of the artist, images of artists at work in their studios, and reproductions of works sprinkled throughout the text.

The work ethic was identified with the market values that were the consequence of all that work. The marketplace even dominated the choice of reproductions in some cases: although Redgrave's daughter included only four reproductions in her text, they are not the popular Victorian genre paintings that had secured Redgrave's fame in his lifetime but suffered declining market value. Instead, she selected her father's lesser-known landscapes, which had a steadier, still brisk exchange value. While she described his techniques when painting some of his most famous works, such as *The Sempstress,* she curiously did not reproduce this work, perhaps determining that her readers in 1891 would have less interest in sentimental narrative than had her father's generation. Of all the authors, she is the least authoritative in art matters, relying heavily on primary documents. She reiterates themes of hard work and sociality and identifies him with middle-class values, citing his refusal of a knighthood, "a title very inconsistent with our mode of life and feelings."[49]

Amy Woolner's biography of her father blended themes of sociality, work, and professionalism. She limited discussion of technical matters to the preface, assuming, perhaps, as most of these biographers seem to have assumed, that readers were not interested in such topics. Members of Woolner's circle included Tennyson, Carlyle, Sir Walter and Lady Trevelyan, the Prinseps, and Gladstone. Woolner's busts of such prominent people (including four busts of Cobden) were liberally reproduced. His love of riding to the hounds was deemed worthy of inclusion, as was mention of his long hours, "killingly busy working all day and half the night." Even more interesting are overt references to money, as in this letter from Woolner to Mrs. Tennyson: "You know that one of the dearest wishes of my soul was to get a house in town where I could also have my studios. . . . I have paid the

49. F. M. Redgrave, *Richard Redgrave, C.B., R.A.: A Memoir Compiled from His Diary* (London: Cassell, 1891), 44–45, 305.

whole of the money £1200 and now you may regard me as a Nabob swelling with importance." A letter to Coventry Patmore on the same subject is also included. Woolner's pride is voiced directly in another of his letters to Mrs. Tennyson: "I knew you would like to know of a bit of good luck in the worldly professional sense—I am to execute the London statue of Lord Palmerston for Palace Yard, the finest site in the whole of London. . . . Any sculptor would have crawled 100 miles on hands and knees to have got [*sic*] this commission."[50]

Amy Woolner herself addressed the issue of how her father made money because others claimed "he dissipated his energies in making a collection of pictures." Although noting that her father's fine collection resulted in his expertise being sought by other collectors, she called his collecting an "expensive hobby," not a source of income, and sought to "correct erroneous statements" that Woolner made his money through dealing and collecting. She insisted his money had come first from his art before he began collecting and that he even undersold works from his collection. Collecting, she insisted, was recreation "after the day's work was done, for Work was his aim in life—the very reason of existence to his mind; Work was almost a religion with him." Amy assured the reader that her father was "a devoted husband and a kind and indulgent father—interested in his children's pursuits and amused at their opinions of men and politics fearlessly expressed. He was very fond of animals." She concluded with Callander Ross's description of Woolner's work as exhibiting "conscientiousness and thoroughness. He spared no pains to get at the heart of his subject and to master every detail. His workmanship was as thorough as his study. . . . There are no pot-boilers from his hand . . . blessed with simple, healthy tastes."[51] Thus his works were always a good investment. Lists of his works and of his writings constituted the appendix. Reproductions included Rossetti's portrait of Woolner; a photo of him among his assistants who roughly carved or cast the work he had modeled and designed and which he then finished; an 1877 photo of the artist with full, flowing beard; and a photo of him in his studio working on the bust of Tennyson. The

---

50. Woolner, *Thomas Woolner, R.A., Sculptor and Poet: His Life in Letters* (London: Chapman and Hall, 1917); see 242, 134; letters are quoted 205, 206, 280.
    51. Ibid., 281–82, 333–35.

remaining forty-eight reproductions were of his works, sketches, a sample of his handwriting, a portrait of his wife by Arthur Hughes, and a drawing of his father done by the artist.

One of the most compelling hybrids is Ford Madox Ford's biography of his grandfather, Ford Madox Brown. Ford's biography was obsessed with details of artistic production and consumption, reflected also in the fifty-four reproductions in the text. He included many of Brown's diary entries, letters, and direct quotations intended for the biography and given shortly before his death. Ford was forthcoming about sale prices and the mercurial relationships among the painter, his colleagues, and his patrons. Paintings were described throughout the text at various stages of their attenuated production. Not only the major paintings but many sketches done for these paintings were included and specially grouped together at the end of the book, as if they formed a small catalog. Reproductions included photos and portraits of family members, wife and children, but only two portraits of Brown, one sketch of him at age twenty-nine and a frontispiece of his portrait done in 1875. Ford relied on Brown's diary, in which the artist meticulously recorded all transactions, his labor, and his often low prices. Although presenting Brown as a professional and a businessman, Ford also detailed Brown's domestic life without mentioning his wife Emma's alcoholism.[52]

Ford provided a great deal of information about Brown's working hours and pay: "From the 15th to the 22nd of October [1865] Madox Brown worked continuously at the *Nosegay*—most of the time in the garden, working altogether fifty-seven hours in the seven days, . . . not an unusual number of hours' work in the week . . . [and] as a rule, devoted the evenings to working at cartoons for the Firm."[53] While decidedly outside the genteel social networks that helped promote the careers of Cope, Orchardson, Redgrave, and Richmond, Brown was nevertheless fastidious about the business end of his artistic career. The visual emphasis in the book was on Brown's works, including preparatory sketches, while the text was dominated by professional experiences and hardships.

52. Ford, *Ford Madox Brown, a Record of His Life and Work* (London: Longmans, Green, 1896), 60–61.
53. Ibid., 208–9.

Against this business-driven model stood the more renegade personae of Edward Burne-Jones and George Frederick Watts. Georgiana Burne-Jones wrote a spiritual and intellectual biography and freely debated issues of art and creativity. Her *Memorials* insisted on her husband's unique spiritual qualities, even within his family. She claimed his father, the senior Jones (the original family name), was not an artist but a mere carver and gilder. She cited a series of secular conversion experiences that marked her husband's progress into art: reading Ruskin, seeing Millais's *Return of the Dove* and Hunt's *Awakening Conscience,* meeting Rossetti, traveling with William Morris to northern France, where they jointly vowed to abandon the church and become artists, finding Southey's reprint of Malory's *Morte d'Arthur,* "his own birthright upon which he entered."[54] In other words, Burne-Jones's "real" or spiritual father was Arthur, not the drudge who carved and gilded and bore the commonplace name of Jones. Other spiritual fathers were Ruskin and Rossetti. Georgiana emphasized her husband's intellect, copious reading, and excellence at disputation with a "strong natural bent towards logic and metaphysics." Unlike most artists of the time, Burne-Jones was very well educated and attended Oxford and thus could develop his bent toward metaphysics. Burne-Jones appeared self-made, even genealogically, renaming and distancing himself from the manual-crafts-worker father, so that father and son were differently inscribed by class, education, and artistic production. No photo of Edward Richard Jones, the artist's father, appeared in volume 1, although Burne-Jones's mother, maternal grandfather, and uncle and aunt appeared in the section of volume 1 on the artist's childhood. A small photo of his father appeared later in volume 2.

Images of Burne-Jones included the portrait of him at age thirty-seven by Watts as frontispiece of volume 1; a portrait of him at age sixty-four painted by his son as frontispiece of volume 2; photos of the artist at ages forty-one and fifty-one; two photos of him in his studio, one in smock and one in dress coat; and one photo of him seated contemplatively in the Castle Naworth garden. We see him at work and in serious portraits during various ages of his life. His wife and children appeared in photos, drawings, and paintings;

54. Burne-Jones, *Memorials,* 1:116–17.

Figure 2. Burne-Jones's house studio, June 18, 1898. Watercolor by
A. M. Poynter, from Burne-Jones, *Memorials,* facing 2:350.

there were photos of his homes, The Grange and Rottingdean, and
of a dining room, and a painting of his studio on the day he died
(Figure 2), implying he worked up to his death. Volume 1 began
with a print of the Birmingham building in which Burne-Jones was
born, complementing the final studio image in volume 2, and thus
framing the biography with sites of his birth and death. Photos of
friends—Ruskin, Rossetti, Morris (twice included), Swinburne—and
his patron William Graham are included, as are various women—
Elizabeth Siddal, Jane Burden, Ruth Herbert, and Georgiana before
marriage.

Georgiana was a dominating narrator. She used the pronoun *we*
often, presenting her husband as part of the marital pair. She filled
her text with descriptions of social engagements and dinner parties
and commented freely on her husband's activities and friendships.
She presented her husband's friends as hers, too ("our very good
friend Mr. F. S. Ellis the publisher"), which authorized her to delve
into their relationships to her husband and to claim some authority

in the professional, as well as in the domestic, sphere. Her anecdotes frequently combined both spheres, as when she quoted the banter among Morris, Burne-Jones, and Rossetti about each other's paintings, a presentation at once homosocial, professional, and quasi-familial. She also interpreted Burne-Jones's art and thus took on authority in the professional sphere.[55]

Georgiana sanctified her husband and his art-making and carefully negotiated his public persona; she never mentioned his notorious affair with Marie Zambaco, for example, nor hinted at his reservations about marriage. She seemed to be a presence in the studio, as well as in the home, and often ventriloquized her husband's innermost thoughts and feelings: "Human beauty especially was in a way sacred to them. . . . [T]he men were as good as they were gifted, and unlike any others that we knew." Her husband's "love of beauty did not seem to me unbalanced [a common charge against Burne-Jones by Victorian critics and by Nordau], but as if it included the whole world." She carefully distinguished Burne-Jones from Ruskin by citing their differences of taste on Italian art. Likewise she was quick to point out that her husband did not follow his best friend, William Morris, into socialism. Her husband was domesticated by virtue of photos of home and studio, humorous drawings sent to his children, and references to periodic cleanings of his "Augean Studio," assuring us that his studio was not an unruly place but as orderly as the home. His domesticity extended to his work habits: he worked "harder than ever and with increasing method and regularity" as he got older. She asserted his love of children and quoted letters that displayed his sense of humor, a trait missing in his paintings.[56]

Finally, she selected reproductions fetishistically to "recall his personality" and to support her contention that her husband was essentially spiritual. Images of his works started with early illustrations done when he was in his twenties. Arthurian subjects included *Launcelot's Dream* and *The Passing of Arthur* placed poignantly in the context of the end of the artist's own life. There was no appendix listing

55. Ibid., 2:40, 76, 66.

56. Mary Lago, ed., *Burne-Jones Talking: His Conversations 1895–1898 Preserved by His Studio Assistant Thomas Rooke* (Columbia: University of Missouri Press, 1981), 10–11; Burne-Jones, *Memorials,* 1:169, 2:79, 2:221, 2:213.

his works and buyers, avoiding connotations of consumption and the market. Rather, Georgiana called patrons "believers" and ventriloquized Burne-Jones's notion of art-making as putting God back in the world. To further mystify his personality in line with the "calling" of art, she asserted that Burne-Jones drew as if he were breathing, naturally and as unstudied "as if his hand were only removing a veil."[57] Despite such spiritual claims, volume 1 concluded with a list of his illustrious patrons and friends: Henry Holiday; Edward Clifford, "one of a new group of Royal Academy students who had discovered and were enthusiastic about some pencil heads that Edward sent to a Winter Exhibition of the Old Water Colour Society"; Henry Wooldridge, "now Slade Professor at Oxford"; Madox Brown; the Howards, "now Lord and Lady Carlisle"; the Greek community in London (Ionides); and Ruskin. Georgiana aligned her husband with the Royal Academy practice of finish and distinguished his work from that of his imitators, a crucial distinction in the marketplace.[58]

Georgiana subtly aligned her husband with conservative Victorian tastes through veiled references to his attitudes toward the newer art styles and toward Impressionism. She outlined his political views, while insisting he had no hope for political solutions to problems: he disliked empire and aggression and disapproved of the Boer War. In his own *alleged* words he spoke his spiritual nature: "I love the immaterial. You see it is these things of the soul that are real—the only real things in the universe." His moral traits, besides hope and love of the immaterial, included refusal to recognize defeat; development in which he grew but did not change; lack of envy; sympathy; and acceptance of hardship without complaint.[59] His character was as aesthetic as it was moral. Georgiana recast his character into the aesthetic mode to fuse it to the idealist contents of his painting and demonstrate that very Victorian virtue of sincerity, which demanded that artist and works share traits. Her strategy separated him from the economics of professionalism, while endorsing the autonomous "calling" of art, all the while undergirded by images of material success—big house and studio, family, many works of art.

57. Burne-Jones, *Memorials* 1:223–25, 295, 2:257, 6.
58. Ibid., 1:302–5, 2:321.
59. Ibid., 2:300, 319–20.

Mary Watts presented a similarly "spiritual" G. F. Watts. In place of the standard genealogy, she quoted Watts's feelings that his family name lacked fineness. He longed for "a long line of worthies" to sustain him. Like Burne-Jones, Watts was not particularly fond of his lineage nor distinguished by it. Both artists preferred to define their achievements as based on merit, not family, unlike their genealogically more blessed fellow academicians. Watts fantasized that he had Celtic blood, romanticizing and masculinizing himself while also risking unrespectable associations with the Irish or, worse, with gypsies or bohemians.[60]

Mary Watts emphasized Watts's character traits: "sentiment, love, honour, patriotism." She even compared him to "the heroes who won Waterloo." Refusing to consider himself a professional painter, unlike more conventional academicians, Watts appropriated a Victorian version of the Renaissance artist. About one-quarter of the way through her biography, Mary cited the moment when Watts's friends began to call him by the Anglicized Italian designation *Signor*, which she then used for the rest of the book. She began each chapter with a quotation from Watts, such as, "I want to make art the servant of religion by stimulating thought high and noble. I want to assert for art a yet higher place than it has hitherto had."[61] She crowned her husband with a halo of patriotism, selflessness, and morality, an artist who donated his public sculptures to the nation. In the Royal Academy he insisted on ethical hanging practices, returned a check for a portrait when it was criticized, hung his own work in a poor spot to accommodate another colleague, and gave a commission to another man, surely proof of sainthood, as if his refusal of a baronetcy were not enough. Two reproduced portraits of him as a young man of seventeen and in 1848 depict a long-haired, tousled youth, one almost Byronic in appearance. A self-portrait done later and now in the National Portrait Gallery shows him in a Raphaelesque bust portrait with a slightly turned head, wearing a vaguely Renaissance cloak and hat.

60. M. S. Watts, *George Frederic Watts: The Annals of an Artist's Life*, 3 vols. (London: Macmillan, 1912), 1:4.

61. Ibid., 1:1, 6, 194.

Other reproductions served to underscore Mary Watts's canonization. While reproductions in volume 1 included portraits, in volume 2 there was only one portrait: a frontispiece of Watts in long smock and characteristic skullcap reinforced the construction of him as self-made, hard working, and dedicated, especially since he stands in front of perhaps his most Smilesian work, *Physical Energy,* a sculptural tribute to British drive, perseverance, strength, work, and power (Figure 3). In four of the five photo images of Watts, he is at work on public sculptures, including his gigantic Lord Tennyson, and always dressed in smock and skullcap, always the Signor. With these photos of Watts coexisted photos of his homes and studios, Little Holland House (where he had a large, airy studio whose space sans artist metonymically concluded the volume) and Limnerlease. Volume 3 was the most "posthumous" volume; consisting of his writings and illustrated by twenty-two reproductions of his sketches, drawings, sculptures, and paintings, it is the most heavily illustrated volume and reveals his conceptual processes and the extensive range of his labor, justifying Watts's own insistence that he be considered an artist, not just a painter.

Contrasted with the educational and career patterns of the academic artists, Watts and Burne-Jones were constructed as self-made men, driven by vision rather than by technique or peer networks, though it was vital to their successes that both had wealthy, prominent patrons. The Prinseps bestowed on Watts living quarters and a studio at their large Holland House for decades. Without this extraordinary gift, Watts could hardly have succeeded. While families of academic artists struggled to maintain the values of art as masculine and businesslike, Georgiana Burne-Jones and Mary Watts insisted on their husbands' otherworldly traits and rejection of the marketplace. Burne-Jones and Watts in their smocks and Orchardson in his suit were workers or gentleman, respectively.

One question, however, still remained even for art's saints: what to do with portrait painting, that lucrative entrepreneurial genre, in which "spiritual" artists participated as did their academic contemporaries. Watts's portraits were cast in the position of being spiritual, of capturing the essence, what his wife called the "transcendental self," rather than being the superficial, merely flattering portraiture

Figure 3. Watts in the garden with his sculpture *Physical Energy*, 1888. From Watts, *Annals*, 2: frontispiece.

of academic painters. Similarly, Georgiana quoted her husband that "the only expression allowable in great portraiture is the expression of character and moral quality." For the "spiritual" artists, portraiture was recast as a moral exercise, not a lucrative business.[62]

The Artist's Body in the Material World

In *The Presentation of Self in Everyday Life,* Erving Goffman examines the role of inference in the presentation of self and the reading of that self by others. Goffman describes an asymmetry of self-presentation between direct and indirect information, the latter including postures, body language, tone, facial expressions, and glances such as those captured by the biographies' photographs. Through these, inferences

62. Ibid., 1:115; Burne-Jones, *Memorials,* 2:140.

may be made about the social acceptability or the greatness of the bio-graphical subjects, which the authors might not wish to state directly.[63] Serious character flaws are absent in these hybrid texts, while minor ones are used to paint human, kindly portraits of the artists. Reproductions provide crucial inferences complementing the narratives. Images of artists at work in their studios or in their well-kept English gardens, or of their famous paintings or sculptures, provide visual material from which the reader may infer the presentation of artists as hard-working, successful, propertied, and paterfamilial. In a social encounter we are inclined to test whether presenters fulfill traditional roles they claim for themselves. Because the role of artists was morally, socially, and economically problematic and bounded by bohemia and modernism on several sides, inferential or indirect cues became all the more important, as "artistness" was differently foregrounded by verbal and visual texts.

Artists produced not only art but their own bodies and images. Photographed images have more objectivity and palpability than words and thus better create what Goffman calls a "veneer of consensus," an acceptable view of the situation. For example, photos of Millais (Figure 4) represent the artist as casual and relaxed, in his leisure garb, or suited in his studio. Goffman points out that the image of a relaxed, comfortable body, displaying "easy control" over the situation, assures the viewer that the subject exists in the situation by habit and by internal sincerity, is at home in the situation, not simply putting us on or pretending.[64] One photo was taken by Rupert Potter, who invited Millais and the Hon. John Bright, M.P., to Potter's country home at Dalguise to go salmon fishing, which Bright and Millais, good friends, both enjoyed. Millais and Watts were both photographed at home relaxing, not painting necessarily, but able to read and contemplate because of the wealth and leisure their work had purchased.

Millais's work and patronage are symbolized in a photo of him in his studio with large portraits behind him, while his success and domesticity are represented by the spacious studio, the large hearth, and the lovely objets d'art placed around the room. Orchardson and

63. Goffman, *The Presentation of the Self in Everyday Life* (New York: Double-day-Anchor, 1956).

64. Goffman, *Relations in Public: Microstudies of the Public Order* (New York: Basic Books, 1971), 248.

Figure 4. Millais at Dalguise, 1879. Photo by R. Potter, from Millais, *Life,* 2:240.

his wife in his studio (Figure 1) declared the intersection of artistic production and domestic order (and indeed Mrs. Orchardson was active in her husband's career as bookkeeper and protector of his time). A photo of Woolner at work in his studio, surrounded by portrait busts commissioned from him, commented on his work ethic and on his patronage by the prominent men whose simulations surround the busy artist. Burne-Jones thoughtfully seated in his garden revealed a contemplative, sequestered artist whose skill is conceptual, as well as manual. Photographs of artists inhabiting their studios and domestic spaces and bearing well-dressed bodies respond to Nordau's charges of degeneracy by a counteremphasis on ordinary physical appearance, rational domesticity, hard work, and masculine roles as father and successful breadwinner: "Success in any field, especially with adequate remuneration, remains a focus of Victorian biographical writing, forming its most consistent theme."[65]

65. Nadel, *Biography,* 44.

While Brown, Burne-Jones, and Watts were distinguished from the entrepreneurial, social-climbing academic artists, all of the artists represented by this genre shared the values of work, productivity, and domestic life, although differently imaged as suited gentlemen or besmocked workers. In addition, they shared a hostility toward French Impressionism, which signified modernity, bohemia, and degeneracy. Orchardson disliked Sargent's painting. Watts hated Impressionism and French art in general. Burne-Jones attacked Impressionists for their lack of beautiful faces and "desirable sentiment"; he called Impressionism an art without ideas while also recognizing its power to affect his sales. Millais warned young artists against studying Impressionism in France, "to escape the grind . . . by studying in Paris . . . 'you want to run before you have learnt to walk.'" According to Millais's son, Impressionism denied artistic labor, "the apparent ease and simplicity of the [Impressionist] works exhibited betraying no sign of the arduous toil by which the artists had attained their skill." This shared aesthetic hostility bound these artists and marked them as English, asserting their identification with their readers. Through this strategy, then, as interpreters and presenters of various selves, the biographers constructed a "working consensus" to substantiate the nebulous, shifting, and troubled category of artist through a shared nationalistic aesthetic, despite differences among these artists: "Real agreement will also exist concerning the desirability of avoiding an open conflict of definitions of the situation," as Goffman points out.[66]

Among the strategies Goffman cites are attempts to humor readers and encourage their catharsis. It may have been more important, as Orchardson's daughter noted, to describe the artist's life outside rather than inside the art world. Presenting artists in varied situations objectified in photos, biographers could reveal artists who conformed to the consensus held by their readers, as in the example of Georgiana describing her husband's sense of humor to permit the readers' identification with a prank-playing, fun-loving subject or with details of his childhood or dinner-party gossip. Constructing an artist biographically was, then, a matter not of defining an essence of artistness but of relating artistness to the "interdependent activities of an on-going social

66. Burne-Jones, *Memorials,* 2:188; Lago, ed., *Burne-Jones Talking,* 2; Millais, *Life,* 2:2; Goffman, *Presentation,* 10.

system" and to the enactment of the rights and duties of that system. Status was conduct and grew out of a performance in which different parts of the self were presented to the audience in a "series of occasions," the faceting I cited earlier by the inclusion of multiple voices and roles. To be cathartic, as Goffman points out, these occasions must unveil circumstantial details of body, clothes, and surroundings that are saturated with character, power, and sanctity. Credibility requires coherence between the subject's appearance and the role's assumed functions, which for late Victorians were ambiguous and debated. Images reproduced in these texts guaranteed, because of their "objective" presentation of details, that artists' appearances were coherent with respectability, which for Victorians superseded professional roles.[67]

What authority did the child or spouse have in this biographical bricolage, after all? The public role of adoring wife or child was the niche the authors inhabited with some small divergences, and these roles guaranteed that their biographies were thoroughly institutional in their structure and in their social veneer. While declaring their inferiority to the artist, the authors at the same time present the "artist" as just one role to be filled by artists. It seems to be a composite role, its moral claims dependent on the artist's fulfillment of familial and social roles. The authority needed to prove they fulfilled these social roles was precisely their authors' domestic authority.

Artists' representations should be further comprehended within the broader field of cultural production. Pierre Bourdieu emphasizes the infrastructural relationships of the art world in contrast to our traditional ideological notions of art as disinterested, unmotivated by personal interests, and the product of individual genius. On the contrary, the artistic field is dominated by concerns with economics. His theory further focuses on the artistic field as a dynamic between producer and consumer. In this regard, artists' autobiographies and biographies, so copious in the last quarter of the nineteenth century, served to cement relations between artists and buyers. The more hierarchical the field, as in this case of academic art, the more material success validated the artist for the role; in reverse, the more autonomous the field (avant-gardism, Pre-Raphaelitism), the more claims for symbolic power validated the artists' fulfillment of their roles. Watts and Burne-Jones,

67. Goffman, *Presentation,* 14–16.

for example, had symbolic capital; their wives overtly denied material values despite their husbands' successes, to maintain the belief that art for them was a vocation, a spiritual calling. Neither Watts's biography nor Burne-Jones's included lists of works and owners and thus their authors avoided allusions to art as property or investment. Nevertheless, photographed images aligned Burne-Jones and Watts with their academic contemporaries while counterpointing the texts. Academic artists adhered to a model dominated by social and economic concerns, so their images complemented their biographical texts.[68]

Thus, the artistic field's contradictions were explored, debated, and masked through the "types" of artists represented in these biographies. However, even for disinterest to be acceptable, it had to accompany success. Success must exist for the artist to reject it (Redgrave, Burne-Jones, and Watts declining knighthood or baronetcy), so its rejection would be a matter not of sour grapes but of the individual's agency in which a disavowal of economic interests was a real sacrifice. In this way the professional status, measured by economic and social markers, was sustained, and the sacrificing, spiritual artist was not seen as an irrational nonparticipant in the social order (like the Romantic or bohemian) but as a professional capable of making an informed decision, opting for "transcendental" values.

Besides contesting constructions of the artist as professional versus idealist, economically motivated versus "called" to art, biographies contested the nature of art. Parallel to Amigoni's examples of literary biographies constituting theories of language (literary, "poetic" and subjective versus historical, "factual," and objective), artists' biographies contended with issues of representation—realism versus imagination, daily life versus dream—as the proper subject of art. Thus, the language of art (realist or fantasy) comes to constitute the person and function of the Victorian artist (academic or idealist). Professional issues about the source of artistic ideas invaded the narrative content of these biographies, forming socio-aesthetic values defining different camps of representation. Georgiana Burne-Jones thematized her husband's description of his inspirational sources ("out of his own head"): " 'the place where I think pictures ought to come from,' said

68. Bourdieu, "The Field of Cultural Production, or: the Economic World Reversed," *Poetics* 12 (1983): 312.

Edward." Hilda Gray defended Orchardson against charges that his subjects were purposeless: "I once asked my Father if Art should be didactic, and if subject were important, and he told me—I do not remember his exact words but only the sense—'that fine art must be fine in subject as well as in manner, that a purposeless picture could not be fine in the full sense of the word; and that what most appealed to him personally was the dramatic moment.'" Orchardson's probing of marital relations and interest in social life united his life (his busy social life; his close bond with his wife) and work, and distinguished him from Burne-Jones, whose life and art were united through values of beauty, "spirituality," and subjects of dreamy nostalgia.[69]

Lists of works and images of artists' bodies and domestic environs conveyed subtexts of productivity and the marketplace and presented the artist as "economic man," not simply as a model of perseverance. In *The Political Economy of Art* (1857, reprinted 1880), John Ruskin argued that the state must control the production and consumption of artists' works by tending to artists' educations and not overpraising or overpaying them, so that they would work happily like children for the state. In these biographies, family authors establish an artistic self that resisted Ruskin's image of the infantile artist: patriarchal, rather than the child Ruskin described; entrepreneurially competent, which Ruskin did not consider a capacity of artists; financially successful, obtaining wealth that Ruskin thought only properly handled by the state or patrons; and socially upper middle class, the gentlemen Ruskin believed artists should be. Artists were represented by their families not as submitting to the state or patron, as Ruskin advised, but as capable of controlling their own production and of channeling, not squandering, profits into spacious bourgeois environs, well-dressed and clean bodies, and socially adhesive relations with patrons with whom they fished, hunted, played, dined, and traveled as equals. Such images also created a cathartic investment for the readers.

By economically rehabilitating the artist's public image, these biographers melded domestic and professional spheres, both inscribed by economic behavior, as Smiles insisted. William Epstein considers the professional biography a response to the hero-worship biography. This professional model could "describe, not only the professional

69. Burne-Jones, *Memorials,* 2:223; Gray, *Life,* 273.

reputation of the character, but also, the means by which that reputation was attained."[70] Artists' biographies evidenced professionalism
in the genteel sales lists with patrons' or buyers' names.

It is worth mentioning the difference between these Victorian
themes and those of the artist's biography in nineteenth-century
France in which the artist "made a 'system,' a 'doctrine' of the
refusal of social determinations, whether they be those associated with
belonging to a social class, those of all the bourgeois maledictions,
or even those of properly intellectual signs." The popular bohemian
stereotype of the French artist's resistance to social integration, though
not in fact the case for many French artists, is what Bourdieu describes as "the aristocratism of voluntary renunciation." While the
French artist, as Gustave Flaubert represented him in *L'Education
sentimentale,* might reject "domestic and democratic virtues" associated with the bourgeoisie, the Victorian artist represented by family
biographers embraced domestic virtues and the bourgeoisie whose
patronage dominated the market. Consequently, the Victorian artist
was represented as rejecting the renunciation and the indeterminacy
of bohemian life.[71]

Amigoni raises several issues relevant to these hybrid biographies
and their possible functions. These are centripetal biographies, to
borrow Amigoni's term, trying to rein in and discipline meanings and
interpretations of the artist, perhaps because of the genre's roots in
the evangelical tradition that Christopher Tolley traces as a source of
family biographies. In several ways they parallel literary biographies
in determining a discipline and being determined by one: both English
literature and art history became bona fide university disciplines circa
1870. Biography served to model behavior for the reader and to draw
the boundaries of professional activity, to define disciplines of literature and history, according to Amigoni.[72] Biography's role in defining

---

70. See Epstein, "The Center for Tomorrow: Disciplining Victorian Biography,"
Nineteenth-Century Prose 22 (1995): 8–24; *Recognizing Biography* (Philadelphia:
University of Pennsylvania Press, 1987), esp. 142–44.

71. Bourdieu, "The Invention of the Artist's Life," *Yale French Studies* 73 (1987):
78–79.

72. Amigoni, *Victorian Biography;* Tolley, *Domestic Biography: The Legacy of
Evangelicalism in Four Nineteenth-Century Families* (Oxford: Clarendon Press,
1997).

"artist" and in performing competing definitions was also reciprocal with a nascent art history. Despite contentions over the meaning of "artist," all of these biographies shared motives of perpetuating market value, delineating production to avoid diluting the market with forgeries, and defining the professional artist as distinct from the amateur and the bohemian. To serve these ends, they incorporated art history's mode of information (cataloging and photographing artworks, citing provenance) to legitimize their own facticity. This "objectivity" and the authors' need for sustained market values distinguished these biographies from other kinds of biographies, including the many brief, popular, journalistic biographies of prominent artists, such as Millais and Burne-Jones, that primarily continued to serve the function of reader edification.

Edmund Gosse referred to the widow-biographer in Darwinian terms as "the triumph of the unfittest."[73] Arguments for the purity of biography, aimed in part at family authors, should perhaps be seen in the contexts of late Victorian and modernist anxiety about competition from women ("scribblers" in literature; "dabblers" in art). In many ways Victorian widow-biographers were the fittest, and their content, while denigrated as trivial in connection with attempts to professionalize and hence masculinize biographical narrative, was crucial to constructing the Victorian artist for Victorian readers and art buyers.

As Judith Butler argues, representations extend visibility and legitimacy to subjects as political subjects while simultaneously serving the normative function of language "to reveal or distort what is assumed to be true," or the norm. Representation lays out the criteria that form the subject, and thus representation operates in the realm of the acknowledged and the acceptable. As these boundaries are socially instituted and intelligible within that set of social institutions, the concept "artist" must be read as legible within whatever historical and social terms are represented. Like *woman, artist* is a term subject to rigid representations whose transgression implies moral, especially sexual, pollution. Both terms are marked by an assumed infantilism and a tendency for practitioners to enact a masquerade that may both assert and threaten the boundaries. *Artist* is performative, whether

73. Quoted in Altick, *Lives,* 187.

represented by its most acceptable performers, such as Millais, or its most threatening, such as Beardsley and Wilde. Like *woman, artist* is defined not only by its deed, but also by the everyday actions and the social imbeddedness of its performers. Indeed, the social web is even more a determinant of the meaning of *artist* than the artworks that are generally read from the life, rather than vice versa, in Victorian biography. By joining the margins of artists' lives with the margins of Victorian sociality, family biographers insured the impermeability of those margins, doubly strengthened against pollution and vulnerability, thus making *artist,* a term that often functions dangerously close to the margins of the social order, less dangerous than it would be if not reinforced by socially acceptable boundaries. Like Goffman, Butler also reads "words, acts, gesture and desire" on the surface of the body. By aligning these gestures with Victorian ideal behavior, the family authors, through photos as well as written text, reinforced the artistic identity they also shaped. If signification is the function of "a regulated process of repetition that both conceals itself and enforces its rules," as Butler argues, then these biographies define the (Victorian) artist within a consistent social framework they all repeat despite differences in their representations.[74]

Bourdieu argues that for each career or biography "each individual trajectory must be understood as a particular way of traversing the social space." Whatever the Victorian family biographers' emphases— economic or idealist—generic hybridity allowed contradictory themes to coexist and overlap: the marketplace, consumption, inspiration, social acceptability, moral character, selfless patriotism, financial success conspicuously displayed, and solid domestic life. Assuming "irrelevant" details are relevant, I argue that heterogeneity offered an opportunity to resist narrative as a simple trajectory. Thus, we can better appreciate the authorial strategies of family biographers who participated in the dialectic between cultural discourse and the image of the artist. By virtue of their social and economic behaviors these artists resisted the dangers of an untamed creativity and inhabited

74. Butler, *Gender Troubles: Feminism and the Subversion of Identity* (New York: Routledge, 1990), 1, 132, 136, 145. See also Mary Douglas, *Purity and Danger: An Analysis of Concepts of Pollution and Taboo* (Binghamton: Vail-Ballou, 1980).

what Epstein calls the "dominant authority structure" without necessarily embracing all aspects of entrepreneurship and commerciality. Thus the authors could claim, to varying degrees, their subjects' difference from, and similarity to, the Victorian social order.[75]

Such negotiations, however, could not prevail for long, as modernists and avant-gardists argued for artists' special status and behaviors: antisocial, apathetic toward economics, sexually undomesticated, contemptuous of the social order despite the reality that avant-gardists could enjoy great wealth (Picasso) or a stable family life (Matisse). The Victorian artists commemorated in these biographies were the last of the English-educated. The next generation of artists learned art in France and then "contaminated" English art with Impressionism, loathed by "true" Victorian and thoroughly English artists. This schism between academic or popular success and rebellious avant-gardism marks the twentieth century's cultural dialectic and ideological masking of the economic reality of artistic production, as it turned professionalism and sociality into polar opposites, at least ideologically (Bourdieu). Artists' biographies written around 1900 may be regarded as valiant efforts to unite artistic claims—economic, social, and professional—for one brief decade before the Great Schism, and their authors may be commended for balancing artists' roles in these biographies through careful negotiations of their own domestic authority.[76]

75. Bourdieu, "Invention of the Artist's Life," 87, n. 6; Epstein, *Recognizing Biography,* 88.

76. I wish to thank the National Endowment for the Humanities for a fellowship in 1992–1993 that enabled me to research the subject of Victorian artists' biographies and autobiographies; the British Art Center at Yale University for a fellowship in the summer of 1994 to examine artists' self-portraits and popular biographies of Victorian artists; and my colleagues who have generously shared their knowledge of these topics with me: Debra Mancoff and Joseph Lamb.

Debra N. Mancoff

Infinite Rest

Sleep, Death, and Awakening in the Late Works
of Edward Burne-Jones

L ate in life, Edward Burne-Jones was haunted by the specter of his own mortality. In his conversations with his studio assistant, Thomas Rooke, as well as in his letters to friends and family, he confessed fears about aging, isolation, and exhaustion. The deaths of his friends—first Dante Gabriel Rossetti in 1882 and then William Morris in 1896—left him with feelings of powerlessness and abandonment. His obsession with his own increasing physical fragility led him to reflect on death, not as a dreaded end, but as a welcome release. In 1897, he seemed ready for the inevitable, telling Rooke, "It's so sad to hear of anyone weeping at the idea of his own death . . . it would be such infinite rest to be no more worried about doing a picture."[1]

Burne-Jones's words, betraying a loss of artistic confidence and identity, are in direct conflict with accomplishments of his late career. The last decades of his life were highly productive; through public exhibitions and lucrative private commissions he established the reputation that defined his legacy for generations. He won long-sought critical recognition and earned the

1. Mary Lago, ed., *Burne-Jones Talking: His Conversations 1895–1898 Preserved by His Studio Assistant Thomas Rooke* (Columbia: University of Missouri Press, 1981), 162 (October 26, 1897).

elusive respect and honors in the art world that he had come to shun. But the increasingly morbid subjects he chose—paralysis at the moment of fulfillment, as in *King Copethua and the Beggar Maid* (1884; Tate Gallery, London); destruction at the hands of desire, as in *The Depths of the Sea* (1886; private collection); death as a refuge from disappointment, as in *The Sleep of Arthur in Avalon* (1881–1898; Museo de Arte, Ponce, Puerto Rico)—suggest that the artist was lost in his own despondency. Unable to challenge mortality, Burne-Jones seemed ready to surrender.

But to read these paintings as a retreat into passivity and isolation is to misread the profound message of Burne-Jones's mature artistic vision. With his heightened awareness of the passage of time, he took up a theme that had fascinated him for decades: that of the sleeper, bound in slumber but destined to wake. And with these works came a new understanding of his mission as an artist. When read in the context of his own personal interests and convictions, his late paintings disclose a profoundly intricate process of mediation, reconfiguring fear into faith. The ideas that darkened his words and his subjects illumined his artistic expression; as Burne-Jones worked to his last days, he used the theme of infinite rest—a theme that testified to his belief in the artist's infinite vision and mapped the course to the attainment of immortality—to transform Thanatos into an angel of deliverance.

Until the last two decades of his life, Edward Burne-Jones worked in relative obscurity. This appears to have been a clear and conscious choice, influenced perhaps by the reclusive example of his friend and mentor Dante Gabriel Rossetti. Rather than expose his works to an uncomprehending critical assessment in public exhibitions, Burne-Jones advanced his career by working on commission for supportive patrons and by providing decorative-arts designs for the firm of Morris, Marshall, Faulkner and Company. He made no secret of his personal distaste for the conventional exhibition practices of his day, confirmed by his own experiences with the Old Water-Colour Society. In 1870, when his depiction of *Phyllis and Demophoön* was excluded on the sole basis that it featured a frontal male nude, he ended a four-year association. Later, in 1866, he wrote to Alfred William Hunt about his continuing sense of estrangement from the restrictive practices of conventional art institutions: "I am not in harmony at all with associations like the Academy and the Old Watercolour Society; my real home would be in a society which embraces and covers all art—everything that art enters into—and the disintegration of art and the development and favouring of little portions of it is a sore matter to me."[2]

The opening of the Grosvenor Gallery in 1877 marked a radical departure from the standard practice Burne-Jones distrusted. Artists participated through invitation, but they were allowed to make their own selections of works. The galleries were large, well lit, and beautifully furnished. Works were given space on the walls, rejecting the long-standing salon-style hanging that presented paintings in serried rows, often crowded, with frames nearly edge to edge. At the Grosvenor, each work was separated from adjacent works by six to twelve inches of space (still short of modern hanging standards by ten to fifteen inches). According to Georgiana Burne-Jones, this eliminated the "patchwork-quilt effect" typical of contemporary exhibitions and allowed the viewer to "take a breath before passing from one work to another."[3]

Burne-Jones sent eight works to the first Grosvenor Gallery exhibition in 1877 and contributed to subsequent shows for the next decade.[4] Although he had been a working artist for more than twenty years, the appearance of his paintings in the Grosvenor—treated by critics like a debut—marked his first public success. Writing in retrospect, his wife, Georgiana, saw this as the turning point of his career. "From this day forward," she noted, "he belonged to the world in a sense that he had never done before, for his existence became widely known and his name famous."[5]

2. Georgiana Burne-Jones, *Memorials of Edward Burne-Jones,* 2 vols. (London: Macmillan, 1904), 2:170.

3. Ibid., 2:69.

4. Burne-Jones submitted the following works to the first Grosvenor Gallery exhibition in 1877: *The Beguiling of Merlin; The Days of Creation; Venus's Mirror; Temperantia; Fides; St. George* (unfinished); *Spes; A Sybil* (unfinished). He sent works to each subsequent exhibition, excluding those in 1881 and 1885, until 1887, when he transferred his association to the New Gallery. For more information, see Christopher Newall, *The Grosvenor Gallery Exhibitions: Change and Continuity in the Victorian Art World* (Cambridge: Cambridge University Press, 1995).

5. Burne-Jones, *Memorials,* 2:75.

Critical recognition led to international fame. He exhibited, by invitation, at both Expositions Universelles in Paris (1878 and 1889) and was awarded the Legion of Honour in 1889. At home, the rush of acclaim seemed calculated to make up for the years of obscurity. An honorary degree from Oxford in 1881, followed by an honorary fellowship at Exeter College, offered a corrective to the abrupt end of his education in 1856. The Birmingham Society of Artists elected its now famous native son president in 1885. In the same year the Royal Academy offered him associate status; he accepted, but his views on conventional art institutions did not change, and he exhibited there only once and resigned eight years later. In 1894, he reluctantly accepted a national honor: the queen granted him a baronetcy, and plain Ned Jones from Birmingham became Sir Edward Burne-Jones, one of the most respected painters in England.

All the honors and attention could not dissuade him from believing that contemporary art was straying from its true course as a search for beauty. He disdained the loose technique and emphasis on colorism—hallmarks of an advanced style pioneered in France and now influencing English and American painters—as sloppy, betraying a lack of finish and commitment. He also lamented the increasing rejection of literary and allegorical subjects in favor of the modern-life genre and emerging abstractionism. On occasion, he expressed his concern humorously, wondering, for example, if Chaucer would approve of his pictures for the Kelmscott publication, or if he would prefer "impressionist ones."[6] But Burne-Jones placed great value on the seriousness of his endeavors in art, and this led him to question contemporary aesthetics and public taste. He testified for Ruskin against Whistler in the notorious libel trial of 1878.[7] He called Edouard Manet and his circle "a set of inferior chaps who do next to nothing but talk about what they do," and he lamented the taste of his own generation: "An age that makes Sargent its ideal painter, what can we say of it?" As the years wore on, his sense of estrangement increased, no matter that his reception and reputation indicated otherwise. He repeatedly

6. Lago, ed., *Burne-Jones Talking*, 44 (September 23, 1895).
7. Linda Merrill offers the fullest account of the trial and its consequences in *A Pot of Paint: Aesthetics on Trial in Whistler v. Ruskin* (Washington, D.C.: Smithsonian Institution Press, 1992). See 171–76 for Burne-Jones's testimony.

voiced fears that he was the last practitioner of exactly the type of art that had led him to become an artist, telling Rooke, "It's such a disappointment to find the future of painting turning in that direction [French modernism]. So opposite of all I've wished and thought. . . . When there's an end of me it won't make the slightest difference to what goes on . . . when I'm over all that I love will be over and no one will be left to care two straws about it."[8]

The pain of isolation and estrangement sharpened as the deaths of friends made Burne-Jones constantly and painfully aware of his own mortality. In October 1881, Dante Gabriel Rossetti canceled a proposed visit, being too ill to receive even a long-valued friend. The older artist's death that following April only served to heighten Burne-Jones's sense of regard. Contrary to his own reluctance toward biographers, he considered writing a memorial to Rossetti but later reflected, "It is nice to be remembering it all . . . only most of it is so indescribable. His talk and his look and his kindness, what words can say them?"[9] Others passed out of his life. He lamented the lack of ceremony at English funerals, first at Robert Browning's on December 31, 1889, and then again at Alfred Tennyson's on October 13, 1892. Ford Madox Brown's death on October 11, 1893, increased his sorrow. In an undated letter to Lady Rayleigh, written around this time, Burne-Jones confided, "Dear Lady, my friends are dying . . . and I want to make a great fuss over the living, and keep them close to me and well in sight."[10]

On October 3, 1896, he suffered his greatest loss. William Morris's death was hardly unexpected. Throughout the summer of that year, Morris's famously vigorous health declined, then disappeared, until he was—in Burne-Jones's words—no more than "a shadow . . . a glorious head on a crumple of clothes." In his sorrow, Burne-Jones overcame his natural repulsion toward corpses and forced himself to look at Morris laid out on his deathbed, but the experience left

---

8. T. M. Rooke, "Notes of Conversations among the Pre-Raphaelite Brotherhood," 4 vols. (National Art Library, Victoria and Albert Museum, London), 310 (December 16, 1896); Lago, ed., *Burne-Jones Talking,* 102 (May 9, 1896); Rooke, "Notes," 213–14 (May 19, 1896).

9. Burne-Jones, *Memorials,* 2:117.

10. Burne-Jones Papers, Fitzwilliam Museum, Department of Manuscripts, Cambridge, 27 vols. xxvi, f. 250.

him cold, disdainful of "all that talk about the beauty of death . . . it's nothing like the beauty of life." Perhaps emulating Morris's own ethic, he sought to lose himself in work, confessing to Rooke, "Things must be done and the living have to live." Yet the feeling of abandonment never left him. Instead, losing Morris rekindled his mourning for Rossetti. In May of the following year, he recalled a line from Swinburne's "A Song in the Time of Order" to illustrate for Rooke the strength of those friendships: "When three men hold together the kingdoms are less by three," and he reflected ironically on his changed situation. "To say 'When one man holds himself together in a very shakey way, the kingdoms are less by one' doesn't sound so well, does it?"[11]

In this spirit of lost agency, Burne-Jones painted *Lancelot at the Ruined Chapel* (1896; Southampton Art Gallery). Alone, and lost in his despair, the flawed and failed knight is shown collapsing outside the sacred chapel that houses the Grail. In the legend, Lancelot's own passion for Guinevere barred him from completing his quest, but in this oil of 1896, Burne-Jones suggests only exhaustion. The guardian angel at the door, raising hands in wonder and sympathy, makes no attempt to wake the sleeper; the narrative ends in oblivion. In his late career, Burne-Jones explored this subject in decorative-arts designs twice: in a stained-glass design for his home in Rottingdean in 1886 and in an 1891 tapestry design. Both works were produced by Morris and Company. But this painting directly recalls Rossetti's version of the same subject from the 1857 Oxford mural. Burne-Jones sat for Rossetti's figure of Lancelot, and, in reviving the image of the knight, with lank limbs, fine features, and gaunt grace, Burne-Jones created an icon of his own lost youth. The elegiac spirit of the work commemorates his lost companions, but it also portrays a man diminished by this loss, for, as Burne-Jones lamented to his wife after Morris's funeral, "I am quite alone now."[12]

Throughout his career, the idea of agency arrested by slumber fascinated Burne-Jones, as can be seen in his repeated interpretations of the Briar Rose narrative, a variant of the Sleeping Beauty legend. In 1862, he created ten designs for tiles illustrating the narrative of "A certain prince who delivered a king's daughter from a sleep of

11. Lago, ed., *Burne-Jones Talking,* 115 (October 4, 1896), 147 (May 29, 1897).
12. Burne-Jones, *Memorials,* 2:289.

a hundred years," part of the furnishings commissioned by Birket Foster from Morris, Marshall, and Faulkner for a new home in Surrey.[13] Burne-Jones returned to the theme in 1869 on commission from William Graham, selecting three subjects—*The Rose Bower*, depicting the sleeping princess and her attendants; *The Council Chamber*, portraying the king and his court; and *The Briar Wood*, presenting a knight encountering the sleeping guards—for reinterpretation as full-scale oil paintings (*The "Small" Briar Rose Series*, Museo de Arte, Ponce).

As soon as he concluded this series, Burne-Jones expressed his desire to do it again, but on a larger scale. He took his plan to Graham, who refused it for lack of space. After preliminary work in 1873–1874—doubling the size of the canvases and adding an additional subject, *The Garden Court*, presenting the serving maids of the princess asleep outside her chamber—Burne-Jones set the project aside, taking it up again in 1884. Even before the completion of the large *Briar Rose* series, Graham negotiated on the artist's behalf with Agnew's Gallery. The completed set was exhibited there in 1890, drawing large crowds and unprecedented critical acclaim. As a result, the four paintings were purchased by Alexander Henderson (later Lord Faringdon) for the saloon of his Oxfordshire estate, Buscot Park. Burne-Jones began a final series on the theme in 1872 and completed *The Garden Court*, *The Rose Bower*, and *The Council Chamber* before ceasing work on the set in 1895.[14]

In these paintings, Burne-Jones made a deliberate choice to depict an unresolved narrative. When asked why he did not paint the awakening of the princess by the knight, he stated, "I want to stop it with the Princess asleep and to tell no more, to leave all the afterwards to

---

13. The Sleeping Beauty tiles were originally called "Of a certain prince who delivered a King's daughter from a sleep of a hundred years, wherein she & all hers had been cast by enchantment." Designed by Burne-Jones and William Morris in 1862–1865, they were possibly painted by Lucy Faulkner in 1864–1865. They are currently in the collection of the Victoria and Albert Museum, London. See Jennifer Hawkins Opie, *William Morris*, ed. Linda Perry (London: Philip Wilson Publishers, 1996), 189.

14. The final set of *Briar Rose* paintings is separated. *The Garden Court* is in the City of Bristol Museum and Art Gallery; *The Rose Bower* is in the Hugh Lane Gallery of Modern Art, Dublin; and *The Council Chamber* is in the Delaware Art Museum, Wilmington.

the invention and imagination of people."[15] This inherent ambiguity has led to multiple readings of these works, all reflecting a desire to cast the artist in the role of reclusive romantic, in surrender to escapism and passivity as much as his characters are surrendered to sleep. Both contemporary and modern critics link the figure of the princess to Burne-Jones's fears about his own daughter, Margaret, a reasonable assumption, for Margaret modeled for the princess in the large version of *The Rose Bower* in the mid-1880s. Georgiana Burne-Jones recorded that her husband harbored a persistent anxiety about their daughter's health, always anticipating an impending illness and early death. Kirsten Powell links this apprehension with an actual bout of illness Margaret suffered in the summer of 1884, noting that she sat for the figure in the following year. Penelope Fitzgerald uses the association of Margaret and the princess as evidence of Burne-Jones's desire to keep his daughter in a virginal state in the face of her marriage to J. W. Mackail in 1888, an interpretation easily refuted by the painter's own studio list, which reveals the work was completed by 1886.[16]

Rejection of the contemporary world serves as the most consistent message drawn from these and Burne-Jones's other images of submissive sleep. Martin Harrison and Bill Waters, Powell, and Larry D. Lutchmansingh all see in the inconclusive narrative various modes of retreat: from current politics, changing society, or modern aesthetics.[17] It is true that Burne-Jones often expressed disassociation with his own times, declaring it a "pity" he was not born in the Middle Ages or "How nice it would be to live for five hundred years, taking less and less part in the world but watching it with big eyes."[18] But to see the *Briar Rose*

15. Burne-Jones, *Memorials,* 2:195.

16. Ibid., 2:146; Powell, "Burne-Jones and the Legend of the Briar Rose," *Journal of Pre-Raphaelite Studies* 6 (May 1986): 20; Fitzgerald, *Edward Burne-Jones: A Biography* (London: Hamish Hamilton, 1975), 226; "List of my designs and pictures when I began to draw," notebook of Sir Edward Burne-Jones, Fitzwilliam Museum, Cambridge.

17. Harrison and Waters, *Burne-Jones* (New York: Putnam's, 1973), 151, 153; Powell, "Burne-Jones," 16–17; Lutchmansingh, "Fantasy and Arrested Desire in Edward Burne-Jones's *Briar-Rose* Series," in *The Pre-Raphaelites Re-Viewed,* ed. Marcia Pointon (Manchester: Manchester University Press, 1989), 123–39.

18. Lago, ed., *Burne-Jones Talking,* 146 (May 29, 1897); Burne-Jones, *Memorials,* 2:201.

series as an escapist's fantasy does not take into account Burne-Jones's own desire that the painted narrative, by design, remain open-ended. With lack of closure, Burne-Jones prompted the viewer to complete the story and thereby actively draw the promise of rejuvenation out of the stasis of infinite rest.

During the years that Burne-Jones worked on the large *Briar Rose* series, his imagination fixed on another unresolved narrative that featured an iconic image of infinite rest. In 1886, he wrote a letter to Thomas Rooke, who was in France on a sketching tour: "But how is it you are in Avalon, where I have striven to be with all my might— And how did you get there and how does Arthur the King? . . . I have designed many pictures that are to be painted in Avalon—secure me a famous wall for I have much to say."[19] Rooke's response has not been preserved, but it is easy to speculate that he smiled in sympathy when he read these words. His travels had taken him to "Avallon," a picturesque old settlement in Burgundy. But the "Avalon" of his employer's reference was the magic island of the Arthurian legend, a symbolic site rich with multiple meanings.

The myths of Avalon derive from twelfth-century accounts of the legend. It was first cited as the land where Excalibur was forged. Popular lore defined it as a real location, the ancient foundation of the Abbey of Glastonbury, where the monks claimed to have discovered Arthur's grave.[20] Avalon also has significance in the Grail legend, as the location of a sacred chapel, the one where Galahad was nourished by the holy vessel and concluded his quest. But most important, in the *Historia regum Britanniae* (circa 1138), Geoffrey of Monmouth described the *Insula Avallonis* as the eternal sanctuary of the Once and Future King, a vale of safety and rest where Arthur's wounds are healed as he waits for the moment of his prophesied return.

At the time of Rooke's travels, Avalon had acquired a physical and personal association for Burne-Jones and his assistant. In 1881, George Howard, Burne-Jones's longtime friend and patron, commissioned a

---

19. Burne-Jones, *Memorials,* 2:169.

20. In 1190, the monks of Glastonbury produced the bones of a man and a woman, claiming them to be those of Arthur and Guinevere. Now believed to be a publicity stunt, these "relics" turned Glastonbury into a popular and lucrative pilgrimage site for centuries. See Norris J. Lacy and Geoffrey Ashe, *The Arthurian Handbook* (New York: Garland, 1988), 60–61.

work for his library in Naworth Castle, Cumberland. Howard gave Burne-Jones the freedom to choose a subject from the Arthurian legend, a mutual interest that united them early in their friendship.[21] *The Sleep of Arthur in Avalon* was planned as a solemn and conventional depiction of the king at rest after his earthly labors, but as the work progressed, the image took on the complexity of a personal testament. In January 1885, Burne-Jones wrote to Howard requesting that he consider accepting a simpler work with fewer figures, allowing him to put aside the original design, reflecting, "One day I would finish it, perhaps."[22]

Howard released his friend from the commission and never requested return of the advance payment. After the artist's death, Georgiana Burne-Jones sent Howard a painting of Saint George to cover the debt.[23] The alternative scheme was never realized, but Burne-Jones continued to work on the large *Avalon* painting. Georgiana claimed that the scope of the endeavor "grew until it ceased to suit its original purpose," being transformed into a "task of love to which [the artist] put no limit of time or labor." The size of the painting—eleven and a half feet by twenty-one and a half feet—required the rental of a special studio. He worked on the painting intermittently for the next thirteen years. He referred to the work and the artistic ideals its represented to him interchangeably, writing to his wife, "I am at *Avalon*—not yet in Avalon. . . . I shall let most things pass me by . . . if I even want to reach Avalon."[24] He put the final stroke on it the day before he died. For Burne-Jones "Avalon" became an amalgam of place, picture, and state of mind. But more than that, it defined his objectives in art through a metaphor that shaped his life.

As with the *Briar Rose* painting, scholars have sought to explain the enigma of *Avalon* through the events of Burne-Jones's life. It has been seen as the ultimate imagined escape, as a lament for lost dreams,

21. Burne-Jones met George Howard (an aspiring painter) at Little Holland House around 1860. A drawing by Burne-Jones of *Tristram* in the Victoria and Albert Museum, London, has a note that Howard assisted with some of the figures. See Fitzgerald, *Edward Burne-Jones,* 102, 287n.

22. Letters of Edward and Georgiana Burne-Jones, Castle Howard Archives, 522/27, 20.

23. Ibid., J23/105/13 [1881] 66.

24. Burne-Jones, *Memorials,* 2:116, 340.

and even as a wish for death. A current and prevalent reading asserts that the work commemorates Morris, with the artist's longtime friend being the model for his king. This claim is easily contested: Morris was in vigorous health when Burne-Jones began the painting. There is no record of Morris posing for the image (and it is absurd even to imagine Morris taking time away from his socialist activism in the 1880s to model as a monarch), and the head of the king was completed long before the artist had the sorry vision of his dying friend reduced to no more than that "glorious head on a crumple of clothes."[25]

Others have seen the image of the artist in the king. A. W. Baldwin purports that when Georgiana Burne-Jones caught her husband napping on his studio sofa "his posture . . . was generally the same as that in which he had painted King Arthur." Jan Marsh suggests that the depiction of "an old man lying surrounded by eight women" offers "an unconscious but transparent reflection of the artist's lifelong demand

25. The notion that *The Sleep of Arthur in Avalon* is a memorial to Morris seems based in imaginative projection. Fitzgerald describes the work as intended to be "commemorative of his (Burne-Jones's) own dead kings and the disaster the world would suffer at their loss" (*Edward Burne-Jones*, 190). This vague analysis likely encompasses Rossetti (and perhaps Tennyson) as well as Morris. But only Rossetti had died when Burne-Jones was formulating the composition, and the figure of the king was long complete before the deaths of his other "kings." In *The Legends of King Arthur in Art* (Cambridge: D. S. Brewer, 1990), Muriel Whittaker extends this assumption. Ignoring the fact that the work had been long in progress, she bluntly states, "Arthur is also his (Burne-Jones's) old friend, William Morris, who died in 1896." As evidence, she cites a visit by Graham Robertson to Burne-Jones's studio, noting that he saw a physical likeness of the dying Morris in the image of Arthur's "glorious head on a crumple of clothes" (258). She does not cite her source for Robertson's supposed observation, and it cannot be verified in his writings on the painting in his memoir of the late Victorian art world, *Life Was Worth Living* (New York: Harper and Brothers, 1931), which does offer his own description and response to the work. From his boyhood, Robertson was a regular visitor to the artist's home and studios, and his reflection on the painting (although not dated) is retrospective: "[The] actual design had never been one of my favorites . . . the central figure of the sleeping Arthur to which all eyes were directed seemed to lack dignity and import. I had looked for a great man in a tiny island tomb; here was a little man in a vast land of rolling hills and vales" (277). And, of course, the description of the "glorious head on a crumple of clothes" was Burne-Jones's, his memory of how Morris wasted in his last days, shared with Rooke on the morning after Morris's death (Lago, ed., *Burne-Jones Talking*, 115 [October 4, 1896]). The argument that the head of the king is a portrait of Morris is simply indefensible, and no amount of misquotation can change the chronology of a work in progress.

for female attention." Mary Lago observed that in Burne-Jones's last year of life all "his energies were collected and directed toward the completion of this picture, and yet he felt that, being finished, *Avalon* would be his own ending."[26] Basing her analysis on his personal commitment to art rather than his private preferences in life, Lago offers instructive insight. And when *The Sleep of Arthur in Avalon* is read within a context of the artist's long fascination with the Arthurian legend, his vocabulary of pictorial symbols, and his own words (which have been sorely neglected as the means to understand his art), an answer arises out of the enigma of the unresolved narrative in Burne-Jones's art.

The Arthurian Revival ran parallel to Burne-Jones's life and, to a very real extent, shaped his imagination. During the artist's childhood and adolescence, the legend emerged as the national epic. In 1842 Alfred Tennyson published his first poems on the subject of the mythic king; these were warmly received, and the public called for more. One poem, "Sir Galahad," inspired the young Jones, as an Oxford undergraduate, to declare his desire to found a modern order, based on the example of the chaste Grail knight.[27] Thomas Malory's canonic *Le Morte d'Arthur* provided a bond of friendship between Jones and his favorite classmate. The wealthy Morris gave the impoverished Jones a copy of the book that he coveted but could not afford. In 1857, as William Dyce carried out a government commission to portray the legend on the walls of the Queen's Robing Room in the new Westminster Palace, Dante Gabriel Rossetti schemed up a rival program for the new Debating Hall at Oxford. Burne-Jones participated in the ill-conceived project; his design, featuring Merlin's enchantment, was one of the few murals actually completed.

Just as Galahad gave Burne-Jones a model of youthful idealism, Merlin provided the icon for his middle years. Unlike Morris, Rossetti, and Swinburne, Burne-Jones never disparaged Tennyson's Arthurian endeavors. *The Beguiling of Merlin* (1874–1876; Lady Lever Art Gallery, Port Sunlight), one of his most important midcareer pictures, owed as much to Tennyson's *Idyll* "Merlin and Vivien" as to the

26. Baldwin, *The MacDonald Sisters* (London: Peter Davies, 1960), 155; Marsh, *Pre-Raphaelite Sisterhood* (London: Quartet Books, 1985), 336; Lago, ed., *Burne-Jones Talking,* 160.

27. Burne-Jones to Cormell Price, May 1, 1853, in Burne-Jones, *Memorials,* 1:76.

medieval *Romance of Merlin* from the *Vulgate Cycle* that inspired the setting of the hawthorn tree as the site of the mage's demise. Shown at the debut exhibition at the Grosvenor Gallery, *The Beguiling of Merlin*—with its electrifying eroticism and it insinuations of gynophobia— was one of the reasons Burne-Jones rocketed to critical notice.

In the last decades of his life, Burne-Jones explored the Grail quest, using it as a subject for stained glass, tapestry, and countless small and personal studies. Although he and Morris never began the illustrated Malory they planned for the Kelmscott Press, Burne-Jones designed the frontispiece and title page for Sebastian Evans's translation of *The High History of the Holy Graal,* published in 1904, six years after the artist's death. Throughout Burne-Jones's life the Arthurian legend provided a thread of continuity; he returned to it repeatedly, always to find it a fresh source of inspiration.

The subject of Arthur's passing was present—and popular— throughout these years. In 1842, Tennyson used it to link his name to Arthurian themes for his public. Of all his early Arthurian poems, the "Morte d'Arthur" proved the most influential. Grand in scope and epic in tone, it cast an indelible image of the Once and Future King for the Victorian audience, and the shadow of that image would hover over all versions of the legend for the duration of the Revival.

It may seem curious that a poet would choose the final scene of the traditional saga to announce his desire to serve as the new voice for the legend. But, throughout the legend's history, that singular part has stood as an emblem for the whole. Tennyson's tale of the king's last battle and his mysterious journey follows tradition. Arthur faces his enemy Mordred on the field; the king slays the usurper but is dealt a life-threatening blow. In his grief and pain Arthur commands his last loyal companion, Bedivere, to return the sword Excalibur to the Lady of the Lake and to tend his wounds until the time of his departure. A boat appears on the horizon, and when it docks, three stately queens come ashore to take Arthur to Avalon, where his body is healed and he rests until his nation calls him forth again. In this way the legend ends in mystery—Arthur's destination is named but not known—and in a promise—the king will survive to return and reign—a promise that closes the legend with the potential for it to begin again.

Artists also recognized the element of iconicity in the story of Arthur's passing. It was one of the first Arthurian subjects to be depicted in the Arthurian Revival, and it was among the last to endure. No other image so richly consolidated the message of the legend for the Victorian era. Proof of Arthur's heroism, the mystery of his destiny, and the promise of his return converged in a single dramatic moment. In the context of the Revival, this subject, rare in medieval art, engaged modern viewers in a powerful—and reciprocal—association. Gazing at the king, separated by a distance that no human being could cross, the viewer became Bedivere, bound to the legend through obedience, association, and memory, pledged to preserve the ideal in the king's absence.

The idea of Arthur in Avalon drew from the whole of the tradition, but in the Victorian era the subject rapidly developed a standard iconography. All the conventional elements may be seen in James Archer's *La Morte Darthur* (1861; Manchester City Art Gallery). Safe from the rugged sea and the sandy shore, Arthur lies in a grassy meadow where his guardian queens keep their compassionate vigil. As the death barge retreats into the distance, the Grail maiden appears, to heal Arthur with the chalice of the holy quest. Like other Victorian artists who portrayed this particular subject, Archer presented the rest in Avalon as an emblem of comfort and assurance to his viewers. Arthur's body is broken, but his gaze—hollow-eyed in a gaunt face— is fixed and vital. He is still in the time of his earthly existence.

At first glance, Burne-Jones's painting seems to conform to conventional depictions of Arthur's rest. In *The Sleep of Arthur in Avalon,* the king reclines on a richly draped couch in a marble cloister. He is sheltered by a bronze canopy, embellished with gilded plaques that tell the history of the Holy Grail. Seated at his head and feet are the guardian queens, keeping their vigil in silent contemplation. Attendants play gentle music to soothe their sovereign's slumber, and, to the right, noble women bear his arms and armor. Guards are stationed at the entries to the cloister. They hold horns and trumpets instead of weapons; they will wake the king at the time of his return. In this tranquil atmosphere, safe from harm and disturbance, Arthur enjoys the sleep of revitalization. His pain has passed; his wounds are healing. He rests content in the knowledge that his former task is concluded and his future challenge is not yet at hand.

But to see Burne-Jones's picture as just an expansion of conventional iconography is to miss his telling details. The boat of Arthur's passage is absent from this image of Avalon. It appears in every other rendition of the subject and functions as the token of linkage between Arthur's life of action and his reward of rest. The sea is not even visible in the distance. The orientation seems different, even wrong. Nowhere is Arthur so firmly set in Avalon, and this emphasis on location signals the selection of a different moment in time. Connected neither to *once* nor to *future,* Arthur resides in the realm tradition has called oblivion. The point of view in the painting takes the privileged viewer beyond the barrier no mortal could cross. This is the sight denied Bedivere, the one that would have assured him that the king would survive to rule again.

The queens, in this instance, are silent. In other interpretations, they play an active role; they touch Arthur, they read and speak to him, they search his face for some indication of his wants and needs. Here they are silent and still. He is touched only at his head and feet, resting in the laps of his guardians. His body is fully displayed, proof of preservation, a spectacular appearance that emphasizes Arthur's whole body rather than its sites of damage. And Arthur sleeps. In other renditions, he convulses in his pain, he moans in grief, he strains toward the image of the Grail. Here, he rests in slumber, and it is significant that Burne-Jones used the word *sleep* in the title. All other renditions betray a shred of doubt by employing the traditional name *Morte d'Arthur,* Arthur's death.

The field of flowers in the foreground also contributes to the unorthodox iconography. Burne-Jones's strong interest in flowers and their meanings dates to his earliest years as a painter,[28] and in 1882, after a year's work on the *Avalon* canvas, he began the series of small, circular drawings now known as *The Flower Book.* This intensely personal project—published only in 1905, *after* his death—added a new dimension to the popular language of flowers. Rather than illustrating the assigned meaning of each flower, Burne-Jones sought to fuse flower, meaning, and narrative into a single image: "I want the name and the picture to be one soul together, and indissoluble, as if they could not exist apart."[29]

28. Ibid., 1:225–26.
29. Quoted in Harrison and Waters, *Burne-Jones,* 146.

The images in *The Flower Book* provide a catalog of the artist's most persistent and charged subjects: biblical, classical, and mythological. There are many sleeping figures, including the princess of the Briar Rose legend and Arthur on his journey to Avalon. In both cases, Burne-Jones's narrative choice signals a drastic departure from the larger, more public renditions. In *Wake Dearest,* the knight revives the princess, echoing the meaning of the Briar Rose, "I wound to Heal," while *Meadow Sweet* portrays Arthur's recent arrival in Avalon and the surrender of his power to slumber, incarnating the flower as the traditional token of uselessness. Complete in themselves, the images in *The Flower Book* lack the enigma of the unresolved narrative. But, unlike the *Briar Rose* paintings and *The Sleep of Arthur in Avalon,* these paintings were small-scale, made for personal expression and private view. And in this lies a telling difference.

In *The Sleep of Arthur in Avalon,* densely clustered blossoms of pink, white, and pale purple meadow sweet carpet the rocky foreground. This message of lost agency is both emphasized and tempered by the tall, proud poppy at the head of Arthur's couch—a similar bloom grows near the king in the versions of *The Council Chamber* in the large *Briar Rose* series and in the projected but incomplete final set of paintings (*The Council Chamber,* Delaware Museum of Art, Wilmington)—revealing that there is consolation in sleep. But rising above the meadow sweet, greeting the viewer in advance of the poppy, are irises. The messenger flower prepares the viewer to approach the king and reveals the narrative moment; the time has come to wake the king and regenerate the cycle. Once the image is seen, Arthur's new era has begun.

In contrast to the tale of the Briar Rose, the saga of King Arthur eludes closure by convention rather than by interpretation. Throughout the legend's history, the king's tragic fate—losing kingdom, companionship, and seemingly his life—is always subverted by his journey to the isle of Avalon. From the medieval era, this mysterious location provided a realm of sanctuary, where the king's wounds heal and he rests until his nation needs him again. Like all messianic sagas, the Arthurian legend is open-ended. A true cycle, once told it begs to be told again.

Burne-Jones's positioning of the viewer also moves the cycle from closure to reopening. Traditionally, Avalon is seen as a theatrical location, defined by a coastline, rugged waters, and a rocky shore. As the legend prohibits mere mortals from dwelling on the island, the viewer must be located in an audience, confined to a passive role of observation. In *The Sleep of Arthur in Avalon* the shore and the waters are not readily evident. But close examination reveals them, in a guard's shield that reflects a changing sky, a rocky cliff, water, and waves. Burne-Jones was pleased with his work on the shield, telling Rooke, "Yes the shield's all right. It will serve as a token of the tone of what the rest should be . . . if the whole of the picture can be brought up to that it will do."[30]

To see the reflection on the shield the viewer must be standing on the shore. And here is the key to viewing—and then drawing meaning from—the painting. First the viewer undertakes the journey to Avalon, landing the boat and coming ashore. Then, passing through the field of irises and heeding their message of the wonders to come, the viewer is ready to gaze upon the king. In the transformation of the viewer's role from passive to active, Burne-Jones passes agency from the viewed to the viewer. But the viewer then must complete the cycle, reviving the king through imagination, reliving the legend, and, with that connection, returning agency to the viewed. And through this engagement Burne-Jones transfers the power of the narrative to what he called "the invention and the imagination of the people," allowing them not just to see the image he envisioned, but to reenact his own process of imagining and experience the way an artist can coax life and vitality even out of enervation and death.

When the large *Briar Rose* paintings were installed in the saloon of Buscot Park, a similar passage through the pictures was established. Entering the saloon from the drawing room, the viewer encounters the knight "who will smite the world awake," and with him moves through the ensemble—stirring the king and his ministers in *The Council Chamber,* then reviving the ladies' maids in *The Garden Court*—to reach the desired destination, *The Rose Bower,* where the knight will wake the princess and the court will spring to life again. As in the *Avalon* canvas, Burne-Jones transfers the power, and the narrative is completed through the process of viewing. Rather than images of surrender, enervation, and paralysis, then, these late works

---

30. Rooke, "Notes," 401 (February 19, 1897).

communicate Burne-Jones's faith in the power of engagement, that the receptive gaze of the viewer would understand his art and ensure his posterity long after he ceased to paint.

In this light Burne-Jones's longing for "infinite rest" was neither escapist nor romantic. It signified his desire to articulate his belief that art knew no death; if fully realized it would transcend time and, like the king, or the court, or the princess, would need only the sympathetic and receptive viewer to open the closed cycle, to set the journey he imagined back into action. Perhaps Burne-Jones hesitated to finish *The Sleep of Arthur in Avalon* for reasons other—and grander—than a fear that "being finished, *Avalon* would be his own ending." He knew it was his culminating statement as an artist. His strongest desire was not to get it done, but to get it right. In *The Sleep of Arthur in Avalon* Burne-Jones told more than a story of a mythic king. Embedded in his narrative was an artistic philosophy: a reflection on the power of the painter to coax resolution out of enigma, vitality out of enervation, life out of death. Through this all-encompassing painting, inspired by his favorite legend, Burne-Jones made his bid for immortality. And through it he designed a role for himself in the story without an end. Like Arthur, who fought for justice to earn his slumber in Avalon, Burne-Jones had pursued his dreams in art and now was ready for the reward of infinite rest.[31]

31. This essay was inspired by Mary Lago's observation on Burne-Jones's hesitancy in finishing the *Sleep of Arthur in Avalon*, that "being finished, *Avalon* would be his own ending" (*Burne-Jones Talking*, 160). The method of inquiry followed was informed by her methodology, using the artist's own words to understand his art.

Anantha Sudhaker Babbili

The Road from Poodur

A Passage to America

> "Fielding! How's one to see the real India?"
> "Try seeing Indians."[1]

I didn't know the name of my grandmother. But it didn't matter.

I must have been six when I made the first journey to my father's village. India, they say, actually lives in the half a million villages on her landscape, not in the metropolitan cities of New Delhi, Bombay, Calcutta, Madras, or Hyderabad. Poodur is a typical village twenty kilometers outside Karimnagar, the nearest district headquarters, and about two hundred kilometers from the big city of Hyderabad. My paternal grandfather had several brothers and sisters whom I never met. I didn't meet him either, because he died two years before my visit to Poodur. He had six children, of whom my father was the fifth. The village was surrounded by hills where once the tigers roamed in a semiarid climate, beautifully green and stirringly lush during the monsoon and winter seasons, desolate and barren during the long summers. Cool breezes sweep across the farmlands, which produce lentil crops alternating

1. E. M. Forster, *A Passage to India* (1924; Harmondsworth: Penguin, 1936), 27; all subsequent parenthetical citations are to pages in this edition.

127

with rice paddies when the monsoons arrive. The village had the good fortune to be connected by a cement and tar road that ran from Karimnagar to Jagtial, a *taluk,* or district, outpost that only the Methodist Missionary Society (MMS) seemed to be interested in visiting.

By the dawn of the twentieth century the MMS had established itself in the remotest corners, touching my grandfather's life and the lives of his children in far-reaching ways that were to transform my history and my family's identity forever. These towns of Karimnagar and Jagtial, and later Medak—the town where my mother grew up— were like satellites revolving around the regal seat of the nizam, the Muslim ruler, in the city of Hyderabad, the capital of Deccan, the urban oasis sprawling amid medieval splendor. For two centuries, and until the mid-1950s, these cities were part of the nizam's dominion; later they became a part of the Telugu-speaking state of Andhra Pradesh in south-central postindependence India, which saw states demarcated by their linguistic character.

Mapping an imagined space and a critical geography was not considered important to my family or to my culture. Whence we came and where we would go didn't matter. Losses and gains went hand in hand, for fate, they said, was nonnegotiable. Mourning the loss of a family member to urban life was not common; but if it came to pass, the family would be quick to note the transition as one's inevitable destiny.

The Hindu name of my family was Bobbili. Most folk in that particular part of India had names that reflected either a region they came from or the identity of a caste, a subcaste, or the stratum of their larger economic activity. My father's family name can be traced to the city of Bobbili, far to the east of Poodur and Karimnagar. Bobbili was just outside the periphery of the nizam's dominion. The Kshatriyas, the warriors of the princely caste, ruled the Bobbili kingdom that reached the eastern coast of India—to the Bay of Bengal—and extended into the Madras Presidency to the south. Manipulated by Britain's East India Company, the French, and the Portuguese colonialists, the Bobbili dynasty waged a brutal war in 1756 with Vizianagaram near the coastal city of Visakapatnam. Bobbili Yuddham (War of Bobbili) would occupy a sad yet proud chapter in the history of the Telugus which the children of the south study in schools even today. The defeat of the Bobbilis saw a massacre of the youth and men inside the fort.

A fortunate few and their women and children fled the fort through tunnels dug earlier specifically for escape. Having fled into the jungles west of the city, the Bobbilis began a century-long migration further inland—almost on a straight path across the sacred rivers of Andhra over a period of several decades until they came upon the village of Poodur and set their roots there. A loss of identity, status, and wealth was both instantaneous and gradual; searching for a meaningful and peaceful life they decided to anchor themselves in each other and in that serene village by the ravine. Settling in the village took several more decades, and rebuilding an identity and developing subsistence farming finally gave the succeeding generations of the Bobbilis a sense of place. Soon the new generations would forget where they came from and why they settled in Poodur, and none of us would ever visit Bobbili. But it didn't matter.

By the beginning of the twentieth century, the Bobbilis had regained their identity, and the respect of the villagers and its elders, and marched into the caste system to stake their claim to the warrior class—only to be rejected by the inflexible upper caste. The Bobbili men were athletes, gamesmen, and good providers. Then came the pilgrim reformers from MMS. The missionaries had left cold, rainy, and sunless London, embarking on a mission to humanize the region and bring civilization and salvation to the heathens, all in one transcendent attempt. It was the secret splendor of India that entrenched them in her soil. They had come, much like their fellow countrymen in the British army, to shape India in the mold of Britain; but they didn't expect to be shaped by India.

"As a matter of fact I have thought what you were saying about heaven, and that is why I am against missionaries," said the lady who had been a nurse. "I am all for chaplains, but all against missionaries." (28)

Nevertheless, it was hard not to respect these pioneer missionaries. The people of Poodur did not know the origins or mission of these people. The villagers were simply amazed by their sense of doing good and, in particular, by their reaching for the Sudras and the

Untouchables from the lower end of the Hindu hierarchy. Having established a mission headquarters in Medak and Dornakal and outposts in Karimnagar and Jagtial, the pilgrim reformers developed programs of charity, health care, and education—all designed in London and carried out by the missionaries in the hinterland. They translated the Bible into Telugu and Methodist hymnals into the vernacular—some carrying the same tunes and others written and set to notes of regional music. The Catholic Church was already a presence in India, but it was located mainly in urban towns. The MMS went into the rural areas where people never saw a visitor who didn't belong to the region, much less a white man.

Medak would soon become a center for a great cathedral built to the design of Westminster Abbey, only smaller. The missionaries created jobs for the masses who toiled all day making bricks and mixing cement. It was their service to the poor with a gentle motive of converting the workers and their families to Christianity. Soon, Medak became a bishop's diocese, the center for theological education and for rural divinity training for young Indian Christians selected by the missionaries. The MMS built hospitals that provided free health care; primary, secondary, and high schools in *taluk* and district headquarters with English as the language of instruction; and nursery care centers for infants.

Ten kilometers from Medak, next to a river's tributary, the twin villages of Gopalpet and Vaadi were to become inextricably intertwined with the destiny of the Bobbilis to the north. My father would be plucked from the village of Poodur, sent to missionary boarding schools in Jagtial and Karimnagar, and handpicked later to attend the Wesley Boys High School in the city of Secunderabad, the twin city of Hyderabad. He was selected again for divinity training at the Serampore Theological College, Bangalore's United Theological College, and at Cambridge University in England. First, in the late 1940s, he was sent to Medak for rural training. While in Medak, he met my mother. By then, he was different from his village brethren; he looked sophisticated in manner, polished in dress, and wise in speech.

My mother was the second of two children of Gordon Anandam, a Christian convert. He was, the villagers of Vaadi tell me, of huge frame, imposing and dynamic, the best soccer player in the region, and possessed of an impressively native intellect. I didn't know who his parents were. Villagers today speak of him as if he were a legend, a man who stood up to the British in his own way, unafraid and asserting his equality with the outsiders who operated in the domains of religion and local governance, revenue collection, and law and order. His wife was, simply, Anandamma—the wife of Anandam; I didn't know her Hindu name or her Christian one.

My maternal grandfather attended the missionary schools in Medak, was a good Indian adapting to the ways of the British, and became the honored scholar to be sent by the church to the University of Birmingham in England in the 1930s. He was the first Christian from the nizam's dominion to receive the queen's scholarship to study in England. Both the church and the governing authorities hoped that he would return with an advanced training in British higher education to educate the masses in Medak and surrounding villages—which he did later, in his own way. He returned from England with the conviction that the British were ordinary people who washed their own clothes, cooked their own food, attended to their children in ordinary homes— much the way Indians did. Why should the Englishmen enjoy such great privileges of having cooks, their own *dhobi* to wash clothes, gardeners, attendants to meet every need of their children, living in bungalows with commanding aloofness? These were, indeed, danger- ous thoughts for an Indian who, educated in England, was expected to be a grateful subject of the Imperial Crown. After all, Indians were imperial subjects, and he was trained to accept the preeminence of the Englishman. Instead, he joined the first Swadeshi movement—not a rejection of the British, but a movement that promoted things that were Indian-made in commerce and trade. He was in his prime and enjoyed good health. His growing indifference toward the church, his gradual rejection of external governance and law and order, and his preference for the rule of the nizam over the British raj as the lesser of two evils would come at a great cost.

On a clear sunny April day in 1946—sixteen months before India's independence—he was found dead sitting in an armchair on the veranda of his modest home. When my grandmother found him he had been dead for some time, for there were numerous ants crawling on his body. No one knew why and how he died, leaving his wife and two daughters behind in a society that showed disdain for widows and their offspring. Even the church would look askance. Village elders of Vaadi and neighboring Gopalpet still hold the view that he was poisoned. Some contend he was a marked man from the time he returned from the United Kingdom, having quickly become a local hero revered for his courage, outspokenness, and political activism. He was buried in haste by the authorities before his colleagues could call for an autopsy. His death coincided with the rising popularity of Mahatma Gandhi, the weakening of the British Empire, and the onset of the demise of the nizam's dominion. Gordon Anandam, properly baptized, educated in British missionary schools and trained in England, was buried in an unmarked grave. He was also the first of our ancestors to reject the caste hierarchy of the Hindu religion, to resist colonialism, and to see more clearly than any of his peers the dilemma of the subaltern and the sovereign.

Anandam's wife was relegated by the church to work in a nursery, away from society's view, as her widowhood was bound to bring ill will to those she would come in contact with. A widow would be an outcast, wear a simple white cotton sari, and discard all jewelry and bangles. In the Christian converts' circle she would be called from then on the Bible Woman, for she was expected to read the Bible in all leisure hours of the day and avoid contact with people outside her family. Her two children, Barbara and Sarah, having just entered adulthood, became the children of the lesser God overnight. Their struggles for livelihood and education would eventually prove successful despite neglect from the church and fellow Christians. Ammamma, as we, her grandchildren, called our maternal grandmother, earned twenty-seven rupees a month as a nursery teacher—barely enough to feed her daughters. My generation was to derive great inspiration from these women who, with true courage and sheer determination, against societal obstacles, would go on to become pioneers in their chosen fields. My Aunt Barbara finished her education at the prestigious Vellore Medical College and returned to lead the nursing corps at Hyderabad's Osmania General Hospital, developing a great respect for the nizam who had built the hospital. Ahead of her time, she left for Australia in the 1950s for a degree in nursing. She later migrated to the United States and received her master's and doctorate degrees, retiring as a medical surgical nursing professor from the University of Akron in Ohio. She never married and looked after us—her younger sister's children—as her own. Sarah, my mother, would meet my father when he was in rural ministry training in Medak after finishing her education at Madras Christian College. She became a schoolteacher and eventually a leader in the Indian Christian Women's Fellowship, which led her to advanced education in England.

In 1948, returning one evening from the day's training in rural pastoral work, my father saw the young Sarah in her backyard and promptly went to Ammamma to ask her younger daughter's hand in marriage. Ammamma, as a widow, followed custom in advising him to seek the permission of her eldest daughter, Barbara, in Hyderabad, at Osmania Hospital. My father, soliciting the help of his younger brother, went to the hospital nursing quarters to see Barbara, who simply asked him: "If you wanted to marry my sister, why ask me? Go ask for my sister's consent." The advice she gave was ahead of its time in India. Families intervened later, however, and set the stage for the arranged marriage for my parents. My father truly talked to my mother for the first time only after the wedding. She would support him throughout his service to the church—all of it in the villages, which culminated in his consecration as the first Indian bishop of the diocese of Karimnagar in the Church of South India, a union of the Anglican, Lutheran, Methodist, and several other missionary denominations in India.

"Why ever didn't you tell me you'd been talking to a native?" (31)

Back in Poodur, the colonial intervention into the destiny of my ancestors would bring about another family tragedy. My paternal grandfather, on a hot and sunny day, had seen a white man wearing a cardboard hat that shielded him from the burning sun come into the village on horseback; he was clutching a crumpled leather book in his sweaty palm. This was not the first visit to the village by this strange-looking man; the reaction of the villagers who were following him on foot on this particular day seemed rather cold and menacing. Soon the crowd had swelled, displaying further hostility toward the white man. They knew he spoke Telugu fluently, but there was something about the book he was holding, from which he preached, that provoked the villagers. My grandfather intervened in the villagers' physical attack on the white man; he had the stature to stop the attack, scold the villagers, and order them to return to their huts. Clearly, he reasoned, they wouldn't have had the desire to hurt anyone or the courage to attack an innocent man if the village's upper-caste elders had not been behind the incident. He took the man to his home and began a friendship with the British missionary from Jagtial outpost that would, in a strange sort of way, alter his future through his eventual conversion to Christianity and his christening as Babbili Jackiah—the process that triggered an irrevocable chain of events affecting many of his people, notably his children, including my father.

After my grandfather was baptized in the village's new church that he had helped build on his own land, his family name was changed ever so slightly from Bobbili to Babbili, as was the custom of the British missionaries, to set them apart from the family members who chose not to convert. The conversion set the village on course for a collision with the church, the harbinger of the white man's god. My grandfather would stand firm in his faith and in his belief that this was his awakening, his calling, his duty, and his destiny to be a good Christian who would reject the caste system and its economic bondage. His elder brother had different ideas about the conversion; not being able to accept his brother's conversion to an alien faith and feeling shamed by the deed, he would hang himself with a jute rope from the village's prominent tree in the middle of an open space by the Karimnagar-Jagtial Road. He was found there swinging in the gentle breeze of the early morning with a scribbled piece of paper in his pocket that said he could not bear the insult conversion brought to his family.

But life for his survivors went on.

In Poodur, where time is of no essence, work often resembles a ritual; the family of my father would tend to the rotated crops of rice and lentils, waking before dawn and working in the fields until the sun became too hot to bear. The men took turns with the women of the household in bringing a lunch of bread made of maize, raw onions and green chilies, and *thaida gunji*—creamy soup—to the fields. The men would till the land until the monsoon rains came, and the women would pluck the blossoming paddy seed to transplant it in rain-soaked *pattas* for the final yield. When the women were in the fields, the men would bring the lunch in a bundle of a cloth, call them over to dry land, and unfold the culinary experience as if it were another ritual. The men would attend to the children playing and singing under the cool shade of the trees nearby. While the children played, the men would gather to smoke the rolled-up *sutta,* dried tobacco in a fresh leaf. The children would watch with great delight how the grownups lit up the *sutta,* smacking two stones with a thin layer of cotton in between that would eventually light up after several attempts. When it was time to quit, the women would wind their way home through the bazaar, picking up fresh vegetables for the evening's meal. Rice and lentils from their own fields stored in tall jute baskets inside the house composed their staple diet. Mutton was reserved for Sundays, and chicken curry for Christmas, New Year's, and birthdays—if they remembered the dates.

Church activity soon became the most significant ritual in Poodur for the converts; they were loathed by the rest of the village but found favor in the eyes of the white man. On Sundays, families would awaken early, take the regular morning bath, and get ready for the church service on their premises. They liked the Telugu hymns and songs sung in church; fellowship and friendships born out of the churchgoing experience brought a special bonding. Marriages for converted Christians would take place only among the families that went to church and believed in Jesus Christ. They perceived kinship, gender, and property rights loosely, which signified the weakening of Hindu custom and resulted in special forms of social engagement. Many children were christened with biblical and Christian names. My grandfather in Poodur, however, chose to name his children by those derived from Sanskrit: Prabhudass (my father's name, which meant Servant of God), Yesurathnam (my uncle), and others. Only one of his sons, Mark, was named after the New Testament. My father would carry on the practice, naming his children in a Sanskritist tradition— Ananda Diwaker, Anantha Sudhaker, Prem Vidyaker, Vijayaker, Kamalini. Only the latter two carried Christian names in addition—Wilfred and Dorothy—that came from my father's mentors and friends in England and Germany. The Indian and Western names could coexist with no difficulty; our cultural identity would take precedence over our new religious identity.

The village had its own invisible demarcations based on caste and hierarchy. The Karimnagar-Jagtial road was not only strategic for the movement of commerce, crops, and people but also cut across Poodur, separating the upper-caste dwellings to the north, with their adequate supply of drinking water and plentiful water for farming, from the lower-caste huts to the south, which had to make do with water shortages. Poor *bastis*—neighborhoods—with no wells were routinely in jeopardy when the monsoons failed. The critical geography of such housing was accepted by everyone in the village, and no one really protested. The trouble came when a section of the village population in the poor *basti* accepted Christianity. The conversion to Christianity gave them mobility; they could now move across the region, from Poodur to Jagtial, where a church, a hospital, and a primary school were built (my father's initial education was there), and to Karimnagar, where the church had built a middle school and a bigger hospital.

The Karimnagar area was, in the church scheme, a pastorate, which enabled the church to establish larger projects in schooling, health care, and religious worship. Highly regarded by Christians, these institutions, however, carefully avoided politicization of caste, creed, and economic disparities. The villagers saw the pilgrim reformer only at the place of worship and in his bungalow, which was surrounded by a garden, servant quarters, and a garage for either his bullock cart or a motorcar shipped from London—invariably, a Land Rover jeep, which doubled as transport for the *thella dora* (revered white man) or for use by the hospital. The church, the parsonage, the hospital, and other dwellings were located in the Mission Compound with a three-foot boundary wall that provided psychological defense as well as spiritual detachment from their Hindu roots for converts. Completely self-sufficient and, in a way, forbidding to the visitor, the compound proved a safe haven. Many Hindus would come to accept the existence of such a social oasis and would also seek the services offered by the hospital staff and schoolteachers. Outside the compound lay the harsh, unseen, quiet violence only the oppressed villagers experienced, the rest living in denial of its existence. After all, submission and acceptance of one's karma still comprised the over-arching principles that people were accustomed to. The *jagirdar,* the *patelu,* the *subedar,* the revenue collector, the nizam, and the British government of India all had an established, burdensome, archaic, and hierarchial governance in the region. While the church quietly ignored the British government of India's profiteering from the caste system that reinforced its own place at the top of the caste pyramid, the British taught their pupils in the village all that was British—the language, the literature, the basic sciences, and, above all, the history and culture of India duly constructed by the Oxbridge-empire connection. Oxford and Cambridge were very much the co-conspirators of the regime that saw great moral conquests of Africa, the Far East, and the Indian subcontinent. The consequences of this regime were to act as an imperative on the Babbili family and to establish a great divide between its Christian and non-Christian members in Poodur.

"I only want those Indians whom you come across socially—as your friends."
"Well, we don't come across them socially," he said. (28)

While the English worldview of the nineteenth century pervaded the missionary schooling ideology, the other dominant influence came from the nizam—the self-proclaimed descendant of the Moguls, who, in turn, traced their origins to the Central Asian Turks. The nizam was the benevolent ruler of his kingdom known as the Deccan. Most south Indian states belonged to Deccan and carried an indelible imprint of the nizam. Hindu maharajas had a place and stature in Deccan as long as the nizam's preeminence was recognized and regular shipments of revenue were sent to his palace in Hyderabad. The system carried similar allegiances and servitudes down the line to the peasant in Poodur. The idea of the ruler's benevolence had a magical effect on peasants who rarely became beneficiaries of his largesse. The Poodur folk never questioned the benevolence—or lack of it—of the nizam and of the viceroy; they accepted it as if it were part of a mythological reality. Meanwhile, in Britain, the war hero Winston Churchill was fighting tooth and nail to deny India her independence—ironic for a Western leader widely perceived as a fighter for freedom and liberty in Europe while he continued the British oppression of the Indian peoples. To Churchill, Indians were half-naked fakirs who should be more than grateful for being accepted as the subjects of Imperial Britain.

For the converts, Christianity was more than a faith; it provided shelter from a caste system; new status in education, health care, and governmental work projects; and mobility—not an upward mobility within the caste system but a sort of physical and intellectual travel to areas and ideas never before imagined. Despite their meager exposure to what lay outside the village, however, peasants could still identify in the backs of their minds the reality that the initial exploration by the British of India culminated in exploitation. They reacted in silent protest by critically constructing a different identity that, while rejecting the hierarchy of the caste system, reconstituted Hindu cultural mythography in folklore and dominant ideas in history—an ideology Christianity could not well accept and attempted to stand in opposition to. Yet Christianity also anchored their lives. Soon it became an established fact that Indian Christians in Poodur moved from alienation to integration, to new forms of fellowship, and to construction of new traditions that only the church could nurture. Erecting a new community did not mean establishing new forms of conduct; it only meant creating new forms of fellowship. The idea of the humble Hindu and the concept of the secular Muslim were never forgotten in this project of creating a new identity. Christians, consequently, came to be a collective bulwark of the Indian conscience during the tragic and turbulent period that saw India emerging as a free nation and being violently partitioned with the birth of Pakistan. The converts soon began to live in imagined communities and developed a benignly revolutionary consciousness. To Christians in India, these two countries of India and Pakistan always remained one at a cultural level; to Christians the divisive vocabularies of freedom used by Hindu and Muslim leaders were self-serving, a display of egos, insecurities, and enigmas of history and, eventually, a betrayal of each other.

My paternal grandfather, the gentleman farmer, never left the village. He was self-contained in his new community, focused on finding employment for Christian converts inside and outside the village. His view rarely projected beyond the village; after his older brother's suicide he became the family elder. He had an enormous vision of his history that was never documented or communicated properly to his children; tradition was strong in the family, but articulation of it was another matter. Normally Hindu rituals at home and in the community would carry the memory of the forebears, but conversion made those rituals meaningless. While the older four of his children—two sons and two daughters—stayed in the village to farm or moved to another neighboring village after marriage, the road from Poodur for his last two sons took a strange and bittersweet turn. My father would go to Hyderabad, to Medak, and then to far away Serampore for theological education; his younger brother, Yesurathnam, would be one of the first Indian Christians to finish a master's degree in English literature at Hyderabad's famed Nizam's College. Other members of the extended family who did not choose either education or farming went to the Singareni Collieries, the coal mines that made the Telangana region rich in industry but dependent on its sibling, the Andhra, rich in agriculture, for food. The Bobbili family members who went to the coal mines maintained their Christian upbringing, holding on to Christian ritual, worship, and faith in the Holy Bible. They grew too old too soon breathing fumes from the heated earth far below the soil of their ancestors as the nizam's machinery was geared up to serve British India. Progress and industrial life transformed the rural landscape into a hotbed of hard labor with minimal respect for workers' health. In the meantime, the region was giving birth to several revolutionary movements—the Communist on the one hand, aiming to shape the outcome of independent India, and the Naxalite on the other, aiming to break the oppressive hold of the upper-caste *jagirdars* on the peasants. Both of the movements had an immensely popular appeal and used song and dance to present their ideologies and agendas in the form of folklore. Only Mohandas Karamchand Gandhi stood in their way with his powerful appeal to nonviolence.

"Do you really want to meet the Aryan Brother, Miss Quested?" (28)

In the meantime, my paternal grandfather died and was buried on the banks of the *kaalva*—the stream—that ran through Poodur. As children visiting from the city at the time, we played in the *kaalva* and caught small fish with our cupped palms, as if pulled by an invisible hand to stay close to his grave. The grave was washed away by the waters that came up during the monsoons in the following years. As an adult, I later went looking for it and could only guess at the exact location of the burial place so that we could build a grave that now withstands torrential rains. My paternal grandmother, who raised six children in a small, frail house built with weak brick, mud, and sand, lived many years after her husband's death, until her face showed deep lines of ripe age. I saw her for the last time when I was a teenager. She was sitting slouched on the cot outside the hut with a contented smile on her face.

The house, a brick-walled hut, still stands. My father's brother Mark and his wife live there as my ancestors did for several centuries. The house was kept clean with *sallu,* a mixture of cow dung and water sprinkled on the floor to keep insects away; the hand-sprinkled, odorless spray acted as a disinfectant as it dried. One could squat on the floor and roll out a broad, thin leaf in front of oneself from which to eat rice, curry, and *dhaal.* Hygiene was important in other ways, too. They would brush their teeth with *yapa pulla,* a small branch from a tree nearby that had a bitter taste. They would chew the corner of the branch until it became a brush and then clean the teeth until they sparkled. Even bathing near the family well was a ritual. Overnight, my paternal grandmother would soak *kunkudu kayalu* in a tumbler of water, a seed with a cracked outer shell that exuded a fresh aroma. By next morning the water had become shampoo, and hair smelled fresh and aromatic after the bath. The bath itself involved drawing water from the family well into a bucket. A brass mug was used to scoop the water and pour it over the body. Children loved it when it was not cool or breezy outside. Women would bathe in the back room surrounded by mud walls normally without a roof and connected to the main house. When my folk returned from the monsoon-drenched paddy fields, they would wash themselves and enter the house with impeccably clean feet. When electricity eventually arrived in Poodur in the 1950s, the house would have one bulb in the front room, and the smoke-filled kitchen would manage without, the open flames on which the food was prepared providing the necessary glow.

Poodur was immersed in tranquillity. For peasants the day would begin before early morning light; the timing of work in the fields, meal break, and the end of the workday involved keeping an eye on the movement of the sun. A full and a crescent moon indicated the passing of a fortnight; Amavasya, the night without the moon, was ominous, and the children were closely watched. Any tragedy the family might face would happen on that night, they believed. Work did not mean accumulation of wealth; none in the Bobbili family in Poodur expected to become wealthy working in the fields. All they needed was what the land offered, and what it offered was dependent on water and on the monsoons. Absence of monsoon rains was often tragic; all the prayers were directed toward good rains and yield enough to live on until the next monsoon period. Nature and the environment were held in great respect. The hills around Poodur, lushly green, would keep the hot breeze of summer away from the village. Children roamed the fields and learned to swim in the wells and in the kalva, to pluck mangoes from trees, and to chide the buffaloes into rage for fun. The sighting of an occasional cobra snake or scorpion provided the excitement for the week. A homemade slingshot would be aimed at every bird the children saw; rarely they hit the target. Some of them would emulate secretly the elders' habit of chewing betel leaves that had no taste but darkened their teeth and reddened their tongues, which they displayed to each other and to their mothers.

"I really do know the truth about Indians. A most unsuitable position for any Englishwoman . . ." (27)

Printed knowledge was kept from the villagers by the upper-caste families who used it for profit, authority, and internal consumption. The *pujari,* the Hindu priest, claimed direct access to the gods and provided the *prasadam* in the temple and read Sanskrit *slokas* from a book that appeared hundreds of years old. Non-Brahmins watched in awe while the *pujari* read and chanted from the book. The village doctor had exclusive knowledge of herbs and ayurvedic cures and was revered by the villagers. Snake bites that modern medicine did not cure, they believed, the good doctor of Poodur certainly would.

The Bobbili family, like others in the village familiar with the spoken word, would construct songs for *burra katha,* a poetic depiction of their past, to resurrect their histories, which they would sing in the front yard late into the evening in the flickering light of the lantern.

Children listened until they fell asleep in the laps of their mothers or fathers or grandparents. Missionaries who used knowledge of the printed word as the sole measure of literacy viewed them as illiterate, unable to measure the villagers' intuitive grasp of history and of the world around them. Knowledge of science and technology was reflected in their sophisticated understanding of the weather patterns, natural fertilizers, high-yield strategies, and tools of farming. No one had the time or the inclination to learn the printed word until my father's generation. Poodur's encounter with the industrial revolution was the inauguration of a mechanized factory that produced pairs of scissors for the region. It would employ about two hundred villagers and stood in direct opposition to their agrarian lifestyle. By the 1960s, electricity had come to the village's north side, opening further the long-established divide between the landed gentry and the peasants to the south.

In the twin cities of Hyderabad and Secunderabad the cartography of the Anglican Church also contained the same elements as the Mission Compound, except the schools were larger and were based on the segregation of sexes. In the early 1900s the Wesleyans started the Wesley Boys High School and Wesley Girls High School in Secunderabad; both had boarding schools for students from rural areas. The Methodist Church started the Stanley Girls High School and Methodist Boys High School in Hyderabad. All had, until after India's independence, British principals and headmasters who aimed to make all Christian youth essentially British. The Roman Catholic Church in the twin cities, in the meantime, became the preeminent provider of first-rate education and social services. The manner and demeanor of the Catholic Christians in Hyderabad were different, in the sense that a pretense of being Anglo-Indian pervaded a major part of their community. It was important to many of them to be recognized as Anglo-Indian, seen as semi-British, sound like the British, talk like the British, and speak their own mother tongue with a British accent. Names such as Brian Alexander, John Comfort, Horace Bradshaw, and Sam Luck were commonplace. Indeed, the identity they opted for also gave them a sense of place and comfort; they had appropriated the unique history of the Anglo-Indian on the subcontinent. The Christian schools in the twin cities had more Hindu children than Christian, for they were the schools of choice for the Hindu families. However, if the converts looked to the missionaries as extraordinary people of God, the Hindu community saw them as *pardesi,* the foreigners. *Desi,* the native, referred to them as sahibs, although the term was generally confined to the military and political representatives of Great Britain. Britain's hegemony of India was, indeed, complete with its extension through these political and military sahibs. Indians rarely saw them grow old because they were constantly rotated and called back to London, thus creating an illusion among the *desis* that the sahibs were supernatural and direct descendants of God himself. Sahibs were never seen in Poodur and the surrounding area. They did their work through the nizam. Poodur saw missionaries only when they were on *yatra,* a retreat, and held extended open-air prayer meetings for village converts during the cool winters.

He had seen the quatrain on the tomb of a Deccan King and regarded it as profound philosophy—he always held pathos to be profound. The sacred understanding of the heart. (21)

Hyderabad is a city with five hundred years of recorded history. Earlier, it was a settlement for the weary beside the robust River Musi. Even now it has a medieval appearance in the midst of industrial encroachment; it contained a feudal society and remained as such for several centuries. The first Indian university to have an Indian language as the medium of instruction was started in Hyderabad in 1908 by the last of the nizams, Osman Ali Khan; it would bear the name Osmania while the medium of instruction was Urdu, only to be changed to English after India's independence. English soon became the lingua franca of commerce in the midst of a thousand languages of the land. My first encounter with the nizam was when I stepped into the Salar Jung Museum on the banks of Musi. I was awestruck with the splendor of Deccan in the form of the art, sculpture, carpentry, clothing, jade, gold and silver, and woodwork the museum held in its dusty premises.

The majority of Christian converts in Hyderabad had moved to the city as second-generation Christians in the 1940s. They settled in the general Muslim area called Sultan Bazaar. My maternal aunt, Barbara, after completing her college education in nursing at Vellore and in Australia, also moved to Hyderabad with her mother. My mother stayed in the rural areas with my father, who was becoming increasingly recognized as a bright young future leader of the church. My parents decided to send their children to Hyderabad to stay with Ammamma and attend the Methodist Boys High School. The early fifties saw the burgeoning Christian population settling in communities much like the mission compounds they left in the villages. The church would be the focal point with Christian houses located around it. The political timing could not have been better because the Christians soon became a buffer between Hindus and Muslims—who were witnessing the last signs of the nizam's reign. The struggle for power in the vacuum to be left by the dethroning of the nizam was afoot. The nizam unleashed his menacing paramilitary force—the Razakars—to continue, albeit hopelessly, holding on to his power. The Razakar movement sparked by those Muslims who sought independence from the British as well as from India was countered by a police action of the Indian government that resulted in several years of bloodshed. Christians came to the rescue of both the Muslims and the Hindus— in the hospitals and in the streets, since they consciously avoided involvement in the sociopolitical life of the new India of the time. The terrorist activity of the Razakar continued for several years and formally ended in 1948 with the liberation of Hyderabad by the Indian army.

The flight of most Christian converts from the village also developed a schism between the rural and the urban. Geographic relocation was perceived as progress from the uncivilized to the civilized. It soon became a matter of shame to be identified with village ancestry. Relatives coming to the city for a visit, although accepted in public, were shunned in private. They were amusingly referred to as "country cousins" who lacked polish, sophistication, and the finesse of the urbanized Indians. The self-concept of these city migrants gradually changed until the villager was perceived as illiterate and unwise while they considered themselves literate and wise. They soon developed

new forms of culture based on the milieu of the city and a consciousness of history that was dissimilar to that of their village brethren.
Economic activity, wealth (even if it wasn't much), and a position in
society—things the families only a generation earlier did not view as
important—became desirable dreams.

The event of conversion continued to have a ripple effect for several
more decades in the middle of this century, changing orientations,
expectations, institutions, and ideologies. It was influenced by and in
turn influenced a matrix of relationships, expectations, and situations.
The Christians never left the scrutiny of the *thella dora,* and the
inscrutable gaze of the *dorasani* (missionary's wife) never eased.
The church, which had rejected the Sudra Christians a hundred years
before due to their lower-caste status, found itself split and multiplied
many times until the dominant denominations organized themselves
as the united Church of South India. The British, by then, had unwittingly contributed to a schism based on class between those who
attended the English service in the church on Sunday and those who
attended the Telugu service—with the English service goers claiming a
higher status. Within several decades, the church was to become more
evangelized and more charismatic in the region. The Baptist Church
of Hyderabad by the late 1970s emerged as the largest and most
influential due to its Bible-based powerful preaching and an emphasis
on Indian music and worship songs. Notably, it would appeal to non-
Christians in ways the ritualized Anglican Church could not. Christians
in Hyderabad, nevertheless, came to be a strong presence in the
city by the early 1960s. Hyderabad, by then, had lost its ruler nizam
and India was very much an independent nation. Christianity would
emerge as a political reminder of the religion left behind by the British
as well as a cultural conscience of the independent India—sustaining
the buffer between Hinduism and Islam. The Christians remained true
to their faith, but many insisted on being Indian in all spheres of life.
Generations of them would revere Gandhi and the socialist Nehru,
the first prime minister of India. The independent India was to be
different, truly Indian, and I believed she would chart her own course
into the future—except I was to be wrong. The political colonialism
ended; but other forms of colonialism were left behind in schools that
would continue to impact my life.

"I've avoided," said Miss Quested. "Excepting my own servant, I've scarcely spoken to an Indian since landing." "Oh, lucky you." (27)

Dad was committed to the service of the church before I was born. He opted to remain in the rural district areas while some of his divinity school colleagues chose to work in the urban areas. My father and mother would bicycle to remote villages to preach the gospel and attend to the needs of the Christian converts. Living in villages, his children would remain unschooled or would be educated in the Telugu-medium village schools. Mummy would go with Dad wherever he was posted. So, the decision was made to send his two eldest sons, Diwi and me, to Ammamma in Hyderabad city. Diwi, eighteen months older, was a quiet, sensitive boy, and we grew up as friends, protective of each other. We were brought to Hyderabad and dropped off at Ammamma's rented house near Wesley Church. Aunt Barbara continued to live in the nursing quarters of Osmania Hospital. I was to be brought up by Ammamma for a better part of my schooling and college life. We would visit our parents in their rural parsonages for summer vacation and briefly for Christmas. The contrast between the city life of Hyderabad and the rural life of my parents was refreshing. My sense of loss today is intense partly because I longed for childhood in the village; imagining village life became my escape from city life.

Ammamma was getting old. She found herself suddenly responsible for two young Babbili children. Diwi was four and I was two and a half when we began our life with her. Ammamma was barely five feet tall, even less; her slight frame was partially distorted by osteoporosis. She wore a cotton sari always, and at her midriff she tucked into her clothes a tiny sack that held coins and a *gavva,* a seashell, for good luck. Once in a while, when she was asleep, I would steal a coin or two from the sack to buy candy at the street-corner store—a transaction I was extremely proud of doing all by myself. Her wrinkled face showed a great deal of pain, but she retained a pretty smile. I remember her getting up early in the morning and standing in front of a picture of Jesus praying, singing, and all the time crying. I didn't know why she wept so much; she never told us. Ammamma was an unselfish person, pious and strict. She was a disciplinarian who set hours for us to study, to eat, and to play. Beginning school in the kindergarten level at Methodist Boys High School was confusing and stressful. We made friends with boys with a similar background—second-generation children of Telugu Christians in the neighborhood close to Sultan Bazaar called Ramkote. All of them lived with their parents; I wondered why we didn't. Friends were welcome at our home as long as they behaved well and were not disruptive of our rigid schedule.

We would wake up in the early hours of morning and Ammamma would give us a bath; I used to shiver during winter, as the water was never warmed except for the Saturday afternoon bath. I can never forget how at the end of the warm bath on Saturdays she would pour cold water on my genitals as the bath concluded. It didn't hurt, but it made me numb. Even now I can't figure out why she did that so ritualistically. Old people did all sorts of strange things in my culture, and we were never told why. She would give us a breakfast of two pieces of *chapathis*—flattened flour bread—no more—and would pack us a lunch of two *chapathis* each with no curry. She would wrap them in a newspaper. The sugar she packed inside the *chapathis* melted with the day's heat by lunchtime. I did not like sweet things even as a child, and I hated my lunches. I would see other kids in school with steel lunch boxes stacked up with portions of rice, lentils, curds, lime, and mango pickles; the aroma itself was fulfilling. I never did complain to Ammamma about it. I ate two *chapathis* with melted sugar for lunch at school for seven years. Occasionally, when relatives from the village visited, she would send one of them to school with a hot lunch of rice and lentils.

The walk to the Methodist school was about a mile from the house Ammamma rented from Muslim landlords. Wearing uniforms, my brother and I would always arrive at school on time, since Ammamma made sure of it. We never missed school even when we had malaria or a fever. One day I walked to school with excruciating pain in my groin and Ammamma walked alongside with a watchful and caring eye to make sure I made it to school that day. Seven periods of different subjects taught by seven different teachers made up the school day. I felt defeated inside, although I didn't know why. After school all the neighborhood kids would walk back home. Sankranthi season meant we flew kites. Winter evenings meant playing *kabbadi* and *kho-kho,* ancient Indian games that relied on physical stamina and finesse. The rest of the year was my favorite—because it meant playing cricket. I was good at it; very good, actually. By the time I was nine I was playing cricket with much older boys and leading the team as an elected captain. I didn't know the game was British, for Indians had long appropriated it as a national pastime. Test matches between Commonwealth nations and India would attract the entire neighborhood and millions around the country to All India Radio for running commentary on the game. I was in bliss when the test season came; it made me forget the pain of living away from my parents. I was recognized by the neighborhood as a budding star of national-level cricket. I possessed a rare combination of several talents on the field: fast bowling, opening batting, quick fielding—an overall menace to the opposing team. And I loved it. I may have been angry at the world and never displayed it. I just took it out on the cricket field. I was a clean player; my team loved my game, and the team we played against would dread me.

The church had taken my parents away from me, and I was resigned to accept it without ever questioning the inevitability of it. Soon I developed nightmares and persistent anxiety. I was four when I developed a secret life—that of a protector to my Ammamma and my brother. Even when I would visit my parents during holidays, I would stay up all night alert to defend the family from all evil. My fears were not totally ill founded. Clergymen were routinely threatened, harassed, beaten, and sometimes killed. Dad was too passive and too oblivious to the dangers of his calling. If he did perceive them, he never mentioned it. I, too, never mentioned to anyone my fear of a family catastrophe. Ammamma's old age and thoughts of her eventual death also haunted me. We would all sleep in one room on the floor. I remember I used to hold Ammamma all night, watching her tummy go up and down with her breathing. As long as she breathed, I was all right. I would watch my brother peacefully asleep, but I would some-how make sure he was alive. I thought if Ammamma died that night for some reason, my brother and I would be left all alone. I couldn't face such a terrible specter. Many nights I slept very little. Sleep came when daylight arrived; daylight meant an unexplained assurance that things would be all right. Soon, I developed the fear of abandonment, the fear of dying, and the fear of rejection that stayed with me.

I was a naughty boy; Ammamma had her hands full with my mischief. The protector of my older brother, I would get into nasty and painful fistfights with older kids just to prevent them from picking on him. Muslim kids in Ramkote were the worst, because they inflicted the most pain on me. Yet I was hurting the most for my parents, but those feelings I didn't know how to express. I grew physically strong to withstand neighborhood bullies; I was a kid other kids learned not to mess with. Older boys called me Sam Luck after the boxing champion of India at the time. My worst sort of mischief as a child was jumping over the wall into a neighborhood performance hall and stealing rubber caps that held a steel chair firmly on the ground. I used to love it because I never got caught like some other kids. I was outgoing, always smiling and cheerful, and was skilled at imitating popular film stars and playback singers. I learned to play conga drums and displayed a sense of humor that bordered on being clownish. I became an entertainer; they said I resembled my mother in looks and possessed her singing talents. All the time, I hid the melancholy and that sense of loss deeply rooted within me. I didn't know at that time why I felt sorrowful and tragic inside. I didn't remember much of my schoolwork until high school; all I remember was that I was the teacher's favorite student in my English class.

As the next three siblings arrived in Hyderabad, it became too difficult for Ammamma to take care of all of us. I was completing my seventh grade, comfortably placed with friends, school, and cricket. That's when my parents started talking about sending Diwi and me to a boarding school in Secunderabad. I was not fully prepared to leave Ammamma. Leave we did when a *tonga,* a buggy drawn by a horse, came to take our trunks of clothing and supplies to Wesley Boys Hostel. It was, by far, the most painful move in my life. The sense of another loss was too much to bear, but I could not speak of it. We arrived in the hostel after dark and were left there with the luggage. I was told the superintendent of the hostel was an uncle of ours; his family would keep an eye on the city kids who would be added to the mix of mostly village boys from surrounding areas of Medak and Karimnagar. I didn't realize that the hostel boys from my father's ancestral area were perceived as brutes with rough mannerisms and unsophisticated speech. These students were some of the best, however, because they had too much invested in successful schooling in the faraway city.

My world turned upside down the first week I was in the hostel; my personality underwent a complete reversal. I probably gave up with this second phase of abandonment. Ammamma would care for the younger siblings at her home until time came to send them away to boarding school. The terrible sense of loss and the feeling of isolation from the family showed up in severe headaches and nausea. Ammamma must have intuitively understood the state of my affairs because she would come to see me during the monthly visiting hours and bring me home-cooked food, vitamins, and even a bulbul sitar, a musical string instrument, to distract and brighten me. It was to no avail. The nurse at the hostel started giving me cod liver oil every morning for what she thought was my vitamin deficiency. Nothing helped. My headaches soon turned into long nights of insomnia and nervousness. Pure trauma accompanied the second transition in my life, and my heart ached for months. My parents were too busy serving the church while we were navigating through the troubled waters of hostel life. It was necessary for them to remain oblivious to our ordeals because the church came first. Service to God, a western God, was the paramount objective. I resented that for years to come.

Boarding school, as in the words of Kipling, was my own House of Desolation. It was started by the missionaries, and the Indian authorities ran it like a boot camp. The rude wake-up call came at five-thirty in the morning, with chapel service at six, a terrible breakfast of *upma* at seven, study hours from seven-thirty until eight-thirty, and the walk along the Pendergast Road to Wesley Boys Multipurpose Higher Secondary School by nine sharp. After school there was an hour of playtime followed by dinner and a study period until bedtime. Every morning, school would start with a prayer session in the main hall. I started at Wesley in eighth grade; two years later when the time came to select the optional subjects for high school I chose BPC—biology, physics, and chemistry. I do not recall Dad or Mom discussing our academic future. It was basically left to us. I decided to follow Diwi, who was aiming to become a doctor, which he eventually did. I had no purpose and no idea of what I wanted to become. I sensed no one cared. But I felt the heavy burden of not letting the family down. Honor was at stake. I had to succeed in school. English remained my favorite subject at Wesley. Purshotham, the English teacher, would find my grasp of Shakespeare uplifting. He would ask me to stand and read my reviews to the class; I didn't particularly like it, but secretly I enjoyed the confidence he had in me. In sports, the most terrible loss I experienced having moved to Wesley was the lack of a facility for cricket and a cricket team like that of the Methodist school. The game, which was my only outlet for emotion, my only passion and pride, washed away along with my sense of belonging to Ammamma.

As he entered their arid tidiness, depression suddenly seized him. The roads, named after victorious generals and intersecting at right angles, were symbolic of the net Great Britain has thrown over India. He felt caught in their meshes. (18)

I was born in 1950, on October 22, at seven-thirty in the morning as the church bells were ringing, Mummy used to be fond of telling me. The one-bed mission hospital in Medak was the same place where Diwi had been born. The British had left India in 1947. Lord Mountbatten hastened the inevitable fact of a free India after four decades of the Quit India movement that held the entire nation together following the call for civil disobedience by Mohandas Gandhi. The colonial masters had gone, and by the next decade or so the missionaries would also follow. But I was to encounter colonial hegemony even after the independence. The new masters were these brown sahibs, the Indians educated by the British and trained to think and act like the British. Schools continued to be the epicenter for their encounter with the society. They continued to hold on to the British pretense— partly because it was professionally lucrative and partly because it was socially rewarding. These new masters showed a disdain for the un-Anglicized Indian. It was fashionable to speak English both among friends outside the home and inside the home with the family. The worst had indeed occurred: the British came in the guise of our own; the new masters would be the extensions of the invisible empire. This cultural imperialism was, in many ways, worse than political and economic colonization, for this sort of imperialism could not be easily identified or understood. Some Indian clergymen also behaved like their British predecessors. My family, however, rarely spoke English at home, and most of my friends were either Telugu- or Hindi-speaking. My parents did not emulate the British in any noticeable manner either.

Poodur and its surrounding villages never did experience the direct rule of the British. Telangana, along with the states of Maharashtra, Karnataka, Madhya Pradesh, and Madras Presidency, was sheltered from the British by the nizam. Consequently, the region retained its cultural identity, unlike the north, where the English were busy leaving their permanent imprint. However, the rule of the nizam meant furthering of the Muslim identity over the native Hindu identity; caught in between were the Christian converts. The nizam, and the partly independent *jagirdars* who nurtured the Deccani rule, provided a juxtaposition to the British rule in the area. In a way, it was worse because things became blurred and confusing to the people. The villagers had heard of the benevolence of the British ruler due to the carefully cultivated propaganda of the empire. The kind and compassionate missionary provided the proof of such compassion. But they did not know the difference between the racist political representative of the Pax Britannia and the zealous missionary of the MMS. In spite of their differing agendas, they all appeared the same to Poodur folk.

In the 1960s my parents were posted in a village called Panigiri (Hill of Snakes) when my transition from Ammamma's place in Hyderabad to Secunderabad's Wesley Hostel took place. Fellow hostellers were, indeed, rough and tough youth. I was twelve years of age, and the experience of living in a boarding school for the first time almost destroyed me. I found myself resenting everything: daily chapel service, Bible readings, regimented successions of chores and responsibilities, gardening knee-deep in muddy waters behind the Junior Hostel building, and food—bitter *chapathis,* and insufficient portions of rice and lentils. Meat was reserved for Sunday afternoon meals after church. Occasionally, the students would find a lizard floating belly-up in lentil soup or a cockroach that fell into the huge pots while the cook prepared supper. The word would go round, but we were too hungry to discard the meager portion of food for the day. I saw a hostelmate simply pick the lizard up by its tail, toss it, and continue devouring his food. We eventually began to look at these matters in good humor, referring to lizards and cockroaches as protein in one's diet. We were hungry all the time; some of us would hop over the wall of a Hindu temple across the street, steal coconuts offered to the gods by worshipers, and eat them as if it was the last meal of our lives. I felt no guilt then, and I feel no remorse now.

Being a year older and ahead in school by a grade, my brother Diwi was placed in the Senior Hostel, while I was placed in the Junior Hostel. Nights were scary, and the cold winters made it uncomfortable. I was awakened to the bittersweet joys of sex there, although girls and a heterosexual encounter were out of the question. Rumors of homosexual experiments in the hostel abounded, but I never paid notice to it—until a senior prefect, a junior hostel monitor, and the chapel monitor tried imposing themselves on me at separate occasions. The chapel monitor would call me into the chapel's vestry on the pretext of teaching me how to play the harmonium and would rub himself against me. Although I was too scared to fight it, my brother's growing reputation as a strong kid and my family relationship with the hostel superintendent prevented their outright imposition on me. Later, I learned its impact on me, for I could not develop trust or feel comfortable with the opposite sex until I was over thirty. I loathed the fact that my father and mother had deserted me there in the hostel; I developed a benign anger against Ammamma for letting all of this happen to me. I became increasingly detached and vulnerable while Diwi was growing in stature for the first time in his life. In Hyderabad, I was his protector; here, in the hostel, he took over as mine. I think it had something to do with his hostel buddies who worked out on the parallel bars next to the soccer field and on weight-lifting equipment. He began to develop a muscular body that prevented older students from taking advantage of him or me. My performance in school slowly deteriorated, and I became weak in my mother tongue, Telugu, but, not surprisingly, more adept at English. The latter fact, and the regaining of my academic standing by my senior year, was to propel me as a valedictorian in the final candlelight service at Wesley Church for graduating seniors four years later. However, the hostel life taught me things I did not recognize then: sustained survival in an unpleasant environment, discipline, and the ability to organize chores and survive anywhere.

The best memories during hostel days were the times Diwi and I would visit my parents in Panigiri for holidays. The worst day was the day of departing from the village to return to the hostel for another year. When we left for holidays, the pleasant train ride and a bus journey put us back in Panigiri. Trains were full of pilgrims going to

Yadagiri Gutta, the holy temple on top of a rock mountain. Shaved heads, brass mugs containing holy water, and a wooden bowl for food given by devotees would identify the pilgrims. Peddlers yelling "drinking water!" and children shrieking, young boys running around the railway station, noisy yells from youth selling *yapa pulla,* "chai, garam chai" (tea, hot tea), coffee, J. B. Mangaram biscuits, bananas, salted guava fruit, boiled sweet potatoes, and freshly squeezed lime juice made up the scene at the train station—much like a microcosm of India with all of its ethnicities, faiths, languages, and attire. One could effortlessly spot continuing British traditions—first-class passengers cordoned off from third-class ones, with separate waiting rooms, wells, and taps for drinking water. The conductor would wave the green flag and blow the whistle, and on went the train until it stopped at the next station with a similar setting. It was a thing to watch, a thing of beauty, for people always fascinated me with their diversity. Diversity was a way of life. The train journey was exceptionally excit-ing because those residents of the Wesley Girls Hostel heading to the Panigiri area would also return home for holidays on the same train. Strong emotions and my complete inability to approach and talk to them baffled me; I would remain the same way even after seven years of living in the United States. Inculcation of Christian ethics, the sense of abandonment by my parents, and the boarding-school experience, combined with my shyness, stymied my outlook on sex and women in general. Throughout, I was reminded by my family, friends, and relatives that father and mother put us in boarding school so that we could receive a good and proper English-medium education.

I was eventually expelled from the hostel during the final-exams week of my final year because I went to a movie; it was considered sinful. It was a disgraceful departure, but breaking the rules was my way of rejecting that phase of my life before it claimed a legitimate place in my life. I had grown tired of that life when I was expelled. My rebellion touched several relatives and caused them unnecessary strife, especially the hostel superintendent's family. But I had had enough of that life and had no desire to make amends afterward. Paradoxically, without the Wesley Hostel experience I would not be where I am today.

The myriad rules and rigid lifestyle that the church and hostel imposed had made me cynical. The church itself had become devoid of any spirituality. Indian Christians in the church formed committees mostly to defame the clergy and create trouble for loyal members. My brothers found themselves fighting for the lives of my parents. *Goondas,* the neighborhood thugs, would gang up on my father outside the church compound and in meetings; we quickly became our parents' defenders and protectors. Diwi was jailed once by the police as a protection from these *goondas.* I hated the violence that became a norm in church life. All the more I found myself questioning Christianity and my family's conversion. We were forcing ourselves to live up to the demands of Christian beliefs and my parents' position in the church. All the good they were doing in their service to the poor, to the lepers, to the homeless and shelterless didn't mean a thing. My mother had suffered a stroke in the middle of a hostile meeting of the pastorate committee that saw a verbal assault on my father's mission work by his own church members. The local Arya Samaj radicals, who wanted the return of Hindu fundamentalism to the region, posed another threat to my father's life, for he was accosted several times by these groups on his way to church, ridiculed, and manhandled for wearing his habitual cassock. In that context, I began to witness the strengths of my siblings: strength and the first-born's sense of responsibility personified Diwi, while Prem grew up in the likeness of my father, tolerant with not an evil bone in his body. Willie was all passion and zeal, fun-loving with a flair for drama; my sister Dorothy was strong like my Aunty Barbara. Reaction to the modern church work in India that focused on the emancipation of women, eradication of poverty, and construction of hospitals and schools was indeed becoming volatile and hostile. The demons lurked within; Christians were becoming their own worst enemy. Egos, self-interest, and the material rewards of belonging to a church were taking precedence over the calling to serve humanity. The language of religion, indeed, emerged with a forked tongue and a twisted logic. My father was witnessing a postcolonial onslaught of a different sort, and it was a far cry from the chorus that called for independence from the British. This was self-destruction. I began to negotiate with any God that listened.

The next few years for me were ones of aimless drifting. I was given a seat in the B.Sc. program with majors in biology, zoology, and chemistry at the Secunderabad Arts and Science College, affiliated with Osmania University. The college was virtually next door to the

Wesley Hostel, but I felt no connection to my past there. I went by the hostel every day on the way to the college, and I never once wished I was there again. By this time, my aunt had bought a house in a government scheme for middle-income earners and had moved Ammamma there. Aunty was, by then, the principal of the College of Nursing of Osmania University. When I was thrown out of the hostel, the only place for me to go was back to where my Ammamma was living. I lived there throughout my college years and during my working days at the *Indian Herald* until the day came for me to leave India for the States. I was a low-key and introverted student during the days of my first college degree in Secunderabad. After I had completed the degree, I knew I could not continue in sciences and ignore my leanings toward journalism. The latter remained my private yearning, although most Indian children are raised with the hope they would become doctors or engineers. Failure to do so would be a family tragedy. In college, too, the Christian boys hung out together. They were good in sports and in music. The natural leaning toward music, I always reasoned, was due to the early exposure to music and musical instruments in the church. They were gifted in voice, too. But my best friend in college was a Brahmin boy named Shekar Subramaniam. He was a day scholar—not a hosteller—in Wesley High School, and we continued a fond relationship through college. Years later I was to find out he had no mother, a mute sister, and younger siblings to take care of. He was the primary caretaker of the family, cooked for them, got them ready for school, and came to college. He was better in sciences than I was. Watching him later, I wondered if my life was any less fortunate compared to his. We never talked about life and feelings; it was simply not done in the culture where I grew up. I remember my first migraine headache, and it scared the wits out of me for years to come. I remember the devastatingly painful headache preceded by a blinding cloud in my vision and then a wave of nausea. They didn't come often; but when they did, I was incapacitated for the day. I thought for several years that I was about to go blind forever. It was frightening. Yet I could not share my pain with anyone. To cry and to admit pain were unmanly, and my ego and a sense of shame would not permit it. Ammamma would bring tea and medicine to ease my condition while I lay in bed. I didn't know then that my fear of abandonment during my formative years made it hard to forgive those closest to me in the family. I was rejecting her nurturing because, I figured, it was too late to receive it. The damage was done.

During the second year in college, my own sense of rebellion was awakened in the political flames that engulfed the region. It was called the Telangana Agitation of 1969. The Telugu-speaking people of the state of Andhra Pradesh in south India lived in three major regions: Telangana, Andhra, and Rayalaseema. The capital city of Hyderabad was located in the Telangana region, which produced coal and anchored the heavy industry. Andhra was the bread basket of the state because it was the rice-producing delta—fertile and rich in yield. Rayalaseema was God's own house of desolation, and it was hard to imagine why people actually lived in this barren area. In 1966, when Indira Gandhi was the prime minister of India, the historical animosities between Telangana and Andhra exploded on the social scene. The former, under the leadership of indignant but selfish leaders, began a movement for separate statehood for Telangana distinct from Andhra and Rayalaseema. The dominant view advanced the notion that Telangana was a victim of Andhra's assertiveness both politically and economically; its citizens held the best jobs in government and industry and occupied positions of intellectual and artistic prominence. They spoke a purer form of Telugu—but we mocked their accent. Telangana had the linguistic influence of the regionally unique Nizami Urdu that combined Telugu with Urdu and Hindi, the language of the north. Telugu itself was a thousand years old and considered the romantic language of India with an illustrious poetry and prose. It eventually accepted the incorporation of Sanskrit, the mother of most Indian languages, while languages like Tamil to the south rejected such a fusion as a corrupting congruence. The migration of the people of Andhra to Telangana's city of Hyderabad provided the spark that eventually lit the fire. Students, under the influence of the leaders, spearheaded the movement to secure jobs and other equal rights. Secunderabad College became the "khathar-nak college"—dangerous—with political activism, hooliganism, and personal rebellion. I seized the movement as a natural outlet for my anger and frustration at the loss of my childhood.

I joined the movement along with friends, participating in the sit-ins, hunger strikes, street demonstrations, and confronting of the police. We were teargassed and shot at. On a fine morning in March 1969 my journalistic impulse was stirred for the first time when I saw several students die in a hail of gunfire by the police in front of the Legislative Assembly. I must have counted ten lifeless bodies, with injured and panic-striken protesters on the streets extending all the way to Nampally Road and Hyderabad Railway Station. The movement's turbulence was mirroring and playing itself out in my own life; I became extremely sensitive to political disparities and economic injustices that confronted common people. During the long hours of curfew my friends and I would gather at one of our homes to talk politics until daybreak, for there was nothing to do the following day. After a boisterous night on the streets while dodging the police I was arrested and taken to a makeshift jail in my neighborhood for a day. Before I was charged with violation of curfew and stoning a police van, I, along with several hundred students, escaped by climbing the wall behind the area policed by the CRP, the Central Reserve Police. Some weren't as lucky; they were beaten in custody and later hospitalized.

Soon I was to realize that we, the students, were simple puppets manipulated by self-serving politicians who held out until rich dividends came their way. Indira Gandhi managed to do that effectively. All colleges and schools were closed for more than a year, and having lost a year, I graduated late; such was the fate of all students. The agitation shaped my journalistic instincts, a sense of social justice, and my conscious resistance to dominance in any form. I guess I have my maternal grandfather in me, for he, too, resisted control. Busy with church work as usual, my parents were not aware of my participation in the revolt; I did not know how they would have reacted if they had known. They never found out. Ammamma was kept in the dark, too. She was getting weaker and slower. With countless lives lost and hundreds of careers ruined, the Telangana agitation failed to achieve its goal of a separate statehood; political leaders who instigated the students to agitate were appeased with the secret deals that were sealed in India's capital city, New Delhi. Almost two years later students went back to the colleges and universities having achieved nothing.

After graduation, I was lucky to get admission into Osmania University's prestigious Bachelor of Journalism program. The B.J. program required passing a demanding entrance examination that involved knowledge of current affairs, general knowledge, and the ability to write under a deadline. That morning on the forty-minute bus ride to the campus to appear for the exam, I read the morning newspaper. I was surprised to see several hundred prospects packing the examination hall; they all had bachelor's degrees that qualified them to appear for the exam. Some had master's degrees in English literature, business administration, economics, history, and so forth. With my persistent inferiority complex, I was intimidated by the sight and size of the crowd. Could I compete with these fellows? Three days later the results came out in the *Deccan Chronicle*. I was among the twenty selected that year. The exam was composed almost exclusively of that day's news events, which a majority of those who took the exam did not expect. Of course, I had to write a news story based on a hypothetical event under a tight deadline. I guess I did all right. I entered the program, and Dad, although proud of my accomplishment, did not know what was in store for me. Neither did I. All he knew was that the entrance exam was notoriously tough and the program was one of the best in Asia.

In early morning I would go into the grand Arts College building on Osmania campus, which the nizam had built in a distinctly Islamic architectural style, and come out only after dark. For several months I did not see the sun; it was my escape from the world. It was there that I developed for the first time a real awareness of women, for there were ten of them in the B.J. program, all from good families and with a good education. Initially shy, I became a favorite among them with my humor and singing talent, and I developed a slight confidence in myself in my interactions with them. The all-India educational journey we took by train as a group was one of the most memorable events. Sleepless nights continued on the trip. It was my first visit to New Delhi and to the country's economic center, Bombay. My mentor was Basheeruddin, a brilliant media studies academician, a social critic, and a Muslim with a degree from Minnesota who had converted to the Hindu sectarian faith of Sai Baba. When we returned to Hyderabad, I knew it would soon be time to graduate and lose touch with the B.J. girls, for we knew they would be married soon, most of them by arranged alliances within their caste. It was saddening to disband as a close-knit group because I had developed strong feelings toward women in general by that time. But my preacher's kid background precluded the possibility of a premarital relationship.

Several days before I graduated with my second bachelor's degree, I walked into the publisher's office of the *Indian Herald* without prior appointment and secured a job in the newsroom as a subeditor. My confidence and calm exterior more than professional acumen had a great deal to do with my landing my first job. It paid two hundred rupees a month, a meager but reasonable salary for a first-time journalist. The newspaper was published in English under another brilliant Muslim editor named Mohammed Vazeeruddin. If I had learned the rudiments of the press under the tutelage of Basheeruddin of Osmania University, I learned the finer points of journalistic integrity from Vazeeruddin, a former *Times* of India veteran with a ruthless and unforgiving demeanor in the newsroom. One learned quickly never to make mistakes in copy sent to him for approval for the next day's paper. If one did something brilliant and imaginative with headlines or a rewrite, he would never look up from his desk to acknowledge it. But one knew he was pleased. I worked nights and early-morning shifts. When I received my salary, the first thing I did was to buy Ammamma's favorite snacks in Ameerpet on my way home; then I gave the rest to the church. To make Ammamma happy was to make myself happy. I was to spend almost three years in the newsroom of the *Herald*. By this time, I was more fluent in English than in my own language. I guess it was at Wesley School that I began losing fluency in Telugu, and I was too ashamed to admit it to anyone, for it was my mother tongue. By late 1973 I was ready to make a move, but I didn't know what it would be.

Aunty Barbara had left Hyderabad for the States for the second time in 1967 and had completed her doctorate in nursing education at Emporia State Teachers College in Kansas. At the time of her departure to the United States, she was the principal of the College of Nursing in Hyderabad. She was frustrated with the politics of education in India— a typical mayhem of corruption in the state secretariat, ineptitude in the state departments of education, coercion by elected leaders to admit their own candidates, and power struggles in the college itself. Having been educated in Australia and the United States, she was frustrated with the quality of nursing education and nursing practice. Although India exported many nurses trained by the state who had exceptionally sharp skills in medical care of patients, she was convinced that the entire enterprise of nursing academia was on a downward spiral. She had seen academia in America with its trappings of power and ineptitude, but the problems there were nothing compared to those in India. So she decided not to go back home and rejoin the college in Hyderabad. Instead, she accepted a position as a professor of medical-surgical nursing at the University of Akron. Diwi had been to the States for his postgraduate education in Emporia, earning a master's in genetics and biology. He returned to India and briefly worked as a lecturer in a private science college in Hyderabad. It was now my turn to come to the States, my aunt informed me, if I wished. She offered to pay for my master's degree and sent me the air ticket.

Leaving India was painful because I imagined nothing would be the same when I returned. I would miss the Hindi film songs, the music, friends, family, and, above all, Ammamma. She was weak and old, but I was denying she would ever die. On a cold December morning I said good-bye to her and boarded the train to Bombay along with Diwi and a friend who came to see me catch the Air India flight to Cleveland. I did not think it was necessary to be sentimental when the time came to depart, but my mother began crying, and my father, with tears in his eyes, was telling me to be careful and hardworking in America. There were rose garlands from friends and jasmine bouquets from relatives and lots of tears at the farewell event at the train station. I did not know when I would return to India and whether Ammamma would be alive then. I just did not want to contemplate her fragile mortality. Then I boarded the train to Bombay (now called by its precolonial name, Mumbai). After reaching the destination fourteen hours later, we were told that Air India employees had gone on strike. Stranded in Bombay for two days without a soul to seek refuge with, we spent nights sleeping on the platform of the Victoria Train Station. Not being native to the city, we avoided Bombay, with its fast-moving vehicles, hustle-bustle of commerce, and people, millions of them, at every street corner. Confidence-tricksters, vendors, kids with all sorts of propositions, and children insisting on polishing shoes, even if one did not wish it, helped the city live up to its abrasive reputation. The city was a film capital of the world that dwarfed Hollywood. It was a spectacle of joy and a bundle of confusion that brought me into contact with people of the richest diversity only India can offer economically, culturally, and linguistically. Sleeping alongside hundreds of people on the platform waiting for the next train, I realized one had to be an Indian to appreciate it—Oriental existentialism at its best. I tried sleeping, but the noise was too much. By four in the morning the sweeping staff had already begun cleaning and sprinkling water on the hot platform to cool it. Thankfully, it was time to rise; I felt tired but happy with daybreak. Insomnia had long ago become part of me, but anxiety was draining my energy. I was sick to my stomach with the thought of leaving India. I wasn't ready, and I wondered if I would live another year because the fear of death was consuming me nightly. Missing the Air India connection through no fault of mine should have made me frustrated. But it didn't. It wasn't time for me to leave India, I figured. I would go back to Hyderabad on the pretext of the airline strike and see Ammamma again; one more time I wanted to hear her voice and see her sweet smile.

"You never used to judge people like this at home."
"India isn't home . . ." (34)

Diwi made the decision that we should return to Hyderabad and wait until the airline strike was over. It was barely dawn when I arrived back at our Hyderabad residence; I went straight to the outside window next to Ammamma's bed and called her. She was stunned and could not believe her ears, for she thought I was already in the States by this time. Before the shock had sunk in, I quickly explained through the curtained window the reason for my return. She had the biggest smile on her face and was indeed happy with my predicament. Two weeks later, however, I had to leave her—this time for almost five years. I was like a child being drawn away from the breasts of a mother. I was also guilt-ridden and strangely confused because I didn't feel the same about leaving my parents behind.

I flew TWA this time and went through Tel Aviv. My paranoia was intense; I imagined the plane would be shot at when landing for the stopover in the Middle East. Wartime security measures were new to me. The security guards at the airport must have sensed my ambivalence, for they quickly whisked me into a curtained area and asked me to strip. I didn't know what it meant. Added to my anxiety was an intense fear that I would be mistaken as a terrorist. I must have looked like a completely helpless victim. After a preliminary search, the guards apologized and ushered me into the lounge filled with travelers with a coupon for breakfast as compensation. It was my first encounter with unpredictable danger, for back in Hyderabad everything was predictable—and relatively safe. Having a passport stamped "journalist" also prompted a thorough questioning at the passport control office; everything appeared to be menacing.

"Assume every Indian is an angel." (181)

I arrived in Cleveland with eight dollars in my billfold and with a friend named Reddy who was on his way to the University of Oklahoma. Aunty picked us up at the airport on a late December morning. We stepped out of the airport and into the parking lot. I never knew cold to be so severe; it was actually deceptive because the sun was shining. Sunshine in India meant intense heat. Reddy was walking ahead of me, and the ground we walked on seemed clear. All of a sudden I saw Reddy fly into the air and land on his buttocks. Aunty and I burst into laughter, and I quickly found myself also flying through the air and falling smack on my bottom. We never knew what happened, never imagining ice to be on the ground. Ice was completely alien to our imagination. We had seen snow in the movies, but ice, definitely not! It was the most hilariously stunning introduction to the American Midwest winter weather. Later in the week I saw real snow for the first time. It looked beautiful until I stepped into it. Akron U. was largely a commuter school, but I didn't know the difference between universities. It looked like an American campus with plenty of resources. Rubber, they said, built the city, and the university carried that working-class character. There were familiar names like Firestone and Goodyear all around. I lived in Aunty's high-rise apartment near the campus, but it made me nervous to look outside the window, for I could see only gloomy days. When it snowed and the winds blew I wondered why human beings chose to live like this. It was sheer misery walking to the campus three blocks away. When I asked one of my aunt's American friends why people chose to live there and why, having sent men to the moon, they couldn't invent completely weatherproof clothing, she promptly bought me a thick winter coat. I felt embarrassed to wear it because it looked unseemly, tasteless, and too practical.

I lived with Aunty until July 1974. During this time I had befriended a Malayalam-speaking Indian couple living in Akron who knew my aunt. They were Christians and volunteered to take me to church on Sundays. I didn't know the difference between the Anglican Church I grew up in in India and a charismatic one. They attended a nondenominational charismatic church next door to the apartment complex where Aunty lived. The preacher there was like none I had seen; he wore smashingly fitted tailor-made suits instead of a cassock; he was tall and handsome and had a powerful voice. He played football for Ohio State, they told me. I imagined soccer. There was no pulpit; he seemed to be walking around on a large stage as he preached. He used an overhead projector, and the lights dimmed and shone with precision as if by divine providence while he wrote the highlights of the sermon on a transparency. It was the first time I heard of Rapture; the concept was new and entirely puzzling. He showed films that depicted the bliss of the Rapture; people, I was informed, vanished without warning when the Judgment Day came. If I believed in Rapture, I wouldn't be caught unaware. If I was prepared for it, I was going to heaven. If I wasn't, I was destined to lurk in the dark corridors of hell forever. Strangely, with all my exposure to Christian faith, I was never taught about this thing called Rapture. The church had a resounding choir with scores of musical instruments. Everyone was immaculately dressed and exhibited great enthusiasm. Impressed and intimidated by it all, I found myself walking to the front as the preacher issued the call for repentance and accepting the Lord as my personal savior. Fear, not a new revelation of my faith, made me join the ritual. Behind the stage, one of the preacher's assistants asked me if I had completely rejected my previous faiths (assuming I was a Hindu from India) and welcomed me with an embrace into the fold. He was glad, he said, that I had finally seen the light. Secretly, I must have been on the journey that had begun inside me to forgive my parents and to make amends with my past. I didn't know it was going to be a long process that would continue another decade. It was intensely scary, and anxiety was becoming a way of life. The Health Center on campus gave me some medication called Barbitol. It made me sleepy and nervous, so I avoided it. In spite of anxiety, I made it through the first semester with straight A's. Aunty was proud. I was a good return on her investment.

I didn't think American schools were particularly challenging. I went to classes from 8 A.M. to 2 P.M. and worked as a dishwasher in the cafeteria until late into the nights. I and several Chinese foreign students hardly talked while we ran this incredible dishwashing machine. We simply had to feed the dirty dishes in one end, and the students on the other end would take clean dishes off the belt and stack them up in specially designed carts. American efficiency, I thought. Pots and pans, on the other hand, were entirely another matter. I never knew what a busboy was; but I soon became one, a promotion, they said, and I would clean up during and after formal evening banquets. I saw some of most elegant, affluent, and well-dressed African American people at the banquets they attended. The banquets were exclusively black or exclusively white. I wondered why. But it never did occur to me that I was far away from the job I was professionally trained to do. I gained a valuable insight into American society then—watching students in their own similar groups, in cafeteria seating segregated by choice, and wealthy people at banquets. None of them showed any visible awareness of poverty around them. Class differences here were based on economics, not caste; on race, not creed. Busboys were invisible to them; no one even gave them a glance. Even the African Americans who attended these lavish banquets, with their history of oppression, acted as if they were above the rest. The amount of food people wasted in the cafeteria was enormous, and it was sinful in my mind to dump it into the wastebin. It was painful to see such lack of awareness that people around the world could have nothing of what these people left behind on their plates uneaten.

Later that summer I left Akron in a Greyhound bus for the flatlands of Oklahoma, where the winter winds, I learned painfully, could cut through your bones. The journey from Ohio across the Midwest to Oklahoma itself was revealing. I saw the America I watched in the movies back home and the America I wanted to see: beautiful rolling hills, green pastures, huge trees, and plenty of water. It could hold and feed the entire world's population, I thought. However, it occurred to me that whenever I saw a majestic crest of a hill there was a tall steel tower eavesdropping on satellites—apparently a military installation of some sort. It was a striking contrast between the Indian culture and the American landscape: Indians would build a Hindu temple on the highest spot, while Americans built military telecommunications installations. Stopping at bus terminals, however, was not too comfortable. The darker side of America came out at night for business, it seemed. All the bus terminals appeared to be located in the most undesirable settings. In St. Louis, I was confronted by two who hardly qualified as gentlemen in the men's room, attempting to sell small plastic packets of what appeared to be white powder. I had to make a hasty exit. Another gentleman came, sat next to me, and asked if I wanted a woman for the night. It would cost me a little more if I needed a motel room, he said. All of this was greatly confusing and provided enigmatic contradictions to my intellectual understanding of America. I did not come to America to pursue a dream; I wasn't even sure I was going to stay. Education was my only goal. My sights were set on the graduate degree the Oklahoma school of journalism offered.

I soon secured a part-time job in a gas station on Lindsey Street in Norman to support myself through school. Aunty was there to send me money if and when I needed it, but I didn't want to burden her. My first encounter with bigotry took place when a car slowed down near me as I walked to the campus and I heard the driver shout, "Camel jock, go home!" I was perplexed, and when I heard it several times afterward I realized they were assuming I was of Middle Eastern origin. The oil embargo of the 1970s evidently fueled more than an economic crisis in Norman; it awakened in some a toxic disdain for all people who looked different. I would attract different sorts of stares, only some pleasant, whenever I went shopping for groceries or to the shopping mall.

The most revealing aspect of American life came my way mainly because I was in Oklahoma: the ritual of American football. Never did I imagine the fervor or the passion people possessed over the game. When I first saw the enormously large stadium with the accompanying display of titles the school had won, I thought it was for soccer. I did not encounter the football season until early fall. One Saturday, while I was pumping gas, I saw carloads of people wearing red clothes, all of them shouting and yelling. I couldn't understand their accent. It was English, that much I knew. But I failed to make sense of what they were shouting. A small transistor radio in the gas station booth informed us, the attendants, how the game was going. I heard the terms "first down," "second down," and "yards to go." "Quarterback snap," "running back," and "defensive end" meant completely different things to me, and all the time I was trying to imagine a soccer game being played. Then I actually went to a game. An unbelievable sight unfolded before my eyes. In a sea of red—Big Red—swarming throngs of people of all ages made their way to their seats. They held large cups of Coke and hot dogs and boxes of popcorn. People were cooking on grills beside their pickups, vans, and cars outside the stadium. Children seemed excited, and women seemed to share the passion of the day. I was in for a big surprise when I walked into the area marked "end zone"—the goal in the soccer field, I told myself. I didn't know why the soccer players dressed the way they did or hopped and jumped on the sideline. The goalposts were strangely shaped. Helmets and pads were out of place. The ball looked like someone had run over it with an automobile. I knew it wasn't soccer when the players charged onto the field with all that combat gear. For the rest of the game I couldn't see the ball; the players simply ran over each other, abusing their bodies and inflicting great and audible pain on each other. The roar of the stadium was deafening, and people were screaming as if for blood. When the game was over I was in a daze; what transpired in front of me that day gave me an entirely different view of the American people. It was hard to believe what I saw was actually a sporting event; it was mind-shattering and alarming to witness something that came close to Hollywood's depiction of a Roman gladiator sport. My idea of America was never to be the same.

On the brighter side, the two years I spent at Oklahoma taught me to live independently. Diwi and his bride, Latha, arrived the following year on immigrant visas—Diwi as a doctoral student and Latha as a registered nurse. We lived in the graduate housing complex on campus. As I was about to complete my thesis defense, my graduate adviser, Jerry Grotta, called me in and asked if I would like to continue studies at a doctoral level. I was touched that he actually thought I was capable of undertaking another level of study. He always remained "Dr. Grotta" to me, although many students called him Jerry. I had a difficult time bringing myself to address my professors by first name.

It would be disrespectful. He recommended me to the University of Iowa for doctoral admission.

I was accepted in the fall of 1976 and arrived in Iowa City with my small savings from the gas station job and with a promise of a teaching assistantship. There I met Professor Kenneth Starck, the director of the journalism school, and my adviser, Professor Hanno Hardt, a Marxist scholar who had emigrated from Germany. They would have a great impact on my life and on my intellectual growth. Retrospectively, there I think I resisted the Western paradigms of inquiry. Although Iowa was known for critical studies and for bringing alternative ideologies to bear on contemporary media and sociological inquiries, I found these ways not critical enough. My postcolonial experience found Iowa intellectually refreshing, yet too linear and too binary in its methodologies. Linking them to the way the Western mind perceived reality, I found myself resisting, much like an Indian under colonial rule, the very instruments of research in critical inquiry. The choice offered was either a Marxist approach or the prevailing empiricist paradigm—nothing in between or beyond. The academic enterprise was bare and naked in its exclusion of Eastern thought. Philosophy was taught as if the West invented it; critical perspectives were entirely European in orientation. Attempts to inject non-Western thought patterns were readily accepted and acknowledged, but quickly brushed aside as a temporary, albeit necessary, inconvenience on the way to real learning. I learned to give what the institution wanted from me, although Starck and Hardt encouraged me to articulate my own perspectives on topics relating to cultural studies and international discourse. Yet, on a different level, what the American academy considered radical and progressive was still British and Western in origin and context. There was little room for inclusivity even in some of the progressive schools; scholarship was oblivious to other ways of human thinking. Many American scholars in media studies claimed expertise of other cultures and routinely passed as bona fide scholars. The Iowa faculty had a history of international study in indigenous settings, but that was rare overall. Not many scholars knew the histories, languages, or cultures of the countries they studied. If they did, they had usually accepted the Western narratives of colonial histories that acknowledged the brutalities of oppression abroad but somehow earnestly believed something good came out of it all. Comparative studies, in particular, compared

Western realities to other cultures based on the same narratives of the West that reeked of Orientalism. Media constructions of the so-called Third World were accepted with little criticism. Gender studies, as an area of inquiry, had built around itself an impenetrable aura of Western superiority that portrayed Hinduism and Islam, much like all other non-Western realities, as inferior, inhumane, and oppressive. To question their validity was to invite the stereotypical perceptions of the East. The non-Westerner was inherently sexist; both males and females just did not seem to be self-aware of their sexism. Comprehension of the Other in the classrooms of the American academy was virtually nonexistent. In the field of international media studies and intercultural discourse, I seemed to represent the Other, a good soldier, a foot soldier bearing the cross of the Third World upon my shoulders. When the time came to defend my dissertation dealing with Third World nationalism and international media discourses, one of my dissertation committee members informed me the night before the oral defense that he would not sign off on my work—although he had seen every page of the draft for months prior to the day and approved them. Only Hardt, himself a German émigré scholar with Germanic tutelage on the pattern of premier Indologist Max Müller, and Starck, a genuine thoroughbred with holistic leanings, would save the day as cochairs of my dissertation.

Yet Iowa was a different experience from Oklahoma and Ohio. Being a radical town shaped somewhat by the 1960s hippie and protest movements, Iowa City carried an aura of great intellect and challenge. It had a well-known international writers' workshop and world-renowned science programs. Courses in Marxist thought ran side by side with the capitalistic offerings of the business school. The town's setting was much more beautiful with the Iowa River flowing right through the campus. I was not fully an introspective person, although I was doing well in classes. My friends were mostly Indian graduate students in engineering and some from social sciences, although the latter were badly outnumbered. I lived in a one-room shack on Burlington Street with no kitchen and a shared bathroom. I carried a grocery sack of Indian spices in my beat-up Volkswagen Beetle and would go to anyone's kitchen that was offered to me for cooking. I had become a good cook after my sister-in-law trained me in Oklahoma. I was the one-man traveling Indian kitchen in a

Volkswagen in Iowa City; now there was an oddity if there ever was one. Students from the Commonwealth nations like me would play cricket in front of the Student Union on Sundays during the summer.

In 1978 I undertook a trip around the world to gather data for my dissertation and visited my folks in Hyderabad on my way. India didn't look the same after five years. Privately, I found myself comparing everything I saw to the United States, and India didn't seem to stack up. I saw my dad and mummy at the airport, and while the whole family and my friends received me with the customary garlands, I looked for Ammamma. She had stayed home, unable to make the trip to the airport. When I saw her at home, I held her tightly and wept.

I returned to Iowa City and finished the dissertation and left for Dallas–Fort Worth after being offered an assistant professorship at Texas Christian University. I had had a strange premonition when I left Ammamma that it would be the last time I would see her alive. It was. By 1982 she was gone. Years later, I would return to see her grave and lay garlands on it. Both Fort Worth and Texas Christian University posed problems for me before and after my arrival. I imagined the Texas city that lay in a southwestern prairie beside Dallas to be provincial, narrow-minded, and full of gun-toting cowboys who worshiped John Wayne. TCU, I figured, would be a one-year stint because I was not inclined to be associated with a school with a Christian fundamentalist character. Soon I discovered I was wrong on both counts. But students on campus at the time were not exposed to other cultures, and if they were, seemed unappreciative and closed-minded. My presence on campus was unique, as there were no visible signs of the existence of other faculty of color. Students secretly ridiculed my appearance, and most faculty across the campus simply ignored my presence. If a woman passed me by on the campus she would clutch her purse tightly; some women would lock their car doors if I happened to walk by them. The fact that I wore a suit and a tie did not seem to matter; only my skin color mattered. On an amusing note, at the faculty luncheon that opened the fall semester colleagues at my round table introduced themselves to each other; assuming they were mentioning where they had moved from after graduate school, I said I was from Iowa. Everyone laughed until I clarified I was originally from India. My department faculty and students were cordial and welcoming, although not without exception. One of the journalism students found it hard to accept me as her teacher. She complained to the department chair that I was ignorant of the field of journalism and categorically stated that I had no business teaching in an American university. The chair secretly confided in me that the student might have been guilty of "innocent racism." I didn't know what that meant. A year later, however, I found myself in comfortable relationships with other faculty members, especially one from the religion studies department who specialized in Hinduism and Buddhism.

My occasional lunch discussions and sometimes heated debates with Professor Andy Fort, a Sanskritist, continue even now; they were to serve me as a mirror for growth, self-awareness, and the difficulties in judging Orientalism among American scholars. He was an exception, I struggled to rationalize. Unwittingly, he became the center of my intellectual and emotional encounter with the West on my journey to understand myself in terms of my postcolonial identity. In a secret way, I had become an Indian nationalist claiming exclusive domain over scholarship dealing with indigenous cultures, and yet I was becoming an American with a degree of psychological awareness atypical of Indians. One could not study other cultural realities and traditions and thought with any semblance of fairness having seen the parochial training of the mind in American schools. But I relaxed my absolutism over such matters. I realized it can be an infinite virtue if one experiences sustained oppression—any sort of oppression—because, strangely, the oppressed seemed to understand the oppressor, and for the reverse to occur was close to impossible.

My encounters with the West happened again when I taught for TCU at several colleges of Oxford University during summer terms; I remember the emotional reaction I had watching faculty colleagues and students going through Oxford's famous Bodleian Library. In a way, I encountered the ghosts of imperialism for the first time there— the ghosts of the scholars who wrote the authoritative history of India and aided the colonial conquest and gave Great Britain the moral imperative for a justifiable oppression for centuries. One summer, the Bodleian librarian gave a lecture on the library's manuscripts using a slide projector. While students listened and watched in awe the presenter slipped in a slide at the end of his lecture that showed an old painting from India depicting a *saadhu,* a sage, sitting under a tree and an elephant with wings flying over the tree. The students burst out laughing when he remarked that while Oxford was amassing these priceless manuscripts over a period of a thousand years, other cultures were erecting native thought that was devoid of scientific logic and reason. American students found it amusing. The point was effectively made for the irrationality of older cultures without a native rebuttal, for no one in the room except me could even perceive that the librarian's juxtaposition of Oxford and India was intellectually dishonest and exhibited the old and not-so-subtle disdain for things non-Western. Proclaiming the virtues of Western thought was one thing; but to resort to it at the cost of mockery and suppression of native expression was typical of British, European, and American academia, albeit with some exceptions. Repressed memories exploded within and outward into painful exchanges of ideas and debates with my colleagues, yet only one or two actually understood my catharsis while I was at Oxford. I have made good friends from Oxford's faculty—after the transformation from personal anger and intellectual resentment to measured forgiveness and guarded acceptance. I discovered that most of what was taught in American academia in communication theory and humanities—the whole dominant ideology itself—was dogmatic and unrelenting in its exclusivity. Any alternative view would quickly be branded as political correctness and cultural relativism, and any attempt at deconstructing what was taught was viewed as radical, reeking with sinister motives. I was appalled at the unwillingness of many faculty in liberal arts around the country to engage in intellectual debates. Most of them seemed to cling to views and rarely imbibed new ideas. My field, in particular, lagged behind other fields like literary studies and religion studies that I considered progressive, more humanistic, and more self-confident in engaging other points of view. To me, deconstruction was an exercise in intellectual honesty— a commodity that was in short supply all around. In a deeply personal way, Andy Fort of TCU and Professor Michael Nicholson of University College, Oxford, both oblivious to the impact they had on me, became partial, but important, catalysts for my secret healing and coming to terms with my identity. The whole cathartic process took about a decade.

My first marriage took place with an American, a daughter and stepdaughter of two faculty members at TCU. She and her family were members of the Trinity Episcopal Church near the campus, and Father Stanley, the rector, was the personification of my dad. I met her first at the church through her mother; she was a sophomore social-work major at TCU who took a journalism course with me during a summer term. Responding to her friendly overtures I found myself willing to be led by her, giving in at every corner and yet unable to achieve any level of emotional or spiritual intimacy. Into my thirties now, I continued to struggle. Both of us were emotionally ill prepared for a marital commitment; she had lost her father to alcoholism while she was a teenager. Secretly, in the act of being rescued I was also becoming the rescuer; seen in a macrocosm, the relationship reflected the meeting of the East and the West, the entire colonial experience re-created at home. The birth of my daughter, Laura Sudha, in 1986 was the ultimate watershed moment that ushered in a new level of self-realization. Laura would have a double identity: she would be an Indian and an American. I feared how she would face the future as a product of two cultures. By the time she was three the marriage was beyond repair, and the five-year marriage ended in 1989.

The next six years of my life were celibate and a time of great strides in personal growth. Events, both personal and intellectual, gave me a chance to face my own past and make sense of what was happening to me. It was time to confront the loss of my childhood, time to forgive my parents for preferring the church to me and to make peace with my past. I learned that there were no mistakes in life; they were lessons. And I had plenty of them to learn from. I went to Co-dependents Anonymous meetings and saw counselors, moving from a male pastoral counselor to a woman therapist. These meetings were of some value, but I could not get what I was looking for in these sessions. I found the counselors well trained, but their experiences were exclusively American. I learned of the Inner Child and Bob's Big Book, Higher Power, the Power Greater Than Myself, and the importance of being earnest in admitting one's own fallibility. Gradually, however, I learned to forgive. My personal growth, in turn, led me into further struggles in the domain of postcoloniality, culture, and religion. In the meantime, I was winning teaching awards and was increasingly becoming visible in the local media as a commentator and speaker at national and local meetings of Indian Americans.

On November 5, 1997, in the U.S. District Court for the Northern District of Texas, after almost two decades of living in the States, first as a student and then as a legal Green Card holder, I was sworn in as a citizen of the United States of America. My path to citizenship was uncharacteristic compared to that of the typical Indian diaspora that usually opts for citizenship for economic benefit and practical reasons. For me, like some others of my background, the step was a deeply emotional one. I finally accepted the fact that by becoming an American citizen, I was not necessarily ceasing to be an Indian; I was simply adding another identity, another self. Nevertheless, I had to be ready. When I eventually decided to seek citizenship I knew the time had indeed come. By then my understanding of first-generation Indian immigrants—mostly intelligentsia and physicians, engineers, computer scientists—was deeply personal and gave me a sense of authority in my lectures and speeches. My speeches relied on self-disclosure. I would go as an invited speaker to the conferences held across the country by the Telugu Association of North America (TANA), by the American Association of Physicians from India (AAPI), and by the Network of Indian Professionals. Affluence, conflicting identities, and fear for their children's future in America were apparent among thousands who attended these conferences. Each person was at a different stage of accepting multiple selves. Depending on age, some would be at the stage of pursuing the American Dream—a dream of economic and entrepreneurial success or professional contentment. Some were at the stage of questioning, some of accepting, their condition. In the lobbies of the hotels in Chicago, Dallas, or Detroit, where some of the conferences of TANA and AAPI were held, one could see enormous tables filled with Indian food prepared by the hotel contractors, makeshift jewelry shops in the lobby, astrology and palm-reading booths, and a "Marriage Bureau" stall that reflected the ambivalent hope of the first-generation Indian immigrants of finding a bride or a groom for an arranged marriage for their offspring. The real challenge I saw was in the dilemmas being faced by the second-generation Indian Americans, children born of the immigrants in the United States or brought to the country early in their lives. They were to be christened as Americans. Although the lure of their native culture would now become merely a cerebral one, it acted as an emotional thorn in the side. The young adults I met who shared my physical identity seemed to be in the benign process of re-creating their cultural identity, accommodating their American self with their Indian self.

I, in the meantime, had a difficult time owning up to the fact that most of the Indian diaspora was exactly that because of British imperialism in India: we were living and thriving in the English-speaking world. We were a hopelessly colonial bunch unable to appropriate the native culture wherever we happened to be: Guyana, North America, East Africa, Britain, Europe, and East Asia. We were cultural nomads by choice, the modern-day Romanies in search of ourselves. The journey, painful and anxiety producing for me for a prolonged period of time, was becoming intellectually addictive and even discreetly enjoyable. I gradually accepted the idea that Indians lived in several millennia of recorded civilization with two major disruptions from Arab and British colonialisms, which were mere interruptions in Indian history in the homeland. These interruptions were not dislocations or upheavals to the common Indian folk; they simply extended their multiple selves further, imbibing some and rejecting some of what the conquerors had to offer. The language of Urdu was an Indian creation of the seventeenth century accommodating Persian and Arabic with Hindi. English, in a strange way, became Indian English. To exist in one or both of these languages was a characteristic of the Indian. Some seemed to marvel and rejoice in them just as multiple selves have coexisted in the Indian for many centuries on the subcontinent. The idea of the feminine—the idea of Mother India and mother goddesses—could coexist within the postcolonial Indian diaspora as much as it did before the foreign invasions. Several identities and ethnicities, languages and cultures, regional and national demands, professions and duties, all had to be accommodated within self on a daily basis.

Heavens behold, the final phase of healing came when Mary Sucharitha walked into my life. Mary, strikingly graceful and Dravidian in beauty, had a background similar to mine, having been born and raised in a preacher's family of village origin. When I met her at my niece's birthday party in late December 1992, I felt her physical warmth and was struck by her spirituality. She was then a student from Hyderabad at Dallas Baptist University, and she seemed, without being conscious of it, caring and affectionate wherever she went. Indian Christians were attracted to her singing of Telugu and English hymnals. Soon, she, along with her older sister and friends from DBU, was visiting my house for social events and Indian cooking. My daughter, Laura, was also smitten by Mary's playfulness and attention. I was becoming attracted to Mary as time went by and began entertaining the idea of having a relationship once again in my life with someone like her. Laura, having grown attached to Mary, asked me one day if I would wed Mary sometime in the future. I was amused at the possibility because I was aware of the difficulties such an alliance would pose for her family, for an Indian divorcé would be the least welcome of choices for an Indian family. She was also younger than I by two decades, even though she exhibited signs of maturity beyond her age. And I was a more complete person now emotionally. I felt a spiritual bonding with Mary, a bonding of kindred souls. I felt the pain of being uniquely in love, for pain reminded me that I had finally found the love of my life. I felt so many feelings for the first time that were new to me, and I felt that the heavens had finally smiled upon me. It has been quite a journey for both Mary and me, and the idea of codependent selves took on a different meaning. I felt that Mary became a part of my being and the essence of what I have become: two bodies attached to each other at a spiritual level and two souls that feed on each other—a sort of common spiritual meal that can be consumed every day and night. Sometimes I see myself in her, but most important, I see in her shades of Ammamma, who must have been like Mary when she was growing up in the village. If this was codependency as the West defined it, I felt strangely comfortable in it. The eventual wedding took place in March 1997 at the University Christian Church with an Indo-American ritual, the *mangala suthra* ceremony, and a distinctly Indian reception. Deep in the heart of Texas, the church was full of people attending the wedding—reflecting numerous ethnicities, attires, languages, and customs. Later in the year, Mary stood in the audience when I took the oath of U.S. citizenship; somehow, she seemed more composed at the time and sure of herself, which in turn was reassuring to me. This marriage was the final phase in my healing and made my spiritual self more complete. She reminded me of my inner contradictions living as an Indian in the United States and made me more aware of my daily negotiation with my multiple selves. I am in a safe place, and I find it peaceful; it seems as though I have found bliss with the soul similar to mine.

My father passed away in July 1996. By the time he retired from the church all of his children had gone away to the United States. Yet he was proud of how we all had turned out. His three-month visit to the United States along with my mother in 1995 was an opportunity for me to regain my dad and reclaim my mother. They were conscious of the childhood I experienced due to their preoccupation with the church in India; but they were not remorseful. To feel remorse would be to regret the lives they had lived. I didn't want that; it was within my power to re-create my selves without burdening them with guilt. All of his children were able to attend the funeral in Hyderabad. His death reminded me that I carry my ancestors—him, Ammamma, my grandfathers, and all the elders who are living—deep within me, for I see them in my daily conduct. Ammamma knew intuitively what was in store for me emotionally and intellectually, and I think she knew my siblings would keep the honor and good name of the family in a land different from hers. I wish I could say I came to terms with her passing away, but part of me has yet to accept her absence in my life. I don't think it is a denial; it is simply that I have not accepted the loss. Laura, my daughter, an American girl with innocent charms and multiple selves, a reincarnation of my ancestors, shows signs of self-confidence and comfort with her identities that I never experienced. She will step into the next century as a child of the diaspora, a mother of civilization and its continuity, and the embodiment of an America that is learning, discovering, vulnerable, yet challenging at all levels. Mary and I have eased into the idea of cross-cultural nurturing of Laura, making her aware at each step, in subtle ways, of the idea of ancestral heritage, the value of cultural hybridity, and the quotidian experience of the social tapestry of a land we have chosen to call our own.

Poodur's trajectory of the Babbili family is now firmly implanted in the Dallas–Fort Worth area. All my brothers and my sister, along with their families, have made north Texas their home; it is not accidental that they settled within a few miles of each other, for deep within all of us the sense of belonging to each other prevails above all else. About twenty thousand of the 1.4 million Indians in the United States who speak in a hundred mother tongues live in this area. They come from all the twenty-eight states of India and from the African and Latin American east Indian diaspora. My extended family members live and work and attend schools in Texas; Christians from Telugu-speaking Andhra Pradesh and Hyderabad, in their own way, have once again re-created the imagined communities of their forefathers in the area. All of them successful in their professions, they meet for prayer meetings every month, meetings that bind them together and foster ties with the members of the next generation. Baptisms, engagements, weddings, and cricket matches are occasions for multiple identities to emerge in unpredictable and surprising detours. Some take it in stride, and others offer an ongoing and benign resistance. Deeply self-aware and in the midst of my own Americanization, I have become more Indian than most urban Indians in India, more nationalistic than most of my people. I wonder if I have the revolutionary spirit of my maternal grandfather in me; if I do, then my father's patience and his ability to balance faith with culture, religion with history, a sense of fairness and treating human beings with kindness and compassion, also seem to reside in me. I guess this is our house of Mr. Biswas, our enigma of arrival, as V. S. Naipaul calls it.[2] Ashis Nandy's exposition of India's encounter with the British pointed to the presence of many personal narratives becoming mythographies in the process of what he calls the loss and recovery of self under colonialism.[3] What I have become is the culmination of decisions made by my paternal and maternal grandfathers in the early part of this century—a narrative that emanates from their conversion to Christianity and that resulted in the loss and recovery of my many selves toward the latter part of this century. The next millennium offers a new hope, a new recovery under new colonialisms—both internal and external—as they continue to exist in one form or another. This is my story, one narrative of the postcolonial India; there are one billion other such stories, other such narratives.

Afterword

This essay might as well be subtitled "an autobiography of an un-known Indian." But that has been written earlier—by Nirad C. Chaud-huri—the sagely expatriate Indian, who retired as the chair of English literature at Oxford.[4] So, hesitantly, I chose the not-so-original but

2. Naipaul, *A House for Mr. Biswas* (London: André Deutsch, 1961) and *The Enigma of Arrival* (New York: Alfred A. Knopf, 1987).

3. Nandy, *The Intimate Enemy: Loss and Recovery of Self under Colonialism* (Oxford: Oxford University Press, 1983).

4. Chaudhuri, *The Autobiography of an Unknown Indian* (1951; Berkeley: University of California Press, 1968).

somewhat appropriate subtitle for this essay, "a passage to America." My thesis here is that my road leads me from—and, more important, to—Poodur, the village of my ancestry in south India, the village I feel I never left. Although I am an American citizen now, my memory and identity draw daily inspiration from Poodur. The narrative here, by necessity, remains an incomplete project. I grappled with the difficult task of the discovery and articulation of my own selves, acutely aware of the fact that introspection, at best, is subjective, and romancing the self can be strangely alluring. The temptation to sentimentalize one's own narrative can be strong. I was taught early in my culture that a conscious exploration of one's past is wrought with indecipherable realities and is rarely conducted in any articulate fashion. One must respect the past, be engaged in the present, and have a sense of responsibility for the future—always seeking to harmonize the three aspects of one's life. I must be forgiven, then, for this attempt at articulation, for it is, in an Indian category, profane to bare your soul. Nevertheless, for the task at hand, I have attempted to do so at the risk of being perceived as essentially Western.

Essaying Biography

The Career of Mary Lago

lthough we cannot hope to emulate her own work as
biographer, this volume would be incomplete without
a glance at the person who inspired it. Mary Lago's
career as a distinguished biographer, editor, translator, and
scholar of Victorian and Edwardian literature had unlikely beginnings. Her first role at the University of Missouri–Columbia
was membership in the "Engineering Wives" (as they called
themselves) in the 1950s. Her colleagues little envisioned that
their hostess Mary, pouring tea or setting out cakes for their
periodic gatherings, was one day to hold the most distinguished professorship in that university's English department,
the Catherine Paine Middlebush Chair of English. How did
Mary gravitate from one role to the other, and what does it
tell us about the shape and significance of her career?

After graduating from Bucknell University with a B.A. in
English in 1940, Mary went to work in New York for Friendship Press, an interdenominational publisher that specialized
in graded books for children, usually with an international
theme. The work was not glamorous: Mary was assistant to
the promotion and then editorial director rather than engaging
editorial work directly, an ironically unanticipatory sign of
things to come. She made time amid work for another of
her passions, music and singing, becoming a member of the

Cantata Singers in New York in the early days of the baroque revival. They performed principally the works of J. S. Bach, as nearly as possible to his original intentions. In New York also, against the backdrop of World War II, she met an electrical engineer working for Bell Laboratories named Gladwyn Lago. They married in 1944, and a few years later, when electrical engineering professors were in great demand to train the postwar generation, they opened a map, considered where they might wish to live, and picked Missouri. "Glad" speedily won an assistant professorship at the principal campus in Columbia, and Mary matriculated as "Engineering Wife." Soon she also gave birth to a son and daughter, staying at home to raise them. Her embrace of traditional domestic roles must have seemed complete.

Nonetheless, the former secretary at Friendship Press blossomed into one of its staff authors. *A Picture Map of Mexico,* with descriptive text by Mary Lago, was published by the press in 1951; *They Live in the City* appeared in 1954, a year after Mary's first child was born. During these years she also organized the Bach Singers, an organization modeled on the Cantata Singers, with vocalists and instrumentalists from the town, the university, and Stephens College. It was, in fact, her passion for music and new knowledge that changed the direction of her life and hence the annals of literary scholarship. A number of Indian students came to Missouri to study agriculture and were befriended by Mary. Having shared with them her interests in music, the students in turn taught her Indian songs. Many of those songs, it turned out, were by Rabindranath Tagore, but memorizing the Bengali was difficult when the words' meaning was unclear.

Mary decided to begin learning Bengali around the same time she determined that, having completed a stint as faculty wife and safely steered her children into school, it was time to resume a career. She entered the M.A. program at Missouri, completing that degree in 1965, and earned her Ph.D. in 1969 with a dissertation entitled "English Literature and Modern Bengali Short Fiction: A Study of Influences." By then she was fluent in Bengali, and she published numerous translations of Tagore's fiction in the 1960s and 1970s. A published scholar as well, she found herself in yet another "traditional" position, the faculty wife who earns her Ph.D. and is marooned in a lectureship at the same institution where her husband teaches. But this lecturer was also publishing books with Harvard University Press: *Imperfect*

Encounter (letters of Tagore and William Rothenstein) appeared in 1972, and *Max & Will* (letters of Rothenstein and Max Beerbohm) in 1975. It was too much to ignore. First Mary was assigned to teach courses that counted for graduate as well as undergraduate credit, and then she was inducted into the ranks of the department's tenure-track faculty. As the dust jackets of *Imperfect Encounter, Max & Will,* and *Rabindranath Tagore* (Twayne, 1976) attest, Mary jumped in one year (1975–1976) from lecturer to associate professor, a rarity in the American academy. Her way was then clear. She edited in succession an abridged edition of Rothenstein's *Men and Memories* (University of Missouri Press, 1978), *Burne-Jones Talking* (University of Missouri Press, 1981), and, with P. N. Furbank, the *Selected Letters of E. M. Forster* (2 volumes, Harvard University Press, 1983–1985). Three years after becoming an associate professor she was promoted to professor (1979), and in 1981 Bucknell University bestowed on her the honorary degree of D.Litt. In 1989 she was named the Catherine Paine Middlebush Chair of English, her department's highest honor.

Mary had written several biographical passages in earlier works—in introductions to or sections within books—but it was only after becoming emerita professor of English at Missouri in 1990 that Mary emerged as an accomplished biographer. Her *E. M. Forster: A Literary Life* (St. Martin's Press) appeared in 1995, and *Christiana Herringham and the Edwardian Art Scene* (University of Missouri Press), the product of some twenty-five years' research, was recipient of the Curators' Award for Scholarly Excellence as the outstanding University of Missouri Press book of 1996 by a University of Missouri faculty member. Mary is currently completing a biography of Edward Thompson (1886–1946), the father of historian E. P. Thompson.

The traditional housewife nurtured the distinguished scholar, only in Mary's case the housewife and scholar were the same person. This paradox is a trope for the significance of her own career: embracing the hallmarks of traditional scholarship led Mary to produce work ahead of its time in relevance and sympathies. That is, by insisting on impeccable accuracy, thoroughness, and rigorous attention to historical detail, Mary was exploring in her scholarship of the late 1960s and early 1970s what would now be labeled issues of postcolonialism, the vexed role of women in postcolonial regimes, feminism, and the politics of the literary canon. In her own view she was simply doing her "homework."

"Homework" in Mary's case meant learning Bengali. In her view this was necessary to sound scholarship. As she remarks in several analyses of the botched translations or readings of Tagore's work in Anglo-American culture, problems usually stemmed from insufficient knowledge of Bengali or of cultural differences, such as the Vaishnava tradition within Hinduism. Learning Bengali enabled Mary not merely to be thorough but also to examine Tagore and his culture from within and without, and thus to exercise the double vision crucial to understanding postcolonialism. Historical accuracy, moreover, meant that she must always remain attuned to the politics of cultural practices, since India's history was inseparable from British imperialism.

Thus, in recounting Tagore's 1912 reception in Great Britain, Mary scrutinizes even William Rothenstein, who brought Tagore to the attention of intellectuals and cultural arbiters in England, for stereotypical responses to the Bengali poet. Her critique of William Butler Yeats, who had himself experienced the brunt of British imperialism, is worth quoting at length:

> The qualities of *Gitanjali* [the book of poems that won Tagore the Nobel Prize in 1913] and of Tagore himself that Yeats found most attractive were innocence, simplicity, spontaneity, and the sense of a mythic tradition, dim, undefined, but certainly reaching back to the unrecorded past: all these were attributes that Yeats was determined to reconstruct for Irish literature. He would have been the first to cry horror at the thought of his having given aid and comfort to England's imperial views, yet a politically useful stereotype obtrudes between the lines of his Introduction [to Tagore's volume]. Tagore is not an ascetic, but he is nevertheless a "saint." The West lacks the "reverence" for its great men that Bengalis seem to have for Tagore. His father had sat immovable in meditation for two hours daily; his philosopher brother Dwijendranath was a kind of St. Francis on whom the birds and the squirrels alighted without fear. Both Tagore and Indian civilization are "content to discover the soul and surrender [themselves] to its spontaneity." Serenity and contentment were what England most coveted for India, whether it was to be found in the soul or elsewhere: Bengalis who sat immovable were less likely to stir up political discontent of the kind that had made the years of anti-Partition protest so turbulent.[1]

1. Lago, *Rabindranath Tagore* (New York: G. K. Hall, 1976), 66–67.

Using the term *multicultural* long before it became fashionable, Mary also asserted two years before the publication of Edward Said's *Orientalism* that "this syndrome—the colonizers' self-denigrating comparison with the spiritual resources of the colonized—is a familiar one in Western writing about the East." Neither did Mary blink away the possibility of Tagore's complicity in colonialism, for she questioned his decision to translate in 1919 a work first published in Bengali in 1906; in 1919 the novel Anglo-American readers knew as *The Home and the World* could support complacent readings of the text as an exposé of "indigenous" problems justifying paternal British oversight.[2]

The link between Mary's commitment to rigorous scholarship and her investigation of postcolonial issues is clear as well in a later essay in a 1989 collection devoted to Tagore. She incidentally articulates her own high standards of research and her dismay when they are breached in "Restoring Rabindranath Tagore," a rare personal glimpse of her working methods.

> Until I took them up, none of the [India Society] papers from 1920 onward, now properly stored in the India Office Library, had been touched by human hands, at least since 1945. I come to this conclusion because those papers were still black with soot from the blitz. I recall how much time I spent running down a long corridor every half hour or so to wash my hands, and everything I wore had to go to the laundry at the end of each day.
>
> Other sources on my list were virtually untouched. Without the least difficulty I saw Macmillan papers, unused in writings about Tagore. Executors for Rothenstein, Brooke, Ernest Rhys, the Herringhams and others gave me letters, manuscripts and photographs never before requested from them. The late Lord Bridges, son of the Poet Laureate, allowed me to see folders of letters used only, so far as I know, by Edward Thompson for his study of Robert Bridges.
>
> Why was I the first to pursue so much crucial primary material, all so readily available? I simply followed what I had been taught was scholarly procedure when dealing with a writer: find the letters to friends and family, find his publishers, find living persons who remember him. How was it possible that, for at least twenty years and undoubtedly much longer, the extensive international

2. Ibid., 28, 68, 122. Edward Said, *Orientalism* (London: Routledge and Kegan Paul, 1978).

literature on Tagore had made no use of such plentiful and fundamental primary sources?[3]

Thus, lack of thoroughness as well as stereotypical thinking (and what today would be called hegemonic ideologies) conspired to produce a representation of Tagore as the "Mystic and the Messenger," an offense both to Mary's sense of justice and to her good scholarship.

Mary's attention to Tagore's representation of women (in a book published only six years after Kate Millett's *Sexual Politics*) is a powerful feminist analysis, all the more useful in that it is situated within Indian traditions *and* colonial rule, the convergence of which offered women new opportunities but also thwarted their realization. *The Broken Nest*, which Mary translated, involves a woman who acquires knowledge and writing skills under the tutelage of her busy husband's cousin, only to be ignored by the cousin in turn when she surpasses her teacher. By the end of the story the woman faces an existence bifurcated between wifely duties and a hidden identity that has no place in her world. As Mary remarks, it is a "story of arrested growth and wasted talents. . . . the irony of [the wife's] situation is that even in her secluded life in *purdah,* she surpasses in achievement both her husband the editor and . . . the college student and would-be writer."[4]

This feminist element in Mary's scholarship, already evident in 1976, is central to *Christiana Herringham and the Edwardian Art Scene.* It is feminist biography insofar as its purpose is to recover a woman whose cultural contributions had been effaced and to situate her life within the constraints she faced as a woman. Mary scrupulously avoids special pleading, but the sense of indignity below the surface is palpable when Mary recounts Herringham's unease as the only woman, successively, on the National Art Collections Fund in 1903 and the provisional committee of the India Society in 1910, and the rhetorical screens of deference and modesty behind which Herringham was forced to retreat while assiduously working to get more women on the committee with her.

3. Lago, "Restoring Rabindranath Tagore," in *Rabindranath Tagore: Perspectives in Time,* ed. Mary Lago and Ronald Warwick (London: Macmillan, 1989), 20–21.

4. Kate Millett, *Sexual Politics* (Garden City, N.Y.: Doubleday, 1970); Lago, *Rabindranath Tagore,* 107.

Here might be the place to mention another connection between Mary's scholarship and her own life. When she offered her first course in Victorian and Edwardian literature in the fall of 1972, she was the sole woman in the department teaching a literature course approved for graduate credit. She was also in a department that had customarily held all-male department meetings. When Mary's colleague and dear friend Winifred Bryan Horner (herself now an internationally known scholar of rhetoric and composition) was granted tenure as an instructor in 1969, she was approached by the department chair, who suggested that it "wasn't necessary for her to attend any department meetings." At first, she didn't. Later, when she and Mary did, they had little encouragement to take active roles in discussion. Mary's custom, according to Win Horner, was to bring tapestry embroidery to department meetings; there she sat, stitching away, and also muttering under her breath, while discussion ensued. She, too, cloaked her singularity under the veil of traditional domesticity. Yet this very act created a disruptive presence—especially if some of those dominating the discussion happened to consider Madame Defarge and her knitting as they glanced in Mary's direction.

In writing the Herringham biography, however, Mary was doing more than finding points of convergence between her life and that of her subject. She was completing a scholarly task she had begun in 1967, when she first encountered Herringham's name while editing the correspondence of Rothenstein and Tagore and was frustrated at the incomplete information available. One of the pleasures of reading the Herringham biography for those who know Mary's prior work is to see how it enters into a seamless web that connects Mary's projects throughout her career. India, British imperialism, and the colonialist reception of Indian art figure importantly in the biography, as they do in her Tagore book and *Imperfect Encounter,* since Herringham, a professional copyist, was determined to copy Ajanta cave paintings that had suffered centuries of neglect and vandalism. The late Victorian art world explored in *Burne-Jones Talking* is mirrored here in Mary's attention to the Edwardian art scene (an emphasis registered in the second half of the book's title). E. M. Forster comes into view in the Herringham story at times, and William Rothenstein is a recurring presence. Even the art (and impasses) of translation enter into discussion, since Herringham's first principal contribution was her translation of a quattrocento treatise on tempera painting, the techniques of which were largely ignored at the time. As Mary observes in a telling aside doubtless born of personal experience, "Translation concentrates the mind wonderfully."[5] Only Mary's interest in music is missing. (That subject is taken up in detail in her prior book, *E. M. Forster: A Literary Life*.)

But *Christiana Herringham* also represents something wonderfully new in Mary's work, a full-scale study of a woman who made things happen but was not always given credit for doing so. And Mary's indefatigable efforts over the course of nearly three decades to retrieve details from the void speak to the commitment she felt to making Herringham's life visible once more. Traditional scholarship and feminism foster each other in the biography, as the traditional and assertive have done in Mary's own life.

Her meticulous scholarship, of course, has also made her the superb editor she is known to be from her work on the Forster letters as well as the Beerbohm and Rothenstein or Rothenstein and Tagore correspondences. This work also formed the professor whose example set high standards for her students, and we want to close by turning to what Mary has meant as professor and mentor to two of her students, the editors of this volume. Both of us have been inspired by Mary's work and teaching, and sustained by her affectionate encouragement, in ways we will never be able fully to articulate or reciprocate. If we share this source of inspiration, we have also found distinctive meanings in our respective relationships with Mary.

Linda Hughes will never forget the first day she surveyed the roster of the University of Missouri graduate faculty when she arrived on campus in the fall of 1970. She had finished her B.A. only a few months before at a state university at which women composed a substantial portion of the English department, including a full professor who had served as acting chair and been recognized for distinguished teaching. As Linda cast her eyes down the roster of some thirty-five names, she was aghast to find not one woman on the list, even though women accounted for roughly half of the doctoral students in the program. She had been accepted for study, but where (to

5. Lago, *Christiana Herringham and the Edwardian Art Scene* (Columbia: University of Missouri Press, 1996), 3, 6.

paraphrase Virginia Woolf) was she to find a foremother? Two years later Mary Lago taught her first graduate-level course, and Linda signed up immediately. From it she gained not only an excellent overview of late Victorian and Edwardian fiction but also the start of her own scholarly career and acquaintance with the professor who was to become a beloved mentor. What impressed her at first glance when Mary entered the classroom, however, was a detail perhaps trivial, perhaps not: Mary, wearing a dress, stockings, and heels, had lovely legs. And Linda was not the only female graduate student who noticed. If their observations suggest complicity in regimes of the female body, these women students were also celebrating the fact that a scholar with immense authority in the classroom was garbed in a skirt rather than in a tweed jacket and corduroys, and that this scholar tacitly communicated to female students that they need not choose between being women and being scholars.

Mary's teaching was innovative in another way that semester in 1972. Although Linda had had excellent seminars with other professors, Mary was the only one to demand original work beyond assigned readings. Rather than requiring students to demonstrate knowledge of the conventions of, or extant commentaries on, Forster or Woolf, she asked students to choose a writer from a list she had compiled of those whose work had hitherto received little scholarly attention; and she challenged students to construct original scholarly arguments about them. After writing her midterm on William Hale White, with special emphasis on *Clara Hopgood,* Linda devoted her semester project to the relationship between that novel and Spinoza, one of whose volumes White had edited. Mary read the paper and suggested that Linda submit it to a journal, a fairly uncommon practice among faculty supervising graduate students in 1972. Moreover, Mary encouraged Linda to send it to the best possible journal rather than aiming for something "suitable" for a mere graduate student. When Martha Vicinus at *Victorian Studies* expressed interest in the article but demanded revision and expansion, Mary made herself available as sounding board and coach, soothing away anxieties and suggesting additional readings. In the end the article was accepted. Linda embarked on her dissertation with new confidence that she could be a professional scholar, and the essay on White entered the scholarly record, showing up some fifteen years later as one of the references in the *Dictionary of Literary*

Biography entry on White. All is traceable to Mary's insistence (born of her own distinguished scholarship while yet a graduate student) that her students, too, could create new knowledge so long as they "did the homework."

Mary was also of immense importance after Linda completed her degree. Through the vagaries of the job market in 1976 (and Linda's dual-career domestic partnership), Linda found herself in a nontenurable position in the English department of a branch campus of the University of Missouri. Only those on tenure track were allowed to teach literature courses or attend department meetings (though, as Linda discovered with some chagrin, her publications were always included in the departmental count of scholarship forwarded to the dean each year). The prospect of heavy teaching loads with no chance to teach in her specialty was not encouraging. But unlike some young professionals in her position, Linda had Mary as a model. She knew about Mary's exclusion from specialist teaching and departmental privileges after earning the Ph.D. at the University of Missouri and then, when Mary's scholarly record had grown so distinguished it could not be overlooked, her elevation to the rank of associate professor. This model inspired Linda not to give up. Although by now, given the grim job market that excises so many from the profession, Linda knows her case has been partly a matter of luck, her persistence and belief that she could succeed paid off. She moved up the ranks—and eventually away from the branch of the state university—to find fulfilling work as a scholar and professor within the academy. Mary's inspiration and model have been crucial at every point.

Joe Law encountered Mary for the first time during his initial semester in the doctoral program at Missouri. She was teaching English 401, the introductory research and bibliography class required of all new graduate students, a course she had quietly modified to make more practical than such courses often are. The first assignment, for example, was to annotate a letter for inclusion in a collection and to explain why certain information had been included and other information omitted. Fledgling scholars were introduced to the mysteries of writing grant proposals as well, and Mary urged everyone to use the final project as a means of exploring a potential dissertation topic. Thanks to that last assignment, Joe was able to see that his initial idea was not suitable, something often learned much later. In a subsequent semester, he took a course called Bloomsbury and the Victorian Background with Mary. As she had done with Linda, Mary encouraged Joe to continue working with his seminar paper, showing him ways it could be revised for publication and helping him place it in an appropriate journal. In both courses, she was an exemplary teacher and mentor.

Yet Joe learned even more from her outside the classroom, particularly by working with her as she completed her part of the work on the selected letters of Forster. Reading proofs and helping with the index gave him a remarkable opportunity to experience how a scholar really works. Anyone who has read Mary's writing admires its clarity and directness. However, the sentences that seem inevitable are the product of countless revisions, made quickly and sometimes ruthlessly. At times, whole sentences were reduced to a salient word or two, achieving economy and grace simultaneously. Every name or date was carefully verified, perhaps for a fifth or sixth time, and the tedium was fully justified by the detection of several errors that would have been perpetuated by subsequent users of her text. At the same time, there was no sense of pressure or impatience. Quite clearly, she was doing exactly what she wanted to do.

On other occasions she made it clear that a scholar could not only make time for other activities but enjoy them. Linda has mentioned Mary's love of music, and it has remained strong. She sang in the University Choral Union almost every semester and attended many concerts on campus. Joe remembers seeing her after a two-hour rehearsal of sections of Bach's B-minor Mass, regretful that it was being sung by so large a chorus but clearly energized by the music. He remembers, with perhaps even more fondness, encountering her in the lobby after a performance of Richard Strauss's setting of Tennyson's "Enoch Arden," a melodrama for speaker and piano. "What a piece of cheese," she exclaimed, still laughing happily.

At other times, the conjunction of music and literature could bring a very different reaction. At least once it inspired a three-day symposium on campus, along with an incidental display of organizational virtuosity. In 1982, Mary had spent the summer in England, working with P. N. Furbank on a two-volume selection of Forster's letters. Among other things, she had interviewed Eric Crozier and his wife, Nancy Evans, about Forster's work on *Billy Budd*. When Mary returned to

Missouri, Joe told her that the music department was producing *Albert Herring* that fall. The libretto of Britten's 1947 opera was by Eric, and Nancy had sung the role of Nancy in the premiere. Mary's response was immediate and simple: "Well," she said, "we must have Eric and Nancy here." And we did. Within two days, with the cooperation of the music department's chair, she had set up a program of events involving the departments of English, music, and theater; obtained funding from several different sources; and made arrangements with the Croziers. The symposium was a success—a lasting success in that it established a link between the University of Missouri and the Britten-Pears School in Aldeburgh that continued for a number of years and is still maintained informally. Mary's generosity in inviting Joe to participate in the symposium has had a lasting impact for him as well. In addition to giving him an opportunity to gain valuable experience in making a conference presentation, she introduced him to people who would eventually provide invaluable advice and assistance on several subsequent projects. To be treated as a full-fledged colleague and to be admitted into those circles also encouraged him to think that he, too, could pursue his interdisciplinary interests professionally. As Joe's and Linda's experiences show, a novice could not hope for a better mentor inside or outside the classroom.

This brief biographical sketch and these recollections should make it plain that the life of Mary Lago is as exemplary as any chronicled by nineteenth-century biographers and their successors. It seems equally plain that she need feel no discomfort if suddenly faced with the question that haunts Jürgen Schlaeger: "And what have *you* done?" At most, Mary would point to a bibliography of her work—if she would do even that much—and it would be an impressive answer. The editors would like to exercise a bit of editorial privilege, then, and amplify that answer. Besides providing a model of traditional yet forward-looking scholarship, she has been an inspiration to her students, showing them how to succeed and making them her colleagues. To her these essays are offered with our admiration, gratitude, and affection.

Publications by Mary Lago

Books

Rabindranath Tagore. Twayne World Authors Series. Boston: Twayne/G. K. Hall, 1976.

E. M. Forster: A Literary Life. London: Macmillan Press; New York: St. Martin's Press, 1995.

Christiana Herringham and the Edwardian Art Scene. Columbia: University of Missouri Press; London: Lund, Humphries, 1996.

Editions

Imperfect Encounter: Letters of William Rothenstein and Rabindranath Tagore, 1911–1941. Cambridge: Harvard University Press, 1972.

Max and Will: Max Beerbohm and William Rothenstein, Their Friendship and Letters, 1893–1945. With Karl Beckson. London: John Murray; Cambridge: Harvard University Press, 1975.

Men and Memories: Recollections of William Rothenstein, 1872–1938. (One-volume abridged and annotated edition of three volumes, first published 1931, 1932, 1939.) London: Chatto and Windus; Columbia: University of Missouri Press, 1978.

Burne-Jones Talking: His Conversations 1895–1898 Preserved by His Studio Assistant Thomas Rooke. Columbia: University of Missouri Press, 1981; London: John Murray, 1982.

Selected Letters of E. M. Forster: Volume One, 1879–1920. With P. N. Furbank. London: William Collins; Cambridge: Harvard University Press, 1983.

Calendar of Letters of E. M. Forster. London: Mansell, 1985.

Selected Letters of E. M. Forster: Volume Two, 1921–1970. With P. N. Furbank. London: William Collins; Cambridge: Harvard University Press, 1985.

Twentieth Century Literature. E. M. Forster Special Issue. Guest Editor, vol. 31, nos. 2–3 (summer–fall, 1985).

Rabindranath Tagore: Perspectives in Time; Papers from the International Tagore Conference at the Commonwealth Institute, London. With Ronald Warwick. London: Macmillan, 1989.

Translations (Books)

Tagore, Rabindranath. *The Broken Nest.* With Supriya Bari. Introductory Essay by Mary Lago. Columbia: University of Missouri Press, 1971; Madras: Macmillan India, 1974.

———. *The Housewarming and Other Writings.* With Tarun Gupta. New York: New American Library, 1975. Rpt. Greenwood Press, 1976.

———. *Selected Short Stories of Rabindranath Tagore.* With Krishna Dutta. London: Macmillan, 1991.

Shorter Translations

Das, Jibanananda. "Five Poems." With Tarun Gupta. *Literature East and West* 4 (1964): 165–66.

———. "Nine Poems." With Tarun Gupta. *Beloit Poetry Journal,* fall 1965, pp. 20–23.

Tagore, Rabindranath. "Two Poems from Kshanika." With Tarun Gupta. *Hindusthan Standard Annual Supplement* (Delhi), pp. 5–6.

———. "Rashmoni's Son." With Tarun Gupta. *Chicago Review* 19 (1966): 5–32.

Bose, Pratibha. "The Family." *Mahfil: A Quarterly of South Asian Literature* 2 (1966): 1–9.

Bose, Buddhadeva. "A Life." With Deepak Majumdar. *Hindusthan Standard Annual Supplement* (1967), pp. 164–78.

Das, Jibanananda. "Two Poems." With Tarun Gupta. In *The Contemporary World Poets,* edited by Donald Junkins, 17–19. New York: Harcourt Brace, 1976.

Articles and Chapters

"The Parting of the Ways: A Comparative Study of Yeats and Tagore." *Indian Literature* [New Delhi] 6 (1963): 1–34. Rpt. *Mahfil: A Quarterly of South Asian Literature* 3 (1966): 32–57.

"Pattern in the Imagery of Jibanananda Das." With Tarun Gupta. *Journal of South Asian Studies* (1965): 637–44.

"Tagore's Temporal Encounters." *Literature East and West,* June 1966, pp. 19–41.

"Modes of Questioning in Tagore's Short Stories." *Studies in Short Fiction* 5 (1967): 24–36.

"Tagore in Translation: A Case Study in Literary Exchange." *Books Abroad* 46 (1972): 416–21.

"Rothenstein, Tagore, and Bangla Desh." *Cornhill Magazine,* spring 1972, pp. 165–76.

"The Essential Tagore: Missing Man in South Asian Studies." *Journal of Commonwealth Literature* 8 (1973): 81–87.

"Campus Problems." *The Author* 85 (1974): 81–83.

"Restoring Rabindranath Tagore." *Encounter* 42 (1974): 52–57.

"A Golden Age Revisited: Edward J. Thomas and the Burne-Jones Centenary." *Apollo* 102 (1975): 358–61.

"Irish Poetic Drama in St. Louis." *Twentieth Century Literature* 23 (1977): 180–94.

"The Fictional Stereotype as Corrective in Tagore's Short Stories." In *Rabindranath Tagore: American Interpretations,* edited by Ira G. Zepp Jr. Calcutta: Writer's Workshop, 1981.

"The Importance of Notes." *The Author* 94 (1983): 83–84.

"Forster on E. M. Forster." *Twentieth Century Literature* 31 (1985): 137–46.

"Max Beerbohm" and "Rabindranath Tagore." In *Oxford Companion to English Literature,* edited by Margaret Drabble. 5th ed. London and New York: Oxford University Press, 1985.

"*A Passage to India* on Stage." *Times Literary Supplement,* February 22, 1985, p. 959.

"E. M. Forster: Novelist as Letter-Writer." In *Essays on Poetry and Fiction: V. A. Shahane Commemorative Volume,* edited by S. N. A. Rizvi. Delhi: Doaba House, 1988.

"Restoring Rabindranath Tagore." In *Rabindranath Tagore: Perspectives in Time*, edited by Mary Lago and Ronald Warwick. London: Macmillan, 1989. (Not a reprint of "Restoring Rabindranath Tagore," above.)

"E. M. Forster and the BBC." *Yearbook of English Studies* 20 (1990): 132–51.

"Edward Burne-Jones: 'King Cophetua and the Beggar Maid' and 'Sir Edward Burne-Jones.'" In *International Dictionary of Art and Artists*. Chicago and London: St. James Press, 1990.

"E. M. Forster: Clapham's Child." *Biography* 14 (1991): 117–37.

"Christiana Herringham and the National Art Collections Fund." *Burlington Magazine* 90 (March 1993): 202–11.

"Visiting Rapallo." *Journal of the Eighteen Nineties Society* 24 (1997): 27–33.

"No Passage from India: William Rothenstein, Tagore, and the Lost Treasures of Temple Avenue." *Times Literary Supplement,* April 16, 1999, pp. 15–16.

Selected Reviews

Dimock, Edward C., trans. *The Maharashtra Purana: An Eighteenth-Century Bengali Historical Text*. Review in *Literature East and West* 9 (1966): 412–14.

———, ed. and trans. *Bengali Tales from Court and Village*. Review in *Mahfil: A Quarterly of South Asian Literature* 4 (1967): 54–58.

———. *The Place of the Hidden Moon*. Review in *Mahfil: A Quarterly of South Asian Literature* 4 (1967): 54–58.

Parry, Benita. *Delusions and Discoveries: The Effect of India on the British Imagination*. Review in *Victorian Studies* 16 (1973): 361–62.

Chakravarty, B. C. *Rabindranath Tagore: His Mind and Art*. Review in *Pacific Affairs* 46 (1973–1974): 595–96.

Chatterji, Bankimchandra. *Le Testament de Krishnokanto,* trans. Nandalal De for UNESCO. Review in *Books Abroad* 48 (1974): 418.

Roy, Manisha. *Bengali Women*. Review in *Journal of Asian History* 11 (1974): 168–69.

Surtees, Virginia. *Charlotte Canning*. Review in *Journal of Asian History* 11 (1974): 168–69.

Thatcher, Mary. *Cambridge South Asian Archive*. Review in *Journal of Asian History* 9 (1975): 87–88.

Dayananda, James. *Manohar Malkonkar*. Review in *World Literature Written in English* 15 (1976): 379–80.

Basu, Romen. *The Tamarind Tree*. Review in *World Literature Today* 51 (1977): 332.

Chatterjee, Enakshi, ed. and trans. *An Anthology of Modern Bengali Short Stories*. Review in *World Literature Today* 51 (1977): 182–83.

Mukherji, P. K. *Life of Tagore*. Review in *Journal of Asian Studies* 37 (1977): 151–52.

Das, G. K. *E. M. Forster's India*. Review in *World Literature Today* 53 (1979): 354–55.

Lipsey, Roger. *Coomaraswamy, Volume III, His Life and Work*. Review in *Journal of Asian Studies* 39 (1979–1980): 839–40.

Lewis, Robin. *E. M. Forster's "Passage to India."* Review in *Journal of Asian Studies* 39 (1979–1980): 839–40.

Bharucha, Rustom. *Rehearsals of Revolution: The Political Theater of Bengal*. Review in *World Literature Today* 58 (1984): 324.

Tagore, Rabindranath. *Poems*. Translated by William Radice. Review in *Times Literary Supplement,* September 27, 1985, p. 1054.

Thwaite, Ann. *Edmund Gosse: A Literary Landscape*. Review in *American Scholar* 54 (1985): 272–76.

Beerbohm, Max. *The Illustrated Zuleika Dobson*. Review in *American Scholar* 56 (1987): 150–54.

Olson, Stanley. *John Singer Sargent*. Review in *American Scholar* 56 (1987): 586–91.

Gupta, Sunetra. *Memories of Rain*. Review in *World Literature Today* 67 (spring 1993): 445.

Borland, Maureen. *D. S. MacColl, Painter, Poet, Art-Critic*. Review in *Burlington Magazine* 38 (January 1996): 37.

Mukhopadhyay, Shirshendu. *Woodworm*. Review in *World Literature Today* 71 (spring 1997): 457.

Radio

"Mrs Max: Florence Beerbohm, in Her Letters." BBC Radio 3 broadcast,
script recorded by Mary Lago and Margaret Robertson, July 18
and November 21, 1974.

About the Contributors

Anantha Sudhaker Babbili is Professor of Journalism at Texas Christian University, Fort Worth. A specialist in international communication, he has published his research in a variety of international journals and is invited on a regular basis to lecture at India's Osmania University, Oxford University, and the London School of Economics. He is also a consultant to the United Nations on issues of global news flow and human rights. His excellence in teaching has been recognized by the Poynter Institute for Media Studies, the Burlington Northern Foundation, the American Society of Newspaper Editors, the Associated Press Managing Editors, and the National Conference of Editorial Writers.

Julie F. Codell is Director, School of Art, Arizona State University, and Professor, Art History and Humanities. She received her Ph.D. in comparative literature from Indiana University, an M.A. in art history from Indiana, an M.A. in English from the University of Michigan, and an A.B. in English from Vassar College. She has contributed numerous articles on Victorian art to *Victorian Studies, Art History, Victorian Periodical Review, Dickens Studies Annual, Journal of Pre-Raphaelite Studies,* and *Victorian Poetry,* and to several books and encyclopedias. She recently coedited *Orientalism Transposed: The Impact of the Colonies on British Culture* (Ashgate, 1998) and is preparing a book-length study entitled "Lives of the Artists: Victorian Artists' Careers, Lifewritings, and Public Image."

Mary C. Francis is a musicologist who specializes in opera and the music of the twentieth century. She is completing a dissertation on the operas of Benjamin Britten at Yale University. A harpsichordist and sometime opera company stage manager, she now works in the music books division of the University of California Press.

P. N. Furbank is professor emeritus of the Open University. His books include biographies of E. M. Forster and Denis Diderot and *Unholy Pleasure: The Idea of Social Class.*

Michael Holroyd has written biographies of Lytton Strachey, Augustus John, and Bernard Shaw. He has been chairman of the Society of Authors in Britain and president of the English branch of International PEN. He is now chairman of the Royal Society of Literature. He lives in London and is married to the novelist Margaret Drabble.

Linda K. Hughes is Addie Levy Professor of Literature at Texas Christian University in Fort Worth. She is the author of *The Many Facèd Glass: Tennyson's Dramatic Monologues,* coauthor with Michael Lund of *Victorian Publishing and Mrs. Gaskell's Work* and *The Victorian Serial,* and guest editor of the special issue of *Victorian Poetry* on women poets (spring 1995). Her essays in books and journals are devoted to Victorian literature and periodicals and to Arthurian studies. She is at work on a biography of Rosamund Marriott Watson.

Joe Law is Associate Professor of English and Coordinator of Writing Across the Curriculum at Wright State University, Dayton, Ohio. He coedited *Landmark Essays on Writing Centers* (Hermagoras, 1995) and *Writing Centers: An Annotated Bibliography* (Greenwood, 1996), which received the National Writing Centers award for excellence in scholarship in consecutive years. He has published essays on writing centers, writing across the curriculum, Victorian literature, and the interrelations among the arts. He is also book review editor for the *Opera Quarterly.*

Debra N. Mancoff, Scholar in Residence at the Newberry Library in Chicago, writes on Victorian art and culture. She is author of *Burne-Jones* (Pomegranate, 1998), *Mary Cassatt: Reflections of Women's Lives* (Francis Lincoln, 1998), and *The Return of King Arthur: The Legend through Victorian Eyes* (Abrams, 1995). Her current projects include *David Roberts: Traveler to Egypt and the Holy Land* (Pomegranate, forthcoming) and *The Field and Flowers of Vincent van Gogh* (Francis Roberts, forthcoming). She is also editing *John Everett Millais: Beyond the Pre-Raphaelite Brotherhood* for the Paul Mellon Studies in British Art series published by Yale University (forthcoming in 2000).

Index